BOOKS BY GEORGE F. KENNAN

American Diplomacy, 1900–1950 (1951)

Realities of American Foreign Policy (1954)

Soviet-American Relations, 1917–1920 (2 vols., 1956–58)

Russia, the Atom, and the West (1958)

Russia and the West under Lenin and Stalin (1961)

Memoirs, 1925–1950 (1967)

From Prague after Munich:
Diplomatic Papers, 1938–1940 (1968)

The Marquis de Custine and His "Russia in 1839" (1971)

Memoirs, 1950–1963 (1972)

The Decline of Bismarck's European Order:
Franco-Russian Relations, 1875–1890 (1979)

The Nuclear Delusion:
Soviet-American Relations in the Atomic Age (1982)

The Fateful Alliance:
France, Russia, and the Coming of the First World War (1984)

Sketches from a Life (1989)

AROUND THE CRAGGED HILL

Around the Cragged Hill

A Personal and Political Philosophy

GEORGE F. KENNAN

W. W. NORTON & COMPANY
NEW YORK / LONDON

The text of this book is composed in 11.5 Bembo
with the display set in Bernhard Modern Roman and Bernhard Tango.
Composition and Manufacturing by the Haddon Craftsmen, Inc.
Book design by Jo Anne Metsch

Library of Congress Cataloging-in-Publication Data
Kennan, George Frost, 1904–
Around the cragged hill : a personal and political philosophy / by
George F. Kennan.
p. cm.
Includes index.
1. State, The.   2. Political science—Philosophy.
3. International relations.   I. Title.
JC251.K46   1993
320′.01—dc20   92-9936

ISBN 0-393-31145-7

W. W. Norton & Company, Inc., 500 Fifth Avenue, New York, N.Y. 10110
W. W. Norton & Company Ltd., 10 Coptic Street, London WC1A 1PU
2 3 4 5 6 7 8 9 0

On a huge hill,
Cragged, and steep, Truth stands, and hee that will
Reach her, about must, and about must goe;
And what the hills suddennes resists, winne so;
Yet strive so, that before age, deaths twilight,
Thy Soule rest, for none can worke in that night.
—John Donne

Contents

foreword

... sad cure, for who would loose,
Though full of pain, this intellectual being,
Those thoughts that wander through Eternity,
To perish rather, swallowed up and lost
In the wide womb of uncreated night,
Devoid of sense and motion?
                    —John Milton, *Paradise Lost*

I approached the writing of this book with much hesitation. I could not have any certainty as to what would come out of it. The undertaking appeared to require—to some extent, at least—abstraction, which has never been my dish. It threatened also to lead me to theory, which to me, as to Goethe, has always been gray, in contrast to the green quality of what he called "the golden tree of life." It had always seemed to me safer, less pretentious, and, perhaps, more useful to illustrate general beliefs through the medium of specific examples, leaving it to the reader to draw his own picture of their implications.

I was far from being alone, I suspect, in entertaining such reservations. I seemed to recall that Justice Oliver Wendell Holmes once said something to the effect that he had never been able to state his own philosophy of the law in any pure form—only through the corpus of his dissenting opinions. And I was reminded of Anton Chekhov, the playwright, who, when asked to explain at a rehearsal in the Moscow Art Theater his interpretation of the way one of his characters should be played, could only say, "Don't you see? He wears checkered trousers."

But I was pressed to recognize that this, in my case, was not enough. A number of recent writers had given themselves the trouble of trying to extract from the welter of my past writings—from lectures on international affairs, from books on diplomatic history, or from cryptic sentences in commencement speeches or other oratorical efforts— something resembling a coherent personal and political philosophy. They professed to have come away frustrated, or at least bewildered. The pickings, they said, were slim, and sometimes even added to their confusion.

What weight there was behind these complaints I could not judge. But I was moved by their effort. It implied a belief, or at least a suspicion on their part, that behind all these suggestive specific examples there must have been something to be said by way of generalization that I had not said but that would be worth my saying.

This foreword, like most forewords, is being written after the completion of the book. (How else could one know to what a foreword should be applicable?) I see, on looking it over, that this work, like all the others I have written, ended up, whatever the original intent, as essentially a collection of critical observations. The difference is only that in this instance I have attempted to take the high ground, avoiding all detailed preoccupation with current problems and trying to stick to the broader dimensions of things—the ones that might still be expected to be visible and significant in future decades as well as years.

Whether the result, bearing this character, represents a betrayal of the original intent to put forward something resembling a personal and political philosophy, I cannot say. But I find myself, at this point, wondering whether any work of personal philosophy, however impressively abstract and theoretical, has not in essence been, or could be, anything other than just such a product of observation and of critical appraisal.

I find sustenance for this questioning in two passages, widely separated in time, among things I have recently read. The first, a passage from Edmund Burke's *Reflections on the Revolution in France,* reads as follows:

. . . I cannot stand forward and give praise or blame to anything which relates to human actions and human concerns on a simple view of the object, as it stands stripped of every relation, in all the nakedness and solitude of metaphysical abstraction. Circumstances . . . give in reality to every political principle its distinguishing color and discriminating effect.

The second of the passages, this one from a recent book review by my good and esteemed friend Stuart Hampshire (a *real* philosopher, as I am not):

We know what we are doing when we actively devise experiments, actively verify and test our beliefs, actively direct our interests and inquiries toward useful and concrete questions. . . . A sequence of abstract thought, and also the stream of our passive impressions together form a sea of ignorance, in which we shall drown, if thought and feeling are cut off from our active interest. . . . Unless we purposefully turn our eyes to look at something that interests us as individuals, we shall literally see nothing in the world, and we shall understand nothing in the real world unless we remember that we freely choose the direction in which to look.[1]

This book represents just such a turning of the eyes to a number of things that interest me as an individual. If the reflections this arouses lack any apparent universal applicability, whether in time or in space, this is because the writer sees little unity in the phenomena observed. But this does not preclude the possibility that there will become apparent to the attentive reader a unity the author himself has been unable to discover. Should this be the case, the effort embodied in what follows will be doubly rewarded.

1. Review by Stuart Hampshire of *The Jameses: A Family Narrative,* by R. W. B. Lewis, in *New York Review of Books,* October 10, 1991, p. 4.

PART ONE

Chapter One

MAN,
THE CRACKED
VESSEL

They sneer at me for leaning all awry:
What! did the Hand then of the Potter shake?
—Omar Khayyám, *Rubáiyát*

*M*an, to the degree that he tries to shape his behavior to the requirements of civilization, is unquestionably a cracked vessel. His nature is the scene of a never-ending and never quite resolvable conflict between two very profound impulses. One of these, built into him from birth and not a matter of his own choice, is something he shares with the animals: namely, the imperative impulse to preserve and proliferate his own kind, with all the powerful compulsions that engenders. The other is the need—a need underlying the entire historical development of civilization—to redeem human life, at least partially, of its essentially animalistic origins by lending to it such attributes as order, dignity, beauty, and charity—this last meaning the love of or at least the respect for one's fellow man, and the capacity for compassion. A central feature of the human predicament is the conflict between these so frequently conflicting impulses—a conflict for which man's own soul constitutes the field of battle.[1]

Let us first look more closely at the compulsion to the preservation and proliferation of the species. This impulse, as I see it, takes two forms. One of these is sometimes referred to as "self-love." Reinhold Niebuhr preferred to use the more gentle term "self-regard," a suggestion I gratefully accept. The second is the sexual urge. And because the latter is the more obvious, the more primitive, and the less subtle of the two, let me turn to it first.

The Sexual Urge

The sexual urge requires no identification—no description. Everyone knows what it is. It attracts more attention than any other aspect of the human predicament. It is the leading theme of most Western literature, inviting treatment both as comedy and as tragedy. Sometimes deplored, sometimes idealized, it is always near the front of the stage in the enactment of human tensions and dilemmas.

It is far from my intentions to depict the sexual urge as a solely negative and reprehensible feature of the human predicament—as something in a state of total conflict with the higher motivations and strivings of mankind. I recognize the interaction of the two sexes as a primary factor in the development of the human spirit and in human creativity, intellectual and aesthetic. I cannot picture art, thought, civilization per se, without it. Goethe had good reason for ending his great creation of *Faust* with the words "the eternal feminine pulls us along" ("Das Ewig-Weibliche / Zieht uns hinan"). And this is only one of a thousand examples of this recognition. It is probably fair to say that no other aspect of the human condition has ever inspired finer or greater manifestations of the human spirit.

Beyond this, it is true that when the sexual urge accompanies and supports deep intimacy and devotion between individuals, it holds

---

1. I am using the word "man" here, and shall be doing so in other obvious instances, as a synonym for "mankind"; and the pronoun will accordingly take the masculine form. I see in this usage no occasion for apology.

satisfactions second to few, if any, in human experience; and it finds, in this way, a redemption from its less admirable qualities.

Yet the relationship of this urge to other demands of civilized life *is* complicated. So far as its contributions to human intimacy are concerned: we must not exaggerate the frequency of such idyllic comings together, or the prospects for their endurance when they do occur. People's physical needs change even when their deeper affections do not. And even these profoundly moving and enriching intimacies can have their ambiguous effects, particularly when they engender proprietary feelings on one part or the other. Men are not generally monogamous in their inclinations, nor are women, for that matter (although their responsibility for children and their greater sense of realism do much to hold them to the monogamous side), And even the deepest personal affection does not assure against the development of such unhappy phenomena as jealousies, suspicions, conflicting loyalties, wounded pride, and tragic unhappiness.

Stripped of its ennobling part in human intimacies, stripped of its mysteries, its multitudinous sublimations, its ornamental trappings, and the higher forms of passion that inspire it, the sexual urge is one of the most tedious, monotonous, at times ridiculous, and least interesting of human proclivities. It is frequently in conflict with the most elementary demands of outward behavior and of inward composure. The act, in its purely physical manifestations, is brief, bestial, and potentially humiliating, so much so as to require elaborate rituals for concealment, disguise, cant, and prevarication just in order to be made even approximately compatible with the decencies of normal social intercourse. Nor is it in any way improved when these unavoidable rituals are neglected or flouted, as occurs in the pathetic bravado and tedium of common pornography.

There is no getting around it: we have to do here with a compulsion we share with the lowest and least attractive of the mammalian and reptile species. It invites most handsomely, and very often deserves, the ridicule, the furtive curiosity, and the commercial exploitation it receives. To highly sensitive persons, it can become a never-ending source of embarrassment and humiliation, of pain to its immediate victims and to others, of misunderstandings, shame, and remorse all around. Not for nothing do the resulting tragedies dominate so much of realistic as well as of romantic literature. Not for nothing has this urge earned the prominent place it takes in the religious rites of confession and prayers for forgiveness.

There is, in short, no escaping it: the sexual urge, the crude expression of nature's demand for the proliferation of the species, enriching, confusing, and tragedizing the human predicament as it does at every turn, must be regarded as a signal imperfection in man's equipment to lead life in the civilized context. It cannot be expected to be otherwise at any time in the foreseeable future.

Self-regard

A similar situation confronts us when we come to the other of man's great imperfections: his self-regard, self-love, egotism, or whatever one wishes to call it. Here, too, we have an endless source of what Sigmund Freud called man's "discomfort" in civilization. The nature of this discomfort is not easy to describe. Reduced to the simplest terms, it consists of the special concern the individual has for the advancement of his own interests and desiderata—but this, in combination with the difficulty he experiences in evaluating his own personality, with the uncertainties and feelings of insecurity that assail him in just that respect, and with his persistent need to seek reassurance in the reactions of others to his own person. We have here, in the interaction of these factors, an ineradicable further source of complexity, frustration, unhappiness, and even tragedy in human affairs—and not just in the affairs of the individual but in those of society as well.

The critical approach to this situation is complicated by the fact that there is one area of human reaction and behavior—let us call it the area of self-respect—within which the special concern of the individual for the self has a natural, necessary, and useful place, not only in harmony with the legitimate interests of society but actually supportive of them. Each of us, after all, inhabits that particular assemblage of physical substances—flesh, bones, fluids, and so on—that comprises his or her own body. Each of us, and each of us alone, has primary, if never complete, control over that body: over what it does, how it reacts, how it comports itself in the face of the endless challenges with which daily life confronts it. However severely habit or the promptings of the subconscious may limit our autonomy in this respect, it is we, after all, who animate many of the physical reflexes of this body and determine a great part of its social behavior. No one else, whatever his power over us, can fully replace us in that capacity. And since it is not only useful but necessary that this control be exercised somewhere and by someone, our exclusive power to exercise it is not just a privilege but a responsibility; and it carries with it, when reasonably and modestly exercised, a certain justifiable dignity.

There is, then, I repeat, an area in which self-regard is not a source of discomfort and trouble in human affairs—or at least need not be and should not be. But it is a narrow area, difficult for the individual to identify and to adhere to. And it is a precarious one, because it is pressed by dangers from two sides: from the individual's underestimation of his own qualities, on the one hand, and from his overestimation of them, on the other.

The Underestimation of Self

Let us take first the rarer of these two phenomena: the underestimation. This can be of two kinds. One of them is what I think of as *real* underestimation, present in the individual's own consciousness. It can be induced by personal failures, by dreadful mistakes, by oversensitivity, or by the pangs of conscience. It can also be induced or promoted by influences from the outside: by evidences of low opinion or contempt for the subject by others—evidences that shake self-confidence. When blows of this sort can be absorbed into an inner humility and can find expression in a reasonable moderation of hopes and goals, they need not, and should not, constitute encroachments on self-respect. But where this is not possible, feelings of inadequacy can assume dangerous forms: excessive discouragement, depression, and despair—conditions that can ruin a life. (The totalitarians, incidentally, were well aware of these realities. It was upon just such vulnerabilities that many of their brainwashing techniques were founded. Their efforts were directed, in the first instance, at the destruction of the prisoner's confidence in himself. Only when this was destroyed and the prisoner had lost all self-respect could they have hope of creating, within the given physical frame, a new personality that would be totally under their control.)

There is also, of course, another kind of underestimation: the feigned one. It takes various forms: demonstrative and insincere self-debasement, exaggerated professions of humbleness or modesty, profuse denials of the value of one's own contributions, and the like. Actually, such behavior is almost invariably motivated by the desire to provoke from the other person some sort of a reassuring denial of the validity of these professions. As such, it is really the evidence of much insecurity, of an inability or reluctance to confront the trials of self-scrutiny, and of a corresponding undue dependence on the reactions of others for the establishment of the image of self.

Anton Chekhov, in a letter addressed to a younger brother in 1879, gave the classic response to the phenomenon of false modesty. He had received a letter in which the brother had signed himself as "your insignificant and obscure little brother." "Do you know," Chekhov asked in reply, "before whom you should confess your insignificance?" And he proceeded to answer his own question.

Before God, if you will, before intelligence, beauty, nature, but not before people. Among people you have to show your worth. After all, you're not a crook, are you? You are an honest fellow, are you not? Well then, respect the honest fellow in yourself, and recognize that the honest fellow is never insignificant. Don't confuse "coming to terms with yourself" with "recognizing your insignificance."

The Overestimation of Self
On the other side of the narrow area of legitimate self-respect lies the far greater and more common danger: that of the overestimation of

one's own worth, or at least the temptation to invite and to welcome the overestimation of it by others. This latter distinction is important; for here, in the thirst for inflation of the ego, is where the reliance upon the reactions of others, as the authentic measuring stick for evaluation of self, tends to be overwhelming. And this is often true not just for the neurotically insecure person but for the normal one as well. The fact is that the ability of the individual to form independently, solely out of the resources of his own judgment and without recourse to the critical reactions of others, a firm, sound, and reliable image of his own worth is extremely small. We all see ourselves in the mirror reflection of the response of others to our personality. Much as we may strive for objectivity in such an effort, we can never entirely succeed; for in this instance the very word "objectivity" is a contradiction of terms.

Not that the effort is entirely useless. There are always things to be gained by the mere effort to take at least a realistic view of oneself, the effort to find some balance between the strengths and the weaknesses of one's own personality. But success in this effort can never be more than partial. The chaotic mix of sensitivities, hopes, expectations, anxieties, uncertainties, temptations to self-admiration, and pangs of contrition that surges back and forth even in the average healthy human spirit, aside from being only partly under one's own conscious control, affords no firm foundation for judgments about oneself. Beyond which there is the fact that man is a social animal; he does not live in isolation. Thus a large part of whatever value his person may possess must lie precisely in the field of its interaction with others and can be judged only on the evidences of that interaction.

This writer can recall his own reactions when, as a poor and very provincial freshman at Princeton, a year younger than most of his companions, he found himself confronted with the greater sophistication and smoother manners of many of his fellow students and was brought to realize that he cut a very poor figure, if any at all, in their eyes. And he recalls that he tried, at one point, to say to himself, "You must not accept at face value the standards these fellows apply to you. You must try to make your own."

It was a brave undertaking. The discipline was probably useful. But in the main, the freshman was reaching for the stars. In the first place, what were his standards? Those, presumably, of his family and his midwestern entourage. But challenges to those standards now confronted him from every side. Could he fully trust them? It was a great wide world, outside of Milwaukee, and he was beginning to become aware of it. What did he have to fall back on?

But actually, he would never be able to establish, and probably never should have tried in the first place to establish, any total independence in this respect. Immature as may have been many of the values the other students tended to apply to him, they were not totally so. He *had* his faults; and the others were probably better aware of some of them than he was. The best he could do, in the end, not only then but even more in later life, would be not to ignore these outside reactions but to try to put them into their place: to distinguish, that is, the kernel of truth they embraced from the injustices and the false standards they reflected, and to learn from them where he could, without establishing them as the sole criteria for self-judgment. For there was danger, too, in a total reliance on the judgments of others. He was to see, in later life, other men whose view of themselves had come to rest exclusively on these outside judgments, and to pity them for the insecurity this reflected.

The conscientious individual is obliged, then, in the effort to evaluate his own identity, to take into account not only his own inner uncertainties but also the evidence afforded to him by the reactions of others to his personality. But in this last effort, he steps out onto a slippery slope, because these evidences are seldom fully reliable. The real judgments of others are not likely to be fully revealed in their outward behavior. Ordinary politeness, including even a certain charitable reticence, can easily conceal feelings of quite a different nature. Outward deference, as everyone knows who has ever occupied a high executive position, easily slips over into unctuousness and flattery.

The observant and thoughtful person, of course, will try to allow for these distortions. But the effort will never be easy. This is so in part because the allowances to be made can never be more than conjectures, sometimes no more than suspicions. But beyond that, and more serious still, the subject's very uncertainty about himself, together with the urgings of his amour propre, will always get in the way. However genuine his private humility, however stern the restraints he tries to place upon himself, however hard he tries to hold only to his own standards, there will always be *some* thirst for reassurance. And there will always be *some* sneaking hope that he will find reflected, in the words and behavior of the other person, a soothing and self-gratifying resolution of his own uncertainties.

And the worst of it is that this thirst for reassurance by the reactions of others can very seldom, if ever, be wholly satisfied. The more it is fed, the greater becomes the appetite. The more the ego is allowed to expand, the more powerful the temptation to reach for even larger expansion.

In its more innocent, and fortunately more common, forms, this tendency to overestimation of the self finds its expression in such very human weaknesses as conceit, ostentation, posturing, and pompousness—forms of behavior that are usually easily seen through by others and, often, find their own punishment in the ridicule they invite. I am reminded of the experienced diplomat at the court of St. Petersburg some hundred and twenty years ago, who, in advising a newly arrived colleague on how to approach the Russian chancellor of that date, said, "Take a viol of the purest flattery and wave it vigorously before his nose. *Il n'aura jamais assez* (He will never have enough)." But this sort of vanity alone, however well it lends itself to humorous exploitation by the novelists and playwrights, can also sometimes produce its full share of real unpleasantness, in the way of humiliation, disappointment, and frustration, for the unfortunate subject. And there are far more serious forms that this indulgence of the ego can assume—ones that can, and do, cause much trouble for the subject himself and for society.

One of these will be found, of course, in the kindred vices of envy and jealousy. These latter, the least admirable of human weaknesses and the ones least likely to enhance anyone's happiness, are also products of the insatiable human ego—the frustrated ego, in this case, denied some longed-for object and determined to see whether the loss could not be compensated for at someone else's expense.

But even more serious, as a projection of the insistent need for indulgence of the individual's self-regard, is the lust for authority, for power, for demonstrated preeminence over others. This urge, assuming an open-ended multiplicity of forms, some relatively innocent and harmless, others more questionable, pervades a great part of personal and organizational life. Sometimes confused with true leadership and prestige, it will be found, for example, in marriages, in families, in youth groups, in social clubs—wherever, in fact, people associate in small ways for personal or other purposes. But much more prominently and ruthlessly does it come to the fore in larger and more formal associations and hierarchies of every sort: professional, military, bureaucratic, and commercial, among others. It finds its acme wherever governmental power is involved, and particularly in politics, which, after all, is simply the competition for the control over the governmental process. (We shall see more of this when we turn to the nature of governments.) This form of self-regard is, in short, a major and unavoidable accompaniment of all organized human activity.

Here again, of course, we find ourselves confronted with the question of degree. What is good in moderation is not good when things are carried too far. Just as there is a reasonable and socially acceptable level of the individual's self-regard, which I have defined as self-respect, so, when it comes to the preeminence of any one person in a group or association, there is a reasonable level of dignity and deference the position of leadership has a right to expect. Where leadership is quietly and unostentatiously exercised, with due respect for those over whom it is exercised, and with a sense of responsibility no smaller than the authority it implies, no exception can be taken to it, and the self-regard of the person who exercises it will suffer no unhealthy inflation.

But these limits are not easy to maintain. Nor are those over whom authority is exercised always willing to accept even the moderate and reasonable exercise of it. Because the authority of the one individual implies the subordination of another, because the expansion of one person's power implies the relative powerlessness of someone else, because the pride of position of the one individual presupposes the corresponding humbleness of place of another, all manifestations of this thirst for authority and power involve rivalry. And all rivalry involves some measure of unpleasantness. The hubris of one person's success is always accompanied, somewhere, by the humiliation of someone else's failure. With the arrogance of power goes the ignominy of unwilling subordination or of frustrated ambition.

It is in this, in the thirst for reassurance through preeminence, authority, power over others, and the forms of exaggerated deference all this engenders, that the weaknesses of human self-regard—its involuntary quality, the inability of the individual to perceive its reasonable limits, and its tendency to feed upon itself—find some of their most sinister expressions. It is here that the conflict between what the individual actually is and what the interests of civilization would ideally require him to be becomes most acute. Here, too, as in the case of the sexual urge, what we have before us is a real flaw in human nature—a flaw which places definite limitations on man's happiness, whether personal or social, the correction of which lies in part beyond the limits of his own powers.

It is with this caveat in mind, then, that I must revert to my original proposition that man—Western man, at any rate—is a cracked vessel: that his psychic makeup is the scene for the interplay of contradictions between the primitive nature of his innate impulses and the more refined demands of civilized life, contradictions that destroy the unity and integrity of his undertakings, confuse his efforts, place limits on his possibilities for achievement, and often cause one part of his personality to be the enemy of another. Whipped around, frequently knocked off balance, by these conflicting pressures, he staggers through life as best he can, sometimes reaching extraordinary heights of individual achievement but never fully able to overcome, individually or collectively, the fissures between his own physical and spiritual natures.

That this is so should not be taken as a reason for despair. The struggle against these handicaps can have, and does have, its glorious moments. And it is, as at so many other points in life and as we shall have other occasions to note, in the inherent worthiness of the struggle rather than in the visible prospects for success that the true glory will be found. But what these considerations should do, as we set out on the unsteady terrain of the search for a personal and a political philosophy,

MAN, THE CRACKED VESSEL

is to warn us against any and every sort of utopian purpose or expectation. Man is not perfectible. These fissures in the human psyche are profound and elemental. As long as civilized life subsists, it will continue to be marked by them and to be limited by the restraints they impose.

The Little Demon

What has been talked about here—the instinctive compulsions that nature has instituted to assure the preservation and proliferation of the human species—constitutes what could be called the demonic side of human nature. And these are not the only examples of it. Others could have been mentioned. There are, for example, the tragic tensions of those—the artists, the composers, the poets—who lose themselves in the creative cultivation of beauty and are torn away from all successful adjustment to the mundane necessities of life. There comes a point, in fact, where beauty, for its reckless devotees, becomes the advocate of death against life.

There are, in any case, few persons who are not touched by one or another of the manifestations of this demonic dimension of human nature and experience. Essentially untamed and unruly, it assumes a multitude of forms, varying with every person. I like to picture it as a little demon companion, in attendance on every civilized person: sometimes representing the sexual urge, at other times the ego's endless search for reassurance, but always constant and persistent, always at hand with outrageous and sometimes positively indecent suggestions, determined to mess up the even tenor of one's life wherever it can, a major nuisance or a minor one, depending on circumstances and on the level of resistance it encounters, but seldom, if ever, to be wholly shaken off. Locked out at the front door, it comes in at the back one or through the window. And if all these entries be closed to it, it presents itself in a variety of the most ingenious and inviting disguises.

People do better or worse in contending with this troublesome little companion: in rejecting its suggestions or, when they cannot be wholly resisted, in concealing the effects of them. There are some who do very well indeed in this last respect, putting on a bold front of serene independence, as though they had all the circumstances of their lives, thank you, well under control.

One would do well not to be too easily misled by those impressive displays of a total personal autonomy. There are few who have not, at one time or another, had to do battle with the little troublemaker; and if there is at the moment no outward evidence of its being a factor in their lives, don't worry: you may be sure it has been there in the past, or soon will be.

But at the same time, one should not be too critical of those who put on this bold front. Once someone has offered as much resistance as one can to the demon's inroads on the good order of his or her life, the best way of coping with the pesky little fellow is to deny it the satisfaction of outward attention by acting, so far as one can, as though it did not exist. The Victorians may indeed have carried these pretenses too far; but that is probably better than not carrying them far enough. A lot of the weight of civilization rests at times on the better of our pretenses. Without them, civilization could probably not exist. "I find this frenzy," wrote Edna St. Vincent Millay, in a sonnet addressed to a gentleman with whom she had evidently been having a less than serious affair, "insufficient reason for conversation when we meet again." Right she was; and would there were more of her!

What, one wonders, is this compulsive preoccupation with explicit sex that marks so much of the American printed word and so many of its displays on the photographic screen? We know the elements of human anatomy. We know how procreation takes place. We have no need for these persistent reminders of what the average schoolchild has usually learned, alas, at the age of six or seven. And as for the intended effect, the impression we are supposed to gain of the boldness and cleverness and daring originality of the writer or film director who dishes out all this muck: I can find in all this only the unintended confession of a serious artistic and intellectual poverty—a desperate effort to draw attention to one's self by pornographic illustration or suggestion when other and more significant means of doing so are beyond one's capacity.

So let us, wherever we can, keep the little demon and its doings in the quiet background of our lives, well removed from all forms of exhibitionism on the façade. The remaining areas of consciousness and activity will benefit from its absence; and it will be forced to recognize, in the very fact of its ostracism, the limits of its power over us.

But the recognition of the part that the demonic powers play in the lives of individuals places two demands upon us. One of them is, of course, that we not go too far in the idealization of other individuals. We must not expect their personality, ever, to be wholly devoid of these complicating factors.

It used to be said, in the days when people had valets and ladies' maids, that no man was ever completely a hero to his own valet. A cruder version of this recognition of human limitations came to my attention when, in one of my younger years, I expressed to my first ambassadorial chief, Mr. William C. Bullitt, my wonder at his lack of any sense of intimidation in the presence of people who were regarded, at that time, as "the great." "My dear George," he replied, "someone once told me that the human body was 97 percent water. Whenever I see one of these illustrious characters approaching, I try to remember that, and I decline to be impressed."

He was both wrong and right. The percentage of water in the physical frame was not, of course, the crucial factor. There were, within such people, things worse than water that served to impair, or to make unreal, their lofty pretenses. On the other hand, there are certain kinds of people in the judgment of whom none of us should be put off by relating their value simply to the physical composition of their bodies, or even to the supposed contradictions of their emotional life.

First, there are the saints. They are the members, presumably, of that tiny elite of human beings who are truly able to control or at least expel from the surface of their motivations and behavior the disturbing little demon to whom reference has just been made. That such persons have occasionally existed and continue to exist, I am glad to believe, even though I am not sure that I have ever met any; and if they, combining this extraordinary personal power with pity and concern for the rest of us, are able to mediate effectively for us in another life, so much the better. But there will never be many of them. And while we others may try to emulate them, we must never expect fully to succeed. Perhaps, in fact, most of us were never meant to do so.

The other category of persons for whom we should not permit our respect to be modified by this recognition of their normal physical and emotional limitations are the truly great. By these I mean particularly the ones—the poets, the composers, the great scholars and thinkers— who find it possible to combine immense intellectual or aesthetic powers with the sense of responsibility toward others which abilities of this order should make incumbent upon them. Such persons, too, have existed; and we must hope that there will be more of them. This level of superiority does not mean, of course, that they have been, or ever will be, immune to the sort of limitations that were discussed above. What it does mean is that they have achieved such unusual levels of accomplishment—levels of greatness, if you will—that in the face of them these normal foibles of human nature become relatively trivial aspects of personality, so greatly overshadowed by other qualities that we are justified in disregarding them or, at least, forgiving them.

And this mention of the word "forgiveness" brings me to the second of the two demands upon us that present themselves when we consider the part played in the human personality by the instinctive, animalistic, and demonic side of man's nature. Since we are all affected by this side of ourselves—since we are all in one degree or another or at one time or another helpless in its tentacles—we ought to acknowledge a certain sense of brotherhood, and reserve some sympathy, for others who are similarly distressed.

Sometimes, no doubt, we do just that. But in other instances our inclination is to say, "Ah yes, but many of these are such disreputable and unfeeling characters that they deserve whatever discomfort or ignominy their confusion brings upon them."

Perhaps—perhaps; but one should be careful. It is of just such assumptions, of just such cheerful and confident moods of disassociation from the weaknesses and miseries of others, that the little demon likes to avail itself, for the achievement of those of its aspirations and purposes that had better been left unachieved. Self-satisfaction in the face of the woes of others is one of those chinks in the door through which this resourceful companion gains entry when other means of access are unavailable.

Heredity and Environment

These limitations on human perfectibility are, of course, not the only qualities that inheritance has to offer us. They are unique in this respect only in that they are universal in their scope, affecting to one degree or another practically every one of us. There are numbers of other qualities—some of them extremely good, others extremely bad, and even more somewhere in the middle—that we also receive from the genes. But these, as bestowed upon individuals, are varied in the extreme, in ways that are often unforeseeable, unpredictable, and surprising.

And the fact that this is so brings us to one more question on which a special word must be said. This is the confusion that reigns in so many American minds over the relative importance of heredity and environment as formative influences on the development of the individual personality. One of the most common features of the American outlook is the traditional belief that heredity has very little importance—that every child born in freedom, regardless of class or race or any of the other distinctions of parentage, is a tabula rasa, to be given its ultimate character exclusively by the postnatal experiences, primarily education, to which it comes to be subjected. Heredity, in other words, is neither here nor there.

I think I can discern the origins of this outlook. We are a nation of immigrants. A great many of us, or our families, came to this country from highly stratified societies, in which the circumstances of a person's life were largely prescribed from birth by the caste or class the person was born into. These distinctions were often seen as unjust, and deserved to be so seen. In the case of many who emigrated from such societies the sense of this injustice, and the desire to escape from it, was often a major factor in the decision to emigrate. One of the attractions of America as a goal of migration was precisely the understanding that American society was devoid of these inherited distinctions and that every child born here would have an equal chance to shape the conditions of its participation in society. This was the foundation for the sense of equality which Tocqueville saw, in the 1830s, as the outstanding distinguishing mark of American society. He regarded it as more important than any other factor in shaping the uniqueness of American civilization; and it provided the very basis for his interest in the country.

But the decision to emigrate was in the vast majority of cases largely or entirely a matter of individual choice and decision. It was often a debatable and even controversial choice, particularly in the eyes of those who were left at home. This being so, it was a choice the immigrant in America often felt a certain pressure to vindicate before those who remained at home in the old country, and before his own conscience. How better to do this than to cite the equality of status that was seen (and not just by Tocqueville) as the outstanding quality of American life? But this required, if only for purposes of comparison, rejection of the value of the inherited distinctions that had been left behind, and demonstration of the virtues of a society where they did not exist. And from this necessity it was an easy step to the assumption that inheritance was a negligible factor—that all that needed to be done for the improvement and perfection of the human species could be done by environment and, above all, by education.

It was never easy to argue against these attitudes, for there was much to be said for them. The earlier allotment of status in life (and with it of the opportunities for self-improvement) solely on the basis of birth and heredity did indeed involve many artificialities and injustices. If superiority in the parent did not preclude superiority in the child, it certainly did not assure it. Many a worthless son was born to an impressive father; and many a potentially valuable one, born to humble parents, had to make his way against the handicaps that this implied. Nature, in her allotment of the various human qualities, good and bad, was capricious and unpredictable. Thus there was indeed much real injustice in any stratification of society based solely on inheritance.

But it was a great and dangerous leap from the recognition of this reality to the assumption that heredity was of no importance at all in the molding of the human personality. The fact that its effects were capricious, unpredictable, and incomprehensible did not mean that they were negligible. On the contrary, a great deal of what the newborn child was destined to be was plainly written into it before its birth. It was simply not true that all were born essentially alike, with similar capacities, inclinations, aptitudes, and traits of character, and that the development of the child as a person and a citizen would depend exclusively or overwhelmingly on the educational influences to which it would be subject. Things were not that simple. The genes played many tricks.

Certainly, the environmental influences were important. The parent, the teacher, the role model, the superintendent, or the schoolmaster: these might be the co-sculptors of the mature personality—the co-sculptors upon whose talents and insights a great deal of the ultimate product would depend. But the material upon which it was given to these co-sculptors to work was prescribed by nature—by inheritance. They could not change it. And, as with every material that was to be sculpted, what could be done to it was bound to depend upon its very nature. There were some things you could make out of ivory. There were others you could make out of wood. But they were not the same things. And in some instances nature, in the creation of the material, had already itself done the greater part of the sculpting.

In short, each of these formative influences, heredity and environment, was important. To obtain a valuable product, both were necessary. The sculpting had to be good; but so did the material. You could not make a good product out of bad or unsuitable material. Yet even the best material could be ruined by unskillful and untalented treatment. What came out in the end was bound to be the result of the interaction of the two factors.

One word more, before we leave these comments on heredity and environment.

We are told by the scientists that human qualities could be artificially shaped by scientific manipulation of the human genes. Something of this sort seems now to be being done in respect to plants and animals. Similar things, we are told, could be done in the case of humans.

Let us fervently hope that this possibility will never be exploited. Just because something is technically possible is not in itself a reason why it should be attempted. The scientists or technicians who would be applying themselves to this task would themselves be the products of the very sorts of genes they would be undertaking to manipulate. Is it to be supposed that the created could be better than the creator?

There are two things human beings should never attempt to bring under their control. One is the weather; the other is heredity. No one who deplores the many bones of contention that divide the human community today, with all the attendant wars and other kinds of beastliness with which people conduct these conflicts, could ever wish upon society the further ones that would develop if ever men were to venture into these forbidden areas. Nature, left with the control of these processes, may at times seem senseless and capricious in the exercise of her powers. But there is at least the saving grace that human beings cannot blame one another when they deplore the results.

The wisdom of the ages has pointed on many occasions, ever since the creation of the legend of Pandora's box, to the dangers of excessive curiosity about mysteries men were clearly never intended to explore. We have already created, with the splitting of the atom, dangers for ourselves and our progeny that are very close to being beyond our control. Let us, for the sake of the future of our children and indeed of our kind generally, finally agree that there are certain stones better left unturned and that, when it comes to the human species, heredity is one of them.

Chance and Mortality

Before we leave the subject of the various limitations on the ability of the human individual to achieve complete self-fulfillment in this world, there is one other such limitation that should not escape our attention. This is the inevitable element of tragedy that attends the life of every individual in the form of the blows administered to him by his own mortality and that of others, and by the crueler vagaries of chance. In the face of these adversities, no one is invulnerable.

There are, to begin with, the accidents of illness. One person, even sometimes the innocent child, is killed or tortured by illness. Another one is not.

There are the various forms of accident—hosts of them, sometimes even fatal, sometimes crippling. Chance, not justice, decides who is overtaken by any of them and who is not.

There is the phenomenon of old age—of declining powers—the humiliation of becoming, in later years, a mere caricature of one's earlier self.

Above all, there is the unavoidable phenomenon of bereavement: the fact that those who are loved do not usually die when the one who loves them dies, so one or the other is normally left in the end in loneliness and deprivation, in spiritual impoverishment, sometimes in at least temporary impairment of the ability to respond to life's challenges.

These things, too, have to be taken into consideration when we reflect on the human predicament. They differ from the contradictions in man's nature that were discussed earlier in this chapter—differ in the sense that whereas in the operation of those other contradictions the individual was an active (if never decisive) partner, the blows just mentioned are ones wholly beyond his control. They do present a further series of tragic limitations on the individual's prospects for happiness in this life. And they do stand as evidence for something that the Marxists and the other materialists appear never to have recognized: namely, that a measure of tragedy is built into the very existence of the human individual; and it is not to be overcome by even the most drastic human interventions into the economic or social relationships among individuals,

How, then, does one come to terms with so grim a state of affairs?

If I had to offer my own short personal answer to this question, it would be: "only by faith." But to leave the answer at that would not be enough. I recognize the obligation to spell out the meaning of the term "faith," as I experience it, at somewhat greater length. For it lies at the heart of a great deal more that will have to be talked about on these pages.

Chapter Two

FAITH

I sing the progresse of a deathlesse soule,
Whom Fate, which God made, but doth not controule,
Plac'd in most shapes; . . .
—John Donne, *Metempsychosis*

There may be some, I suppose, who will say, Why, these limitations you have been talking about, these imperfections and contradictions in the nature and situation of the human individual—these are merely expressions of "original sin," of the ineradicable taint imposed upon all future humanity by the disobedience of Adam and Eve in their tasting of the forbidden fruit that offered the knowledge of good and evil.

This is a thesis I cannot accept. Whatever else might be attributable to original sin, the limitations I have been discussing are not. They consist, for the most part, of the conflict between two sides of man's nature. One of these he inherited from the animals along with his physiological nature. It was something that had existed long before there was any *genus humanum* to experience its influence.

The Emergence of the Soul

In the case of the other side—the spiritual side—of his nature, things are of course more complicated. There must have been a crucial time in the development of the human race when men were subject to a change that none of the other animals experienced. The nature of this change is difficult to describe. I can only say that there evidently developed in man at this point a capacity for self-awareness, for self-scrutiny, and for consciousness of the moral qualities of his own behavior, and indeed a certain ability to perceive and to hold in mind the distinctions between right and wrong. None of these qualities were present in the beasts, of which man had been one up to that time. None are present in the beasts today—at least not in any degree comparable to that of the development of man. If the passages in the biblical account about the tree of the knowledge of right and wrong were taken only symbolically and not literally, there might indeed be said to be some connection between the concept of original sin and what I have been discussing. But it would be at best a faint and partial connection. Not for a moment could I concede that the limitations I have pointed to are the expression of some congenital moral delinquency in man's makeup—a taint imposed upon him in perpetuity by the transgression of remote ancestors. Modern man was not his own creator. What he is, in large part, is what he was created, by the hand of whoever created the physical universe, to be. He cannot change it. He can only make the best of it. And in that effort to make the best of it there lies most of the drama, the tragedy, and the glory of civilized life.

One must not, of course, be too dogmatic about this change in man's nature and the distinction it created between man and the other animals. It had no neat and clear parameters. It must have been a very gradual change; perhaps in some respects it is still in progress. It certainly affected people in varying degrees and at different times. But its significance was not diminished by this lack of tidy limits. And this significance was overwhelming. It would seem to me to have been the greatest single thing that ever happened to humanity.

And the fact that this change did occur is, to me, extraordinary to the point of mystery. Why to man and to none of the other animals? Here, if anywhere, one senses the intervention of a divine hand. For what was happening was, in effect, the birth of the human soul; and for this I, at any rate, am unable to perceive any purely physiological cause.

This is, perhaps, as good a point as any other for recording my own conviction that the soul has an existence wholly separate from that of the body. It has its seat, of course, in the body—is in one sense the prisoner of the body so long as the latter is alive. But it is not of the same substance as the body. And this being the case, there is no reason why it should share the body's mortality. Whether it had an existence before the body did; whether it inhabits, over the ages, only a single body; or what becomes of it when the death of the body has deprived it of this particular habitation: these are the mysteries, obviously not for men to solve. But that the soul is something more than the body it inhabits seems to me unchallengeable.

There is a point, at the end of the Russian Orthodox funeral service, when the casket has just been closed and the body is being carried out of the church, where the choir, in one of those magnificent musical passages that are the glory of the Orthodox service, "sings" the immortal soul out of the now lifeless body and frees it for the pursuit of its passage to whatever awaits it in the afterlife. This image rests, in my mind, on a profound insight—an insight derived from the heart and not from the head. I accept it unquestionably.

This is not just a matter of faith. I have seen (and I am surely not alone in this observation) manifestations of love and concern for others on the part of elderly people, themselves sick and near death, for which no conceivable physical processes in the body could have provided the motivation. This same reality becomes evident wherever real, outgoing love for others, self-denying and self-sacrificing, makes itself felt in human affairs. It is clear that man does not, indeed, live by bread alone, or exclusively by those bodily functions and reactions that bread sustains. There is plainly something else there for the existence of which the body alone provides no explanation.

Let this affirmation of belief in the soul's uniqueness and independence, as something wholly distinct from the physical frame it inhabits, serve as a suitable point of departure for an inquiry, so far as this writer is capable of such a thing, into matters of faith.

A Personal Creed

I regard myself, if anyone wants to know, as a Christian, although there are certainly others who would question my right to that status. Even from the standpoint of the purely secular historian, untouched by any question of his own faith, I would find the appearance of such a figure as Christ on this earth, at the place and the time of which history informs us, a most remarkable occurrence, bordering on the miraculous. The striking nature of his conflict with the Jewish religious establishment of his time; the impressive and startlingly realistic touches in the accounts of his death; the unmistakable profundity of his belief in his own filial relationship to God; and finally, many of the statements imputed to him in the various Gospels—statements destined to affect the lives of large portions of the Western world for some two thousand years into the future: these alone should suffice to persuade the skeptical historian that Christ's passage across the face of world history was an event of extraordinary significance. But on top of all this, there are the evidences of the profound impression his person seems to have made, quite independently of the various miracles, on people of that day. The Gospels are full of such evidences. They are borne out by the endurance and acceptance of these impressions in the decades immediately following his death. I personally find their most striking reflection in these words of Saint John the Evangelist: "And the Word was made flesh, and dwelt among us, and we beheld his glory, the glory as of the only begotten of the Father, full of grace and truth." Nothing in the remainder of the Gospel of Saint John would suggest that these words (aside from giving us, in the King James Version, one of the most beautiful sentences in the English language) were anything other than a faithful description by some serious and observant contemporary (there is much uncertainty about who this really was) of the impression the memory of Jesus was still capable of making on people of a time some forty years after his death.

But it is not on any of those observations that my own religious feeling is based. Nor should it have been. Christ himself would have been the first to maintain, I suspect, that calculations of that sort were wholly inadequate to any serious religious conviction. What he asked for was faith; and I am glad to give it: faith in the man himself, as Christ's image has come down to us in the understanding, perhaps even in the creative intuition and imagination, of people of later ages—faith in the silent suffering Christ who, when Herod questioned him, "answered him nothing"; faith in the equally silent Christ who, in the imagination of Dostoyevski, responded by a kiss of forgiveness to the vainglorious and cynical visions of the Great Inquisitor; faith in the Christ whose own faith was so real and so human that he could find, in his agony, no other final words than a call for forgiveness for his executioners and torturers ("for they know not what they do") and, at last, the desperate and oh-so-human words "My God, my God, why hast thou forsaken me?"

For the belief in this man I need, then, no historical evidence or explication. Faith suffices. But does this faith make me a good Christian? Many, I suspect, would deny that it does. For I have great difficulty in reconciling the figure of the almighty God, the presumed creator of our universe, with that of the supposedly loving and benevolent God to whom we are taught to pray. This latter God was presented to us, after all, as a compassionate one, aware of our problems, concerned for our success in meeting them, prepared to help us to the extent that we were prepared to accept his help. But how would this image fit with the all-powerful God who, if he was truly the creator of our world, must have included in his creation, along with the phenomenon man, the very handicaps—the fractured state and the tragic burdens—with which, as we have seen, that phenomenon is so sorely encumbered?

I can make this point clearer, perhaps, by explaining that I can perceive, on the map of my cosmology, two discrete and quite dissimi-lar features, between which I can find no unity.

The Primary Cause

One of these features is what I might call the Primary Cause of the universe. It is this, as I see it, that brought into being the universe we partially know, with all those qualities the scientists are beginning to recognize in it. Such image as we are able to form of this universe is incomplete, and can, of course, never be otherwise. However persist-ently we pursue it, it inevitably recedes at some point into the unfath-omable recesses of infinity—infinity in time or space or (since they may be the same thing) both. These recesses defy not only our knowl-edge and our powers of comprehension but even our powers of con-ception, of imagination, and of language. And any view of the origin of the universe consists, for this reason, not of any definable or imagin-able object but rather of an assumption—the assumption of the exis-tence of something we cannot see, will never see, and were presumably never meant to see.

It was this Primary Cause, one must suppose, that not only created the Big Bang or whatever it was that brought the universe into exis-tence but also created whatever caused *that,* and so, farther and farther back, as far as you will, as far as imagination stretches, into the forbid-den and impenetrable recesses of infinity to which I have just referred.

Now, whatever else may be said about this Primary Cause, I am most reluctant to believe that it, in fashioning this universe and subject-ing it to the rather relentless laws by which its further development seems to have been governed, was greatly concerned about the well-being of so infinitesimally tiny, remote, and transitory a feature of it as the passage across the face of one of its multitudes of planets, at a time some untold trillions of years *then* in the future, of a curious animal species known to itself as mankind. What we know of the process by which the universe has developed suggests to me nothing whatsoever in the nature of such a concern on the part of its creator. It suggests rather, so far as we are concerned, the prevalence on that creator's part of a supreme and very natural indifference. The Primary Cause must, after all, have had a great many other things to think about. There was at that time, or so we must suppose, nothing remotely resembling a human being for the Primary Cause to have in mind.[1]

Even less plausible is the suggestion that this Primary Cause, having created such an order and laid down the laws of its development, should, in response to the prayers of creatures such as ourselves, interfere currently, on a day-to-day basis, and in greatest detail, in the working of those laws, thus vitiating the very concept that lay behind them. There are other ways, and other agencies, by which certain kinds of human prayers can, in my view, be responded to; and to these we shall turn shortly. But we must concede to the Primary Cause a greater seriousness, and a greater consistency of design and execution, than would be compatible with the suggestion that all of the multitudinous details of our lives are subject, day by day, to its benevolent attention, and are shaped individually, without reference to the rest of the grand design, by its whims of the moment.

Hence my conclusions as to the nature of the Primary Cause. Almighty? Yes, presumably, so far as this physical universe is concerned. Benevolent? Unproven and most unlikely. And certainly not identifi-

1. I was amused, some time after writing the above, to come across in Page Smith's biography of John Adams (Garden City, N.Y.: Doubleday, 1962), 1:29, the following paragraph, dealing with the residence of the young Adams in Worcester, Massachusetts:

There were few if any in Worcester to dispute such a formulation. The debate came over whether God was an active force in the universe, directing and superintending the operation of His natural laws and the particular destinies of men, or whether, as the Deists argued, He was simply the designer and builder of the universe—the "First Cause," the Prime Mover, who, having put together a system of infinite complexity, wound it up, so to speak, and left it to run by the mechanical principles which He had devised for its proper functioning. This view, moreover, left in doubt, if it did not entirely banish, any concept of life after death, or a future state of punishments and rewards. John Adams was as determined to hold to the reality of a personal God and life beyond death as he was to eschew Calvinism's insistence on predestination, infant damnation, election, and other tenets held in strictest observance by his Braintree forebears.

able as a person, with a human gender and a human appearance, in whose image we could possibly have been created.

Such reflections are, I know, far from being original with this writer. Henry Adams, after watching the painful death (from tetanus) of a greatly beloved elder sister, rejected the very idea that any personal Deity could "find pleasure or profit . . . in inflicting this torture upon a poor woman." For pure blasphemy, this, he wrote, "made pure atheism a comfort. God might be, as the Church said, a Substance, but He could not be a Person."[2]

The Merciful Deity

Let me then turn to the other of the two features which, as I said, stand out on the map of my cosmology. I spoke above of what seems to me to be the miracle of the emergence in the human species, at some point in its development, of something that we can only call the human soul. It has been there ever since, in at least a good part of humanity. I see it not only as a sort of self-awareness that was not present in the animal, but also as the emergence in individual man of a certain moral autonomy—an ability to make choices and to design, within the limits of his mortality and his semi-animalistic nature, his own path. With that ability there came, of course, a commensurate measure of moral responsibility, unknown to the purely animalistic species. This sense of responsibility was in conflict with the purely animalistic aspects of the human personality; and so bitter was this conflict, so irreconcilable were the two within the confines of a single human frame, that the individual needed outside help, which could only be the help of faith, to make it endurable.

Simultaneously with the emergence of the soul there seems to me to have become evident the existence, and the involvement with human life, of a Deity of another sort—not the Primary Cause, this time, but something quite different: a Deity filled with understanding and compassion for the agonies inflicted on man by the conflict between his two

2. *The Education of Henry Adams* (New York: Modern Library, 1931), p. 289.

natures, unable, to be sure, to spare him the realities of the animalistic one, but ready to help him, and capable of helping him, to come to terms with it. The Deity could do this only by becoming a part of man's consciousness, by giving him an awareness of the divine presence, and by rendering him capable of the act of faith. We can only conclude that this Deity, if not indeed the creator of the innovation in man's nature called the soul, was and is the companion to it—in this case the loving and caring companion, as the Primary Cause was not, and more than the companion: a part of the human person itself, sharing in its trials and dilemmas, and lending the strength necessary for their endurance.

There are, of course, a number of ways in which this Deity may be conceived. The customary one in Christian Scripture is the paternal image—"Our Father which art in heaven . . ."—to which countless millions of us have prayed. To many in the Middle Ages it was largely, if not entirely, the maternal imagine—the Virgin, the Mother of God—to which, in the first instance, faith was directed. I am not sure that these differences are important. Perhaps the Deity is to each person what that person most needs, and what he or she conceives it as being.

I, in any case, conceive it as a Substance, a Spirit, as Jesus himself is said once to have described it.[3] It is essentially what is referred to in the Nicene Creed as "the Holy Spirit, the Lord, the Giver of Life." But what, to me, distinguishes this Spirit from the all-powerful Deity of established Christian doctrine is precisely the fact that the Spirit bears, in my view, no responsibility for the natural order of things in which the human individual is compelled to live. It regards that order as a "given" factor in the defining of the human predicament—as one of the inalterable terms of the human problem; and it starts from there in the search for a response to that problem.[4] The problem itself, then, is

3. John 4:24.
4. I am reminded of General George Marshall's injunction to those of us who worked under him: "Don't fight the problem." By this he meant, I am sure; Identify those terms of the problem that are not "given"—that are susceptible to being affected by your action; address your efforts to them and do not waste time or energy struggling against those that constitute the very structure of the problem.

reduced to the question of how, within the framework of a natural order already established, the individual is to conduct himself in a manner consistent with the divine purpose. It is here that the intercession of the Spirit occurs, here that it is required, and here, when suitably asked for, that it will, in my deepest conviction, be forthcoming. For the Spirit is not, as I sense it and conceive it, some distant and all-powerful authority, standing wholly outside our predicament and disposing autocratically over all the factors affecting our lives. It is rather a participant in our struggle—a Spirit infused with understanding of and sympathy for our situation, involved as we are in the conflict between our physical and our spiritual natures, and prepared to give us such assistance as we deserve and can accept.

The Divine Injunction

And what might this assistance consist of?

I know of no way to make clear my idea of the answer to that question other than by recording what I seem to hear the Spirit saying to me as I turn to it for help: I, the Spirit says,

am a part of you. I am partly outside you, but also partly within you.[5] I am, of course, not all that is within you. There is also your physical frame, which confronts you with both limits and demands. To some extent these limits and demands are imperative, flowing as they do from the natural order. I did not create this order, and I cannot spare you the necessity of coming to terms with it. I can only help you to live under its shadow, and to a degree under its discipline, but to do this without sacrificing too much of the other side of your nature.

In all of this I can help you, of course, only in the degree that you would welcome the help and put forward your best effort to help yourself. It is in fact you who, by the dimensions of your own effort, define the limits of my usefulness.

5. Note Christ's words to the Pharisees (Luke 17:20–21): "The kingdom of God cometh not with observation. Neither shall they say, Lo here! or lo there! for behold, the kingdom of God is within you."

And what help can I bring? I can bring, first and foremost, understanding. Remember that I, being a part of you, am a fellow sufferer in the face of your vicissitudes. I know the way you take. I know the progress. I also know the failure and reverses. I suffer from these latter just as you do. What I can give you is the awareness that in the most bitter struggles you are not alone.

I can also give you understanding and, to the extent that you deserve it, compassion. Where you do not deserve it (and there are such instances), you will not receive it; for it could then be of no help to you.

Finally, I can give you a certain strength that you, alone, do not and could not possess. For I am stronger than you are. You, in your present incarnation, are timebound and, in part, fleshbound. I am neither. Your efforts, without me, would be limited by your mortality. With my help, they can extend beyond that.

Not all of this will be entirely intelligible to you. Some of it will have to be taken on faith. Indeed, it is offered on the assumption that faith is forthcoming. It is important for you to recognize that, notwithstanding all the preoccupation with the scientific probing of nature that dominates the society of your time, life still has its mysteries (your own identity is one). Some of your hope must lie in your readiness to allow for the reality and the power of these mysteries. Recognize, then, that you were not meant to understand everything; and have the modesty to accept the limits that implies. Do what you can. Leave the rest to faith.

Such, then, is the moral instruction I fancy myself to receive from the Spirit whose nearness to me, and partial presence within me, I so clearly sense. It differs little, I suspect, from that which my father derived from his repeated reading of the Bible. The principal deviation would have been that from the Book of Job (his favorite work of Scripture) he presumably accepted the admonition to regard the ways of God, however inscrutable, as not to be questioned—even in their cruelest and most incomprehensible manifestations (of which he himself experienced no small number). In respecting this admonition he was, of course, accepting the identification of the Primary Cause with the loving and caring God in which so many of us have been taught to believe. This I find it difficult to do. And if this, in the eyes of some, be blasphemy, I would ask it to be noted that in denying to the Primary Cause the quality of being a caring and merciful father to us all, and in charging it with nothing more reprehensible than indifference, I am also absolving it of the charge, to which it might be otherwise vulnerable, of being a capricious and unfeeling tyrant.[6] At the same time, I am absolving the merciful and beneficent Deity in which I do believe from the onus of creating as heartless and relentless a physical environmental as that in which human life is obliged to exist.

The Church

What I have described above is, of course, a purely personal view of a religious commitment. It purports to define the relationship of a single individual, alone and unaided, to the questions of faith. There will no doubt be readers who will say, Yes, but where do organized religion and the religious community come in? What about religion as a bond among large numbers of believers? What, in short, about the church?

To those questions I can only say this:

I am well aware that for the vast majority of believers the manifestation of faith has been a collective, organized effort, normally put forward under the sort of leadership we have in mind when we use the word "church." And I think I understand the very good reasons why this is so. Among them are the strengthening of the religious commitment by association with others in its various manifestations; the need of a great many people for an external spiritual discipline; the need for authoritative explication of the respective faith by persons schooled in the understanding of it; the need for discipline in personal behavior as in worship; the need for the performance of the sacraments by persons whose own professional-religious commitment gives them the stature and authority to fulfill this function; the value of the symbolism involved in organized worship; and so forth. I can understand that there

---

6. I am reminded, here, of Gibbon's disgust with the Ascetics, whom he saw as inspired "by the savage enthusiasm which represents man as a criminal and God as a tyrant." See Gibbon, *Decline and Fall of the Roman Empire,* chap. 38.

are a great many people who are not entirely clear in their own minds what it is that they believe, or to what it commits them, and who need the sort of leadership and support only the church can give them.

I do not regard myself as being above these needs. I, too, welcome the chance to affirm my faith among numbers of others. I, too, welcome particularly the acceptance, implicit or explicit in most Christian rituals, of the equality of all naked human souls in the eyes of God. I, too, welcome the opportunity to participate in that acceptance by kneeling, together with anyone else who consents to kneel with similar humbleness, before the various symbols of faith. I find in this last, as do so many other people, support in the exercise of humility, which I regard as perhaps the greatest, certainly the closest to uniqueness, of the Christian virtues. So I do not view myself as being in any way above the need for much of what organized religion has to offer.

Nor do I have any negative feelings toward any of the great branches of the Christian church. I see greatness in them all. No one, in this respect, could be more ecumenical than myself.

I admire the Russian Orthodox church for the profound emotional depth of its religiosity; for its ready acceptance of the mysteries of faith; for the solemnity of its service and the great beauty of its ritual and its music. I see in it the nearest thing (except perhaps the Armenian church) to early Christianity.

For the Roman Catholic church I have feelings (at this point some of my ancestors will turn over in their graves) of high respect and, in some instances, of admiration. I respect it for many of its qualities: for its grandeur in scope and concept; for its very catholicity; for its paternal understanding for the needs of humble people everywhere; for its recognition of the values of order, and even hierarchy, in the spiritual guidance of great masses of people; for the commitment it demands of its own priests and other servants; for the rich and comforting intimacy it encourages, through the confessional, between saint and sinner. I respect it, too, for its part in the tremendous cultural advances of earlier ages—the great art and architecture, the religious music and literature, that have grown up through it and around it. It surely deserves to be seen as one of the greatest institutions of Western culture. And much of this goes as well for some of its partially rebellious children—outstandingly, the Church of England.

I do not omit, in this listing, that major component of the Christian faith that takes its departure from the Jewish religious culture in which Christ's own life, albeit partly in a dissident posture, was rooted. How could I? Many of the elements of Old Testament faith and wisdom (I think particularly of the Books of Job, Proverbs, and Isaiah) are too much a part of Christianity itself, and especially of the faith of my Protestant forefathers, for me to deny my own debt to them. I recognize, in other words, in the origins of the Jewish faith of our own time, a very considerable part of the origins of my own.

I look, finally, sometimes with amusement and exasperation but never without deepest reverence and even emotional involvement, at the religious ways and convictions of my Protestant ancestors—Presbyterians, for the most part—at the simplicity and, in some respects, the purity of their commitment, and at their readiness to accept the utmost personal responsibility in the enactment of it. I can see how the sterner challenges of nature in the northern latitudes of Europe threw them back upon themselves—and how their own efforts bred in them certain qualities of independence and self-reliance, made them resistant to the authority of great, distant, and, as they saw it, more worldly spiritual powers, and moved them to see their relationship to God in their own way.

I can idealize none of these great ecclesiastical establishments. For all their greatness, they were and are intensely human institutions. I can see in all of them at one point or another manifestations of bigotry, intolerance, narrowness, sometimes even cruelty—manifestations that certainly had no place in Christ's original teachings. But I also see them all as leading institutions of Western civilization and accept them all in the spirit of Christ's reminder that there were, in his Father's house, "many mansions." I am grateful to the several of them that have given me, over the course of a life so largely itinerant as my own, their hospitality and have allowed me to share in their worship even when I could not fully share the form of their commitment.

I recall that my father once expressed to me (in a letter, I believe) in his old age the hope that, whatever life might still bring, I would always continue to go to church. I detect, in retrospect, a certain desperation in that appeal. He sensed, I am sure, the advance of a more skeptical and secular spirit, particularly among the youth. And the church meant so much to him. It was, in those dark final years, all he had to hang on to—the sole and final repository of hope in a life that otherwise offered little sustenance for it. He thought that someday it would be the same with me. I have respected his wish, wherever I thought I could, in the ensuing decades.

Nevertheless, all of that being said, the problem of religious faith has remained, for me, essentially an individual one: the effort of a single man to establish his relationship to forces beyond the reach of his own rational perception—forces upon the interaction with which he knew the ultimate value of his own life to depend.

Ethics

There remains one matter to mention before we leave the questions of faith. That is the subject of ethics.

The word "ethics" has a number of meanings; and since certain of those meanings are related both to philosophy and to faith, this is probably the proper place to consider them.

If the term "ethics" is taken to mean a system of ideal values purporting to be applicable to the conduct of men everywhere and in all times, then the discussion of it has no place in this book. To me there are no such things as abstract and universally applicable rules of ethics. There are certain qualities—notably, courage and loyalty—which, when taken in the crudest sense, the chauvinists of almost any country or society would readily claim as their own virtues. But both of those terms have broad spectra of meanings. Courage can be moral courage; it can also be physical recklessness. It can be the courage of terrorists and assassins. Similarly, there can be loyalties to flashy dictators, to fellow conspirators, and to criminal associates. But there can also be loyalties to standards, to values, to families and friends, to professional associates, to institutions. These are, in short, generally regarded as ethically admirable qualities; but their cultivation can and does take forms many of us would find it shameful to be sharing.

In large part, of course, what most of us would regard as ethically commendable values and virtues are culturally and sometimes religiously conditioned—culturally, even by those who are scarcely conscious of their own cultural inheritance; and religiously, even by those who would scoff at the mere suggestion that religion had anything to do with their reactions. I would attribute my own ethical values, for example, very prominently to the cultural-religious climate, inherited from long lines of Scottish and English ancestors, in which I was raised. And very ordinary values they would be, if one set out to list them—ordinary to the point of banality. They would include, in the outward sense, such things as generosity, kindness, courtesy, understanding, patience, and certain kinds of loyalty. In the inward sense they would include such things as modesty, self-control, self-discipline, sensitivity to the dictates of conscience, awareness of one's own imperfections and the effort to struggle against them, humbleness in the face of one's failures, and, finally, willingness to accept the trivia of life and to deal with them in the manner least offensive and least annoying to others. These are ethical commitments shared to one extent or another by a great many other people. But they will serve to illustrate what I deeply believe to be true: that the ethical values accepted and cultivated by the individual, aside from being partly culturally conditioned, are an intensely personal matter. They are in essence the subject of the individual struggle with the two conflicting sides of man's nature, as described in the first chapter. This is a struggle in which, despite occasional setbacks, one can at times have the feeling of holding one's own, but in which there can be—for most of us, at any rate—no sensational triumphs. I am glad to say that, looking about me within the circle of my own friends, I have the impression that most of them (and this is the source of my affection for them) seem, in the face of these problems, to be doing their best. I would hope that the same might be said of myself.

Chapter Three

ON GOVERNMENT
AND GOVERNMENTS

> Cromwell, I charge thee, fling away ambition;
> By that sin fell the angels; how can man then,
> The image of his maker, hope to win by't?
> —Shakespeare, *Henry VIII*

The Necessity

Government is a universal feature of civilized life. Whatever the form
it takes, however liberal or oppressive it may be, however large or
small the community to which its power extends, government is an
absolute necessity. Its adoption or acceptance is not, therefore, a matter
of deliberate choice. The only conceivable alternative would be a state
of anarchy which would constitute self-destruction for the community
in question—which is, in effect, no choice at all.

Now, it is only where choice is involved that the question of morality enters into human action. Thus the institution of government bears,
in essence, no moral quality. It could be said to be morally neutral.[1]

---

1. Again, after writing the above lines (which I have left unchanged), I was startled to come
across, in Sebastian de Grazia's excellent *Machiavelli in Hell* (New York: Harvester Wheat-

And the same could be said of most of the functions served by a national government: such functions, for example, as the maintenance of law and order, the external representation and defense of a national community, or the concern for its health and welfare, the administration of justice, and the regulation of competing and conflicting economic interests. These, too, are necessities, in their way—necessities that have to be served, whether one likes it or not. They are, for the most part, rather sad necessities, flowing from the inability of men to govern themselves individually in a manner compatible with the interests of the entire community. But necessities they remain.

Government has no need to make excuses for the fact that its functions are so largely riveted to these rather uninspiring purposes. Precisely because these services are necessary, they are useful and morally acceptable. But what this *does* mean is that government, while worthy of respect, should not be idealized. It is simply not the channel through which men's noblest impulses are to be realized. Its task, on the contrary, is largely to see to it that the ignoble ones are kept under restraint and not permitted to go too far.

Efforts may be made, from time to time, by individual politicians or statesmen to use government (or to pretend to use it) for the achievement of what appear to be glorious ideals. But then the uses to which they are professing to put it are ones not inherent in its basic purposes. They usually lend themselves poorly to such exploitation. And the motives for their employment cannot be seen as admirable.

Government deserves to be valued and respected, in short, for what it is, and sometimes, when it is at its best, even admired for the manner in which it performs its essential tasks. But the tasks themselves are uninspiring ones; and the service it renders to their completion can scarcely be more glorious than the ends they are intended to serve. The

sheaf, 1989), p. 76, the following passage: "Another passage in the *Discourses* approaches the question of morality more generally: 'Men act either out of necessity or out of choice.' Without pausing for nuances in such an assertion, we may simply recall that it fits the position of both Aristotle and Augustine that only with choice can an act be moral."

people who want government's head to be in the clouds should remember that its feet are mired, understandably but inevitably, in the clay.

The Power-Hungry Individual

In addition to the uninspiring nature of its basic origin, there is another quality of all government that serves in no small degree to restrict the hopes and enthusiasms it deserves to attract. It is this: government always implies and involves power. No government is without it. No government *can* be without it. It is government's most essential attribute. It lies in the very definition of government that it represents the greatest center of power in any national community.

Now, power is not, in truth, a nice thing. It is very heady stuff. It engenders an excitement which, like some radioactive field, infuses the entire atmosphere in and around any place where it is centered. It is probably not too much to say that all those who become involved with the power of government, whether in the competition for its acquisition or in the enjoyment of it when once acquired, are affected by this excitement, usually quite severely and never very attractively. We saw, in the first chapter of these reflections, how vulnerable is the self-regard of the individual to inflation by the enjoyment, or the prospect of the enjoyment, of a position of authority and superiority vis-à-vis others. It is here, in and around government, in the competition for just such a position and the enjoyment of it, once attained, that the human ego becomes most deeply and helplessly engaged. And it is idle to attempt to measure whether the effect of this is greater upon those who are involved in the competition for political power (which we call politics) or upon those who already enjoy its delights, brief or precarious as these may be. In either case, it inflicts upon those involved in it a peculiar species of agitation, unlike any other—an agitation that distorts not only the person itself but sometimes the entire pattern of external personal relationships.

Particularly dense, of course, is this atmosphere in the immediate proximity of those individuals who occupy, personally, the highest pinnacles of power. I have seen, and I am sure others have, individuals who show signs of a real intoxication of the spirit simply from being in the physical proximity of persons of high office. Anyone who has ever had to talk personally with great heads of state, even without aspiring to any share of their power, knows how hard it is to avoid falling under the spell of the aura in which their persons are enveloped. This will be confirmed by anyone who has had the experience of trying to say to an exalted personage, be it president or crowned head or mighty dictator, things one suspects beforehand that he or she will not want to hear. One is deterred by the feeling that to do this would be an encroachment not only on the dignity of the person but on that of the office as well.

But this, of course, is only an extreme case. The excitement of power envelops the entire entourage, and even the would-be entourage, of great authority. It inflicts, I repeat, a form of distortion of personality that affects not only values but also relationships. It was from experience in government, and not from Henry Adams, that the writer of these lines first gained his appreciation for this distortion; but no one, to his knowledge, has ever described it better than did Adams, in his intellectual autobiography.[2] "The effect of power and publicity on all men," he wrote, "is the aggravation of self, a sort of tumor that ends in killing the victim's sympathies; a diseased appetite, like a passion for drink or perverted tastes; one can scarcely use expressions too strong to describe the violence of egotism it stimulates." And it was Adams, the grandson of one president, great-grandson of another, and a man who throughout his life was exceptionally close to a number of men in power, who pointed out that this distortion of personality affected not only the subject's relations with competitors in the power struggle but also his ulterior friendships. A friend in power, he insisted, was a friend lost.

I write all this not in any spirit of reproach to all who fall under this particular spell. I am aware that many of those who have set out to pursue a good cause have soon been made aware that the cause in

2. *The Education of Henry Adams* (New York: Modern Library, 1931), p. 147.

question could be effectively advanced only from a position of power, and that it was for this reason that they entered, albeit reluctantly, into the competition for its acquisition. I do not blame them for doing so. But that they, once involved in it, remain wholly unaffected by the distorting discipline it exerts, I must be allowed to doubt. In this sense it could perhaps be said, to use a religious simile, that such men have taken upon themselves the burden of sin (in this case, the sin of ambition) in order that the rest of us might be protected in our relative innocence. However that may be, the fascination, the headiness, and the other distorting effects of the possession or the proximity of power, or of involvement in the quest of it, remain, affecting the idealistic as well as the cynical among those who suffer the exposure.

These observations relate not just to the phenomenon of power in government but to power in any organized form, wherever it accumulates in significant measure. Its effects can be observed in business firms, in educational institutions, in private associations, wherever authority exists and wherever it is asserted through hierarchy. Rare is the wielder of authority whose self-regard is not agreeably inflamed by it. I suspect that there are moments when even the most saintly mother superior (and the same would be true of her male counterpart) cannot escape twinges of satisfaction over the authority she exercises and the marks of deference her position arouses in the institution she heads. Such conflicts between the inflamed ego and the conscience are particularly excruciating, of course, where a religious dedication implies commitment to the virtue of humility.[3] In the case of governments, even this restraining commitment is lacking. Here the virtue of humility, pursued beyond a point, can even be a serious obstacle to success.

3. I am reminded, here of an episode recounted (I cannot remember where) involving a Reverend Buckminster, who was pastor of the church, in colonial Massachusetts, of which certain of my ancestors were members. The pastor was addressed by one of his flock, on a certain occasion, in terms that he felt were insufficiently respectful of his ecclesiastical dignity, and he put to the man the colonial counterpart of what today would be the question "Who do you think you are talking to?" When the answer came back—"To a poor worm of the dust, like myself"—the pastor, burying his face in his hands, is said to have replied, "Ah, I know it, I know it."

This being so, it must be recognized as one of the uniformities embracing all governments, democratic and otherwise, that they attract to themselves, and function within, an atmosphere of inflamed ambitions, rivalries, sensitivities, anxieties, suspicions, embarrassments, and resentments which, to put it mildly, seldom, if ever, bring out the best in the personalities involved, and sometimes provoke the worst. Government, in short, is, for unavoidable and compelling reasons, an unpleasant business. It cannot be otherwise. And we find in this fact another reason why, whatever else one may think of government, it should not be idealized. Its doings are something that should be viewed by the outsider only with a sigh for its unquestionable necessity, and by the participant only with a prayer for forgiveness for the many moral ambiguities it requires him to accept and for the distortions of personality it inflicts upon him.

The Political Clique

What has been spoken of above had relation only to the reactions and tendencies of individuals involved in the governmental process. But there is also something to be noted in connection with the similar role and behavior of political groupings. The competition for power is conducted not just by individuals acting in loneliness but more often, and for very good reason, by groups of persons pooling their efforts at least momentarily with a view to achieving positions of dominant influence. Groups thus motivated will be found in the vicinity of the power center of every political regime, authoritarian or democratic. Wherever the dominant personality in the regime is a very strong one, possessing in one degree or another dictatorial powers and able to act largely independently in the selection of his ministers and other assistants, the efforts of these competing groups will normally be directed to the cultivation of his favor. In more democratically organized regimes, particularly in parliamentary systems where political parties play a dominant role and where political advancement is possible only through their mediation, the competition of groups of persons for power takes place, in the first instance, primarily through the inner-party struggle. It is only when this struggle has produced its winners, when intraparty leadership has been established, and when the party has succeeded in capturing the dominant strategic position in government, that an inner group, comprising normally only a tiny elite of the party, emerges at or near the center of power. Here this group will be found to be bringing to expression a wide variety of motivations, including the individual political ambitions of its various members; the interests of the group as such; the interests of the party; and finally, no doubt, such of the national interests as do not conflict too sharply with any of these more burning incentives. One will almost always find at or near every center of power, democratic or authoritarian (and here is where the uniformity comes in) a single group of this nature, momentarily successful, installed (however precariously) in the positions of influence to which it has aspired, and controlling most, if not all, of the instrumentalities of power. It is this, as a rule, that we have in mind when we refer to a "regime."

I stress the words "momentarily successful" and "however precariously." No regime lasts forever. Human mortality assures this even when the hazards and vicissitudes of political life do not. In this sense all political regimes are only temporary occupants of the heights of power to which they have climbed. None is entirely secure. None lives in a complete political vacuum. The heights each occupies always become, sooner or later, a besieged fortress. Every one of them is confronted by others anxious and striving to occupy those heights in its place. And awareness of this fact is what causes each of them, whether brought into power by democratic processes or by other ones, to constitute to some extent, psychologically, a conspiracy against all that lies outside its own ranks and presents a real or potential threat to its power. This last can mean, in the case of the dictatorship, the mass of the population, and particularly the better-educated and politically active parts of it. In the democracy, it will include not just the overt political opposition but all those elements that are susceptible to influence by the opposition.

Government's Two Voices

In the calculations of every regime, of course, the interests of the populace, as a whole, or what the regime conceives to be these interests, play some part. In the case of the democracy, it will be largely a legislative body that is supposed to reflect those interests, and to the demands and reactions of which the regime is supposed to give heed; but there will also be the press, the media, and the opinion polls. Even in the dictatorship, popular opinion will have to be at least taken into account. (It was, I believe, Machiavelli who once pointed out that the interests of even the most despotic tyrant will always to some extent coincide with those of the people over whom he rules.)

Yet the interests of the populace at large will normally be no more than a secondary consideration for those in power. Closer to the heart of any governing regime will normally be its own political fortunes, actual or potential, in the face of whatever significant internal-political opposition it confronts or fears to confront. However seemingly securely installed at any given moment, a governing regime is always only one of the players in the internal political power game, and never forgets it.

It is important for outsiders to hold this reality in mind when attempting to judge a government by its words and its behavior, including the positions it adopts on international questions. These words and this behavior may, of course, at times reflect, particularly at moments of great national danger, the national interest as the regime sees it. But this will seldom be all that is coming to expression. Along with it there will always be reflected, to one extent or another, the competitive domestic-political interests of whatever group or individual occupies at the moment dominant positions of internal power.

The result is that what one is normally hearing, when one listens to the publicly expressed voice of a government, particularly in matters of foreign affairs, is actually a mixture of two separate voices: on the one hand, the voice of the interests of the entire country, as the regime perceives them, and to the extent it chooses to defer to them; and on the other hand, the voice of a single political faction, deeply concerned to serve its own fortunes in the face of whatever domestic-political competition confronts it and threatens it. Those two voices may at times fully coincide, but they do not usually do so; and there is no reason why they should. This being the case, the experienced statesman or student of international affairs, in attempting to interpret the motives of a government on the basis of its various pronouncements, will always be on the lookout for both of these voices and will judge the significance of what is done or said by the probable predominance, at any point, of the one consideration or the other.

Forms of Government

So much, then, for some of the uniformities that link governmental establishments of all sorts. They stand as evidence that the distinctions among governments are never, or almost never, absolute. There are certain reactions and proclivities (the ones we have just seen are examples) in which all governments, fulfilling what is essentially a common function and faced with similar problems, tend to resemble one another.

But this is not to say that there are not also highly significant differences among governmental systems. And before we turn to these latter, there is one phenomenon which I should like to dispose of and to eliminate from further discussion at this point, for it is of such abnormality that it could only confuse whatever else is said on this general subject.

What I have in mind here is the phenomenon of twentieth-century totalitarianism, as manifested by the Stalinist and Hitlerian regimes of recent memory in the peak years of their atrociousness. These regimes differed in certain essential respects from all the other variations of government that the history of Western civilization has to offer. History provides many examples of highly authoritarian or despotic regimes which proceeded with harshness and cruelty against those who were conceived to have broken their laws or to be endangering or challenging their authority. Where these two truly totalitarian dictatorships differed from the other tyrannies was not only in the sheer dimensions of their cruelties (affecting millions of people, whereas the victims of the others might have run to hundreds or, at the most, thousands) but also, more important, in the fact that the victims of those cruelties were, in overwhelming proportion, the innocent rather than the guilty. Millions of people were persecuted and punished under these regimes for what, by no fault of their own, they *were,* or were thought to be, rather than for what they *did;* or, again, for what they were suspected of thinking, rather than for anything they actually thought or said. In many instances, the motivation for their mistreatment would appear to have lain partly in the calculation that it would serve as a useful form of intimidation for others. It was deemed useful that others should know what *could* happen to you if you incurred the regime's disfavor. And if persecution of the innocent could further that impression, why not? Thus the reason for the abominable cruelties inflicted upon millions of people lay not necessarily in the impression that they had, individually or collectively, done anything wrong, but simply in the unfeeling calculation on the part of the respective dictator that their punishment might be in some way advantageous to him from the standpoint of his security or his political purposes.[4]

So extreme, so unprecedented, so clearly pathological in motivation were these and other qualities of the two great dictatorships in question, so much were they the product of their own time and so little are they likely to be reproduced anywhere in ours (or, as I think we may hope, at any other time) that I would ask the reader to regard them as excluded from the scope of the general observations I shall now have to make about the distinctions among governments.

In many respects, as has just been said, governments tend to resemble

4. These were not the only aspects of uniqueness that characterized these two regimes, the Nazi and the Stalinism. Among the others that might be mentioned was the cynical exploitation of the various vulnerabilities of mass psychology, and particularly the whipping up of hatred against the very elements they had selected as their innocent victims. It is only regimes of this nature that I have in mind when I use the term "totalitarian." There is a great difference between these regimes and what one might call normal forms of dictatorial authoritarianism.

one another. But there is one fundamental distinction that runs through the entire spectrum of governmental systems and exceeds all others in significance; and that is the one that would probably be best understood, particularly in the United States, if it were described as the difference between "democratic" and "nondemocratic" governments.

Personally, I dislike seeing the term "democratic" used in this connection. It was not, in the first place, the term most of the founding fathers of our republic would have used to describe the system they were creating. Even in their time, the word "democracy" accommodated a considerable number of meanings and could even be employed in a pejorative sense by people who were strong supporters of a system of representative government. And more recently it has been so widely misused as to have lost much of whatever meaning it once possessed. It has been extensively and cynically appropriated, and introduced into their titles and constitutions, by a number of regimes, particularly Communist or pseudo-Communist ones, that had no intention of conceding to their peoples anything in the nature of genuine popular self-government. The words "democracy" and "democratic" have, in short, been so extensively abused as to be deprived of any very clear meaning; and the employment of them in public discussion merely encourages the sloppy imprecision of language that runs through so much of American political discourse and literature.

Faced with this confusion as to what is meant by the word "democratic," I have cast about for a better designation for this fundamental distinction among governmental systems that I have in mind and to which I attach unique significance. I have thought of saying that it was the difference between, on the one hand, systems where the mass of the people were given the assured power to throw out of office, within a reasonable span of time, any regime that no longer met their expectations, and to replace it by another that did; and, on the other hand, systems where this was not the case. But this formula, enticing as it was for its brevity and simplicity, left out a number of important specifics. It recalled, in particular, too many historical episodes in which governments were removed, and replaced, by urban mobs purporting to repre-

ON GOVERNMENT AND GOVERNMENTS

sent "the people" but having no clear patent for doing so.

I am reduced, therefore, to describing what I would regard as a proper system of self-government as one that embraced and respected what is in this country the traditional division of governmental powers into the executive, legislative, and judicial, with both the executive and the legislative branches being subject to some proper form of electoral control. Where such institutions are realities—where their integrity, that is, is not impaired or threatened by irregular bodies of armed men or by regular armed forces that step out of their normal constitutional role, or by some other irregular means—there we have before us, I would submit, a fundamental distinction, separating such systems from those that do not meet these criteria at all.

Into this latter category—that is, the category of the "nondemocratic" governments—would fall, I suspect, a large proportion of the entities that figure today as sovereign states. This, however, is almost the only quality these latter have in common. They embrace a wide variety of governmental systems, running over the entire spectrum from mock democracy, through traditional conservative authoritarianism, to unstable military dictatorships and primitive tribal chieftainships.

It is on this "nondemocratic" side that the majority of states, members of the United Nations, would today, I suppose, be found. Most pay lip service, of course, to what are commonly held to be democratic principles, but offer in reality few effective limitations on arbitrary personal or oligarchical power.

But to say that is not necessarily to condemn them all indiscriminately. Some of them, no doubt, correspond closely to the customs, perceived requirements, degree of enlightenment, and expectations of the respective societies. In this sense they probably represent just about the best that circumstances will permit. And this I find neither distressing nor surprising. I know of no reason to suppose that "democracy" along West European or American lines is necessarily, or even probably, the ultimate fate of all humanity. To have real self-government, a people must understand what that means, want it, and be willing to sacrifice for it.

Certainly, many of these "nondemocratic" systems are inherently unstable. But so what? We are not their keepers. We never will be. They need not greatly concern us, except where the lack of self-government is linked, as in the recent case of Iraq, with the maintenance of unduly strong armed forces and with a power-hungry and essentially aggressive leadership, and where the combination of these two factors comes to constitute a threat to the peace of the region. Otherwise, let us, acting on the principle that peoples tend, over the long run, to get the kind of government they deserve, leave the peoples of these "nondemocratic" countries to be governed or misgoverned as habit and tradition may dictate, asking of their governing cliques only that they observe, in their bilateral relations with us and with the remainder of the world community, the minimum standards of civilized diplomatic intercourse.

But what, then, about the countries we are accustomed to think of as "democratic"? The advantages of those qualities that I have seen as essential to any proper system of self-government (the separation of the essential powers, and the safeguards against any vitiation, by intimidation, of the regular governmental functions) are so basic that the differences among "democratic" governmental systems seem quite secondary. But such differences do exist; and one or two of them might be worth a word of mention.

First, there is the difference in the relationship between executive and legislative branches that distinguishes the American system from the European parliamentary democracy. Under the American system the chief executive, embracing the offices both of chief of state and of what, in European usage, would be called the prime minister, is directly elected, and this for a fixed term, by the populace. In the European parliamentary democracy all this is different. Here the offices of chief of state (president or royal figure) and prime minister are not combined. The chief of state may be a crowned head, inheriting his title and office and retaining it normally for life, or, if the system is not a monarchical one, he can be a person popularly elected to the office of chief of state for a given term, but incorporating in his person, so long as he occupies that position, the dignity of the sovereign entity over which he presides, and fulfilling the representational and protocol functions inherent in that office. The powers of such a monarchical or presidential figure vary greatly from one country to another; but seldom, under the European system, is the person in question charged with responsibility for the day-by-day running of the government. This last is the task of the prime minister. And the latter is normally dependent on the continuing support of a parliamentary majority. Upon losing this support, he falls from office, whereas the office of the chief of state remains unaffected.

Each of these systems—the American one and the European parliamentary one—has its advantages; each has its drawbacks. Viewed abstractly, the European system seems to me to be the preferable one, partly because it assures at all times a workable relationship between the political head of the government, the prime minister, and the legislative branch the confidence of which he is obliged to retain; but partly, too, because I think the burden borne by the American president, being, as he is, at one and the same time the protocolary head of state and also, in effect, the prime minister, and sometimes the party leader in the bargain, is really too much for any one person. Anyone obliged to confront this plethora of duties could cope with them, as indeed our presidents have come to do, only by a corresponding bureaucratization of his office.

But to say this is not to advocate any change in the present American system. For one thing, the advantages of any governmental system lie largely in the degree to which the people who live under it accept it, are accustomed to it, understanding its workings, and know how to express themselves through it. This advantage would be forfeited in any effort to turn the American system into a parliamentary one. But beyond that, any change in the American system would necessitate constitutional amendment; and anything of that sort, our country being what it is, would hold unpredictable dangers. It has been evident ever since the adoption (and later abandonment) of the Eighteenth Amendment (Prohibition) that a considerable body of the American public has a very poor idea of what a constitution really is supposed to be. Instead of recognizing it as a document defining and prescribing the institutions under which a political system is to function, they seem to regard it as some sort of a super legislative body, and consider the possibility of amendment a device whereby a piece of legislation that finds their favor could be adopted and anchored in such a way that its removal by the normal legislative process would become extremely difficult. This expedient would constitute, as it did in the case of the Prohibition amendment of 1919, a serious abuse of the provision for constitutional amendment. But so strong are these tendencies, as illustrated by the recent agitation over abortion, that there seems to be a real danger that any attempt at all to make further use of the power of amendment would merely open the way for heightened demands that this possibility be exploited for what are essentially purely legislative purposes. What a pity—that the reasonable intentions of the founders should be so frivolously distorted!

Alexis de Tocqueville, in the second volume of his great work on democracy in America (a volume that was actually addressed primarily to the qualities of egalitarianism in general rather than just in America), voiced his apprehensions lest democracy lead to an excessive centralization of power in the respective country. What he feared primarily was not that the central power would become a cruel despotism, harshly mistreating the respective people, but quite the contrary: that it would spoil them by catering assiduously to their material needs and thereby dulling in them the consciousness of the responsibilities of citizenship. It would, to be sure, give them occasional opportunities to sanction, by some sort of plebiscitary voting, the power it exercised over them. But by taking care of them so well in the material sense, it would deprive them of all individual challenge or responsibility, and thus make them into compliant tools of the central authority. And in this vision he thought he perceived ultimate dangers to human liberty greater than any presented by the aristocratic society into which he had himself been born. In that society the powers of the king were limited, after all, by the established positions and privileges of the nobility and the landed aristocracy. In the democracy no such barriers to the accumulation of power in a single center would exist.

While the relative power of the federal government in the United

States is certainly greater than it was in Tocqueville's time, his fears appear to me to have been seriously overdrawn, primarily by his underestimation of the restraints imposed on the central executive power by the judicial power and by the legislative branch. On the other hand, one has to go far back in history to find any central powers as extensive as those conceded to the American president in time of real or perceived national danger or even of extensive overseas military involvement. Beyond which, the failure of a great portion of the American public to vote in presidential elections does suggest a strong sense of indifference or of real helplessness on the part of the individual voter in the face of the remoteness of the Washington bureaucracy from his or her person and concerns.

We will return to this question when we come to the United States and its problems. Suffice it to note at this point that not all of Tocqueville's fears were wholly without foundation. Democracy, too, in all its modern forms, and particularly as it now exists in the United States, is not the final answer to political problems. And if it is true that only a portion of Tocqueville's fears has stood the test of time, that is no reason why the other part of them should not receive our respectful attention.

Human Rights

There is one phenomenon of recent years that does not fit neatly in the dichotomy of "democratic" versus "nondemocratic." That is the promotion of the idea of a universal obligation to the accordance of "human rights."

The elements of this subject are well known. On December 10, 1948, the General Assembly of the United Nations approved and issued a document entitled *The Universal Declaration of Human Rights*. The reader will note the word "universal" in that title. What the Declaration set forth was not, we are allowed to infer, just a recommendation to governments—something to be adopted and implemented by them at their own discretion. It was seen, at least by the official American establishment of that day and this, as an obligation resting upon all governments by virtue not just of the respective Assembly resolution but by the force of "natural law"—a law regarded as already implicit in the inalterable terms of the human condition, and one that every government, regardless of its own policies and decisions of the moment, was supposedly under obligation to respect.

Now, the plea for observance by individual governments of certain elementary standards of humanity in the treatment of their citizens falls in the same category as the plea for the respect of motherhood, in the sense that it is something to which no right-thinking person can be on principle opposed. This, presumably, was the reason why the Declaration in question was accepted by the General Assembly without a single dissenting voice (though there were a few abstentions). No more than any others could this writer oppose the advocacy of so worthy a cause. He does, however, have certain reservations about the way this objective is brought forward in the Universal Declaration and in the policies and utterances of various American and United Nations officials.

The idea of a "natural law" has roots of great distinction running back through the entire history of Western philosophy. I am impressed with the eminence of the personalities and the institutions that have supported this concept over the centuries. But I find the various expressions of it confusing, sometimes contradictory, and, in any case, unconvincing. The idea of a "law" meaningful to man and subject to his interpretation, yet remote from human authorship, leads me into philosophical thickets where I cannot follow. I can see that some portions of mankind, departing from man's fallen and fractured state, have indeed worked out, with a view to his own safety, comfort, and peace of mind, admirable ideas as to what governments ideally owe to their subjects or citizens in the way of forbearance, humanity, and respect for the dignity of the person. I can see that the inspiration for some of these ideas lay in religious faith—an inspiration I fully respect. I can welcome the sponsorship of these ideas by governments and individuals as a great and noble service to the advancement of civilization. All this I can see; but natural law?—no. Alone the multiplicity of ideas about the meaning of "natural law" and the abundant contradictions among them would suffice to arouse my skepticism.

I have particular trouble with the concept of human "rights," as such. Rights before whom? Before God? In the Christian sense—impossible. The individual Christian is at liberty to hope (or so Christ tells us) for God's mercy; but how could he assert a "right" to anything in the face of God? By whom was he supposedly made? By whom, if not by God himself, could such a right have been bestowed upon him? And to whom, then, could he have recourse if he considered it to be violated?

It is argued that this "right," albeit of natural or divine origin, is a right before any government. That is all very well; but by whose authority is it conceived to exist? And is it considered, then, to exist without any corresponding duty or responsibility? Can there be, in other words, any such thing as rights devoid of some equivalent obligation? I had come to believe, over the course of the years, that freedom was something definable only in terms of the restraints that it implied. Could it be otherwise with rights?

Article 25 of the Declaration says that "everyone has the right to a standard of living adequate for the health and well being of himself and his family, including food, clothing, housing, and medical care, and necessary social services. . . ." Is this, too, really to be without obligation on the beneficiary's part? Is he really to be at liberty to spend his life going fishing, or taking his ease in others ways, and still be entitled to demand that he be provided with all these things that Article 25 assures to him? And if so, who is supposed to pay for them? I would submit that the concept of rights as something wholly unrelated to duties is unrealistic.[5]

5. I realize that one of the paragraphs of Article 29 of the same Declaration contains a laconic and ambiguous sentence to the effect that "everyone has duties to the community in which alone the free and full development of his personality is possible." Is it the duties, or the community, "in which" this development of the personality is possible? Even if it should be seen as the duties that are going to make possible "the full and free development of the individual personality," this last is not quite what the right prescribed in Article 25 pertained to. The dedicated fisherman might find ample opportunity for contemplation "useful to the development of his personality" just in the indulgence of his hobby; but someone else would still have to pay for the remainder of the blessings associated with that idyllic life.

I am also intrigued by the fact that the extension of these rights is something demanded from all of the world's governments without regard to their institutions and practices in other respects. The demand, that is, is addressed to dictatorships and other nondemocratic governments as well as to democratic ones. And here I am struck by the difference in vocabulary between the time of World War I and our present day. The world Woodrow Wilson hoped for was one that would be made "safe for democracy." Not "safe for human rights," mark you, but "safe for democracy."

Perhaps this change in concept is all right. If, like myself, one holds no high hopes for the development of a world consisting only of democracies, perhaps reason could be seen for addressing the plea for greater humanity to all governments alike, ignoring the degree of their commitment to popular representation. But this does seem to me to raise the question as to whether we have dropped what I understood to be our traditional opposition to benevolent despotism. And it raises, too, a question as to whether a favorable momentary response by a nondemocratic regime to the call for "human rights" would always be enough. Arthur M. Schlesinger, Jr., in the final passages of his excellent book *The Age of Jackson,* observed that "freedom does not last long when bestowed from above." Is there not, then, something missing when we demand from oppressive and undemocratic regimes the respect for rights that fit very poorly with their treatment of the individual in other respects?

Finally, I am afraid that demands on other governments raised in the name of human rights grate on my sensibilities as a historian. I was once obliged to point out, in lectures delivered long ago,[6] that in the demands we placed upon the great European powers, in the name of the Open Door principle, in connection with their policies in China at the turn of the last century, you had an example of the satisfaction many of us Americans derived from demanding of other governments policies consistent with what we liked to believe to be our own cherished

6. I have in mind the Chicago lectures of 1951 published in the volume *American Diplomacy* (Chicago: University of Chicago Press, 1951).

national virtues, even when there was no serious prospect that the other powers in question would or could do what we were demanding of them, and even—in some instances—when we ourselves apparently had no very serious intention of living up to these same demands. In many American minds, the mere fact that we had stated these admirable principles, and had demanded respect for them, and had done so in ways that would allow our government to appear in noble posture before world and American opinion, was felt to be quite enough. Whether any actual good came, or could have come, from this demand was beside the point. Our statesmen, it was understood, had made a high-minded gesture. It "sounded good." They had received the appropriate domestic-political applause. What more could one want?

The reader will forgive me if I sense a certain whiff of this same sanctimoniousness in American statements and demands about human rights. I sense here the same implied assumption of superior understanding and superior virtue on our part. I sense it in the anxious inquiries as to whether the "human rights record" of this or that government is found, upon lofty inquiry, to be adequate or inadequate from our standpoint. I sense it in our inclination to rate other governments, independently of their remaining practices, outstandingly on the basis of our judgment of their performance in this one particular field.

Having said all this, I must now do penance by recognizing that the worldwide effects of the human rights movement in which both the United Nations and the U.S. government have invested so much of their energies and enthusiasm have been in a number of respects beneficial. A useful influence seems at least to have been exerted from time to time on regimes whose practices are far from lending themselves to classification as "democratic." Even where these regimes have by no means been able to show a perfect human rights record, there has at least been inflicted upon some of them a certain self-consciousness before world opinion—a certain reluctance to be caught out in the more flagrant abuses of human freedom and dignity—which otherwise would have been lacking. Numbers of nondemocratic regimes, including those of Russia (in the pre-Gorbachevian era) but right-wing dictatorships as well, have put forward patently specious claims that they were extending human rights to their peoples; but I do not recall instances where they denied the obligation to extend them. This would suggest that in certain circumstances there may be greater value in these human rights demands than I have been inclined to attribute to them. I still find myself wishing that we could be a bit more discriminating in the choice of our official language, and a bit more demanding of ourselves in bringing gesture into some sort of a visible relationship with reality.

Chapter Four

THE
NATION

What is beyond doubt is that the [nationalist] doctrine
divides humanity into separate and distinct nations,
claims that such nations must constitute sovereign states,
and asserts that the members of a nation reach freedom
and fulfillment by cultivating the peculiar identity of
their own nation and by sinking their own persons in
the greater whole of the nation.

—E. Kedourie, *Nationalism*

There seems to have been, from time untold, a universal need for
people to feel themselves a part of something larger than themselves,
and larger than just the family. Sometimes, in the more distant past, it
has been the tribe, or, in other instances, the native valley, or a religious
association, or membership in a given caste. In the modern world it is
the nation—the country—the social, cultural, and political unit in
which one was born and brought up or in which, by the force of
circumstances, one has been extensively acclimatized. For most of us,

particularly in America, it seems self-evident that the nation is the entity in which all political life should proceed—that it is within the national framework that the process of government should take place.

These assumptions, I repeat, are widely regarded as self-evident. But are they?

What, after all, is a "nation"? On the basis of what criteria do we call a body of people a nation? This question has always defied the lexicographers. For here a number of factors may play a role: among them, history, tradition, geography, religion, and, above all, language. Not all of them are present in any individual case; and even where some of them are, the mix is never quite the same.

Furthermore, things have not always been this way. Nations existed before there was any such thing as the national state, and before people thought of the national framework as the be-all and the end-all of political organization and government.

The Emergence of the National State

A hundred and fifty years ago, things looked very different. The international community was then composed of a few great empires and kingdoms, ruled by emperors and kings who alone were generally entitled to the designation "sovereign"; and then, beyond and under them, a great heterogeneity of smaller and weaker political entities, the very variety of whose titles reflected the wide variety of status they enjoyed in the eyes of the remainder of the world. There were, among others and just to mention a few, principalities, duchies, grand duchies, tributary states, protectorates, confederacies, personal unions, condominiums, paramountcies, suzerainties, sultanates, emirates, palatinates, colonies, and dominions. The only quality these political entities had in common was their subordination in one form or another to one or another of the great imperial or royal sovereigns of the time. In many instances they enjoyed a high level of internal autonomy; but there were certain things, usually taxes and military support, that they owed to the great imperial center, and certain benefits, usually military protection and the privileged access to that center, that they derived from this connection.

In a number of instances these subordinate entities consisted of what we would probably today regard as "nations." But it was not considered to be normal that all political power should be concentrated within the national context. A great part of it was always exercised by the imperial center, to which in a sense, these "nations" belonged. And it was through the intermediary of that center that they related to the world outside the limits of the empire in question.

While signs of change were becoming evident even prior to the end of the eighteenth century, it was the French Revolution that produced the idea of the concentration of all power within the nation, and the appearance on the world scene of the nation-state as an independent and sovereign entity. And an essential part of that concept, as it emerged from the French Revolution, was the voluntaristic quality of this new sovereign entity—its connection, that is, with the modern concept of self-government and democracy. We are talking, then, of a concept—that of the nation-state—the emergence of which as the normal and prevailing form of independent political organization was roughly coincident with, and not unimportantly influenced by, the establishment of our own independence (which had preceded the revolution in France).

Nationalism

The recognition of the national state in the quality of it that we have just observed, and the sense of belonging to such an entity—of giving it one's loyalty and indeed of accepting citizenship in it as a part of one's own identity—these attitudes, in combination, make up the frame of mind that we now refer to as nationalism. It offers a very powerful way of looking at one's identity, at one's center of loyalty, and at the source of the governmental discipline one accepts.

In the course of the two centuries that have passed since its emergence, nationalism has developed into the greatest emotional-political force of the age. In the Western world, and in part elsewhere as well, all other forms of collective self-identification, including those based on religion or class or dynastic loyalties, have been swept before it. It has triumphed most decisively, in particular, over the radical Marxism that loomed so large as an emotional-political force for a time in the early decades of this century. And even moderate and humane socialism has been able to come to terms with it only by associating itself with it politically.

But it is a mark of the emotional intensity of nationalist feeling that it has divided people very sharply, largely on the basis of their respective temperaments, in point of their reactions to it. At the cost of a certain amount of oversimplification (because people sometimes vacillate between the two outlooks and there are always the normal individual peculiarities of feeling), one might say that nationalistic reactions fall into two categories, highly different and usually clearly distinguishable one from the other. We could call them two different ways of looking at one's country and defining one's relation to it.

The first, which I shall call natural and legitimate nationalism, could also be called patriotism, but only in the best sense of this latter term. An outstanding feature of it is, together with the acceptance of a national framework as the definitive determinant of civic identity, a genuine affection for the country in question.

This is sometimes an *amused* affection, born of a familiarity with the country's failings as well as with its virtues. The moderate nationalist knows what to expect of his country; and there is a unique sense of reassurance in the fact of those expectations. He sees its absurdities as well as its strengths. The strengths enlist his pride; the absurdities, his understanding, sometimes his pity. But whatever these feelings are, he relates to the country for what it is—and for what it is to itself, and on its own terms, not for what he would like it to appear to others to be. He is not obsessed with efforts to compare it with other countries. He hopes that others will perceive its virtues together with its faults; but his feelings toward it are as little affected by their admiration as by their contempt. He hopes that his country will bear itself decently and generously in its relations with others. He is proud when it does and saddened when it doesn't. But the balance of wisdom and folly that he sees in its behavior is only part of a larger picture; and his views do not stand or fall with any of the details. He is not ashamed of belonging to this particular country, but he does not feel himself greatly enlarged in his own eyes, or entitled to enlargement in the eyes of others, by the mere fact of his membership in it. He may view with regret and even sadness his country's occasional military involvements, seeing in them the culmination of many misconceptions and errors; but if asked by decision of elected public authority or by his own conscience to march with the others, he does not decline to do so, aware that for better or for worse, this being the country he belongs to, he must shoulder the burden of its mistakes as well as of its achievements. What we are talking about, in short, is a brand of national feeling that responds to a natural need, brings harm to no one else, and deserves the adjectives—"natural" and "legitimate"—that I have ventured to apply to it. Let us call it, simply, love of country.

The other of the two possible attitudes of the citizen toward his nation is something decidedly different from what has just been described. It takes its departure from the latter, to be sure, and tries wherever it can to borrow from it something of its legitimacy and respectability; but actually it is a pathological form of it—a mass emotional exaltation to which millions of people, particularly in democratic societies, appear to be highly susceptible. It could be called chauvinism, and this would not be wrong. But that term fails to bring out the full complexity of the state of mind in question. It has sometimes been referred to as romantic nationalism: and for this there is some reason, for it represents the carrying over into the collective national dimension of the self-idealization of the individual that was a striking feature of the philosophy of the romantic cultural movement of Europe in the early nineteenth century. Where the cultural romanticist glorified the individual human personality (glorified it, in fact, to the point of an absurdity which, being himself humorless, he was unable to perceive), the political romanticist performs a similar distortion on the national society, building it up imaginatively into a state of grandiloquence that is usually as ridiculous as it is unreal.

In many ways, this pathological form of nationalism is the exact opposite of the normal one described above. Where the normal nationalist, the proper patriot, sees the absurdities of his society as well as the strengths, the chauvinist sees only the latter. Where the view of the former combines the pride with the pity, the chauvinist experiences only the pride, and this in exaggerated form. Where the normal nationalist sees his country simply for what it is to itself, the chauvinist— always self-conscious, always posing—sees it primarily in its relationship to others, in the competitive and comparative aspect of its qualities. He is in fact extremely sensitive to this aspect of it. It is not enough for him to affirm the superiority of his own nation; others must be brought to acknowledge it. The same sense of insecurity that prevents the individual romanticist from having confidence in himself, and compels him to rely on the outward deference of others to establish his personal self-regard, arises here once more to determine his attitude toward the collectivity; for it is in the membership in this collectivity, and here alone, that he finds reassurance as to his own worth. If his own view of himself is to find enlargement, it can only be, as he sees it, through the enlargement of the collectivity of which he claims to be a part.

Hence many facets of his behavior. Hence the frequent demonstrational quality of his patriotism: the flag-waving, the sententious oratory, the endless reminders of the country's greatness, the pious incantations of the oath of allegiance, and the hushed, pseudo-religious atmosphere of national ceremony. Hence the self-righteous intolerance toward those who decline to share in these various ritualistic enactments. Hence the extreme national touchiness, the preoccupation with the outward symbols of national honor, the truculent sensitivity to the views of others. Hence, finally, and more serious than all the rest, the fondness for seeing the country's superiority made manifest and confirmed by military posture or, if possible, on the field of battle. Hence all that goes with that frame of mind in real war or in cold war: the demonization of the real or imaginary opponent; the hysterical search for secret agents of the opponent in one's own midst; the subordination of all other values to the military ones; and the fatuous dream that at the end of this sacrifice of the cream of one's own youth—and the enemy's—there will, or can, be such a thing as a glorious "victory."

What we are dealing with in this morbid form of nationalism, and have had to deal with periodically over the past century and a half of the development of Western civilization, is a real and terrible disease of the human spirit. The damage it has done is appalling. It was one of the two fundamental causes of the First World War (the other being the failure of statesmen and of educated opinion generally to recognize how modern industry and technology were affecting the usefulness of war as an instrument of national policy). And the First World War was the great formative catastrophe of the European civilization of this century, not only impoverishing in the most serious way the societies of the principal participants but also becoming the true source of the two great totalitarian movements of midcentury—the Soviet Communist and the Nazi. But beyond that, nationalism of this sort has, in combination with the militarism it encourages, eaten deeply, down to the present day, into the spirit and the consciousness of millions of people, distorting their images of external reality and of themselves, sowing a foolish and suicidal destructiveness among peoples—peoples who are now going to require the greatest of their resources of strength to confront successfully, even in the absence of any military effort and sacrifice, the social and environmental dangers by which their civilization is now assailed.

It would be wrong to assert that this diseased form of nationalism is the inevitable product of the modern national *state* as an institution. But the two are closely connected. It is a disease of the national society, not an essential concomitant of it. But it is an illness to which members of the modern national community are peculiarly and dangerously susceptible. It is comforting to note that in certain of the greater European countries, where a century ago this disease raged in its most virulent form (in France and Germany, in particular), it has markedly declined in the decades since the Second World War. It seems to be the smaller and newer countries of eastern and central Europe, particularly those that have acquired, or are acquiring, their national identity in the present century, that are now most susceptible to it. But even in the larger and older countries, where the spirit of this unhealthy nationalism seems happily to be on the decline, dangerous remnants of it remain in the addiction of their economies to the maintenance of large armed establishments, in the continued cultivation and proliferation of the weapons of mass destruction, and in the truly senseless, vicious, and indefensible massive export of arms to other parts of the world.

The susceptibility of Western societies to this diseased form of the national spirit is not a reason for wishing to abolish the national state entirely; indeed, we have nothing with which to replace it. But it is something to be borne in mind when we consider the future of this central entity in the organization of international life, particularly in the light of the rather unreal theories of total equality and total sovereignty on which the concept of the national state has been allowed to rest. Let us hope that as these exaggerated concepts of national dignity and these excesses of collective self-admiration decline, there will decline with them the dangers that this particular form of political association has carried with it.

The Political Collective

I am aware, in completing these comments on the two kinds of nationalism, that implicit in them is also a comment on two kinds of human reaction: the personal and the collective. In writing of the moderate and realistic form of nationalism, which I have called the normal and the legitimate one and with which I have associated the term "patriot," I have had clearly in mind the thinking, or at least the possible thinking, of a single person, confronting the problem of his relationship to the nation in the privacy, the autonomy, and the loneliness, if you will, of his own thoughts. And what I have written is conceived as no more than a suggestion of the way many of us, as individuals, approach this problem, realizing that it is in the nature of such personal thinking that no two approaches to it could, or should, be exactly alike.

But when it came to the diseased, chauvinistic form of nationalism, this was different. Here, although here too I ventured to cast the reaction in terms of the outlook of a single individual, I was aware that what I was envisaging was actually a *collective* reaction—the common emotional compulsion of a great many people—the force of which, as they saw it and felt it, lay precisely in the fact that it was shared among so many of them. This form of nationalism was essentially a mass hysteria; and it was precisely from this quality that it drew its power. That "we" were so many, and that "we" all thought the same thing, was, in the minds of its devotees, adequate evidence that "we" must all be right. And these reflections lead me to certain observations about individual versus collective reaction which do affect such philosophical attitudes as I might be said to possess, and of which this is probably as good a point as any other to take note.

Wherever, as so often occurs and as we have just had occasion to note, the reactions of the mass represent essentially an effort to transfer an individual reaction to the collective dimension, the collective version of it is invariably an oversimplification and a vulgarization—in any case, a distortion—of the individual one. Essentially emotional rather than intellectual, sometimes reflecting generous emotions but never ones well thought through, the mass reaction cannot help embracing all the weaknesses of a least common denominator.[1]

The mass, the broad public, the people, or whatever you would like to call it, may not be the "great beast" that some have seen it to be; but collective psychology, particularly in its exalted and demonstrational manifestations, is a much more dangerous phenomenon than individual psychology. Humorless, unreflective, anxiously conformist, it sometimes reveals certain of those qualities—self-centeredness, persecution mania, and uncontrollable suspiciousness—that, when encountered in the individual, we would associate with real mental disturbance. But even where these extremisms are lacking, the collective understandings and expressions of any serious social or political ideal are apt to be at best a caricature of the original. I cite this as the basis for my own extreme dislike of all masses of screaming, chanting, flag-waving, and fist-shaking people, regardless of the cause that may have enlisted their

1. Note the view of Reinhold Niebuhr: ". . . collective man always tends to be morally complacent, self-righteous and lacking in a sense of humor." See *The Irony of American History* (New York: Scribner's, 1952), p. 169.

enthusiasm. They may not always be entirely wrong in whatever it is that they are trying to bring to expression; but you may be sure that what they are crying out for, in their slogans and banners, is oversimplified and largely devoid of serious merit. So strong is my conviction on this point that if ever a mob of this sort were to be found chanting what purported to be a version of any of my own thinking, I would be appalled, certain that I was being (and that it could not be otherwise) seriously misunderstood and misrepresented.

I mentioned, above, the ballot box. This has, of course, no relation to what I have just been talking about. Here, in the use of that box, people are normally being asked not to try to express collectively a view on a great problem but to choose a representative or, if what is involved is some sort of plebiscite, to give their own personal and individual opinion on a certain question at issue. In either case, they are not acting under the influence of the curious emotional states that overcome people when they are gathered together physically in some public place. In either case, they are being confronted with a specific problem; and none of what I have just said applies to such a means of expression. I readily concede that ordinary people, challenged in this way, occasionally show more good sense than many of the intellectuals who write or speak about the same questions.[2] In any case, what they bring to expression at the ballot box is a more useful reaction, and what they are saying is more significant and far less dangerous, than what comes out of them when they link arms with other people and march down the street, trying to impress everyone else with how many of them they are and how violent are their feelings about this or that.[3] And nothing, it

2. There will be occasion, in another section of this work, for me to express the limitations I see in the usefulness of the plebiscite as an institution. I still prefer this mode of expression to the effusions of the street mob.

3. It might be held that the substance of this passage was controverted by the masses of people, many of them young, who came out onto the rainy streets of Moscow in October 1991 to argue with the tank crews and to defend Yeltsin's "White House." But things were not quite that way. These people were not marching arm in arm, brandishing fists, and shouting slogans, to impress others with how many they were, and how angry. Theirs was a more serious and businesslike task—to build defensive barricades around the "White House" and to persuade soldiers not to shoot. And this they were doing not out of any

seems to me, has brought more mobs of this nature out onto the streets in modern times than the dizzy exaltation of the national collectivity. This—the very collective nature of the reaction and the emotional states it produces—is the reason why I view it as a form of contagious hysteria to which certain kinds of people, citizens of the national state, are peculiarly susceptible. This emotional fragility of the national society, and particularly of the new and inexperienced one such as those now breaking out of the Soviet and Yugoslav states, may, if not corrected, turn out to be the greatest danger to which the stability of international life is subjected in the final years of the century.

The International Community

We have taken note, now, of the wide consensus that nationality, more than any other quality, should be taken as the established basis for the organization of political power in separate entities across the globe. We now have to consider the significance of the fact that it is only in this form, in the form of a full-fledged national state, that any body of people can now hope to relate itself independently to the remainder of the world community. For new states, in particular, the path from dependency to independent participation in the world community leads almost exclusively through membership in the United Nations.[4] And it is not without significance that the very name, United *Nations,* implies the quality of that organization as an entity composed exclusively of *national* states. For any body of people seeking world recognition as an independent state, membership in the United Nations is the

---

hysterical enthusiasm for Yeltsin or any romantic hopes for an early triumph of achievement under his leadership, but because they valued the freedom they had recently acquired to think and speak and act for themselves, and because they recognized that if they did not do as they were doing, the alternatives would in all probability be much worse.

4. In the formal sense, membership in the United Nations is not absolutely essential for recognition as an independent country. Switzerland has remained outside the UN, as have, to date, the two Koreas. And there are four very minor entities which, although admitted by themselves and others to be too small to shoulder even the minimal responsibilities of UN membership, seem nevertheless to be generally recognized as independent states.

only way to go. No other choice is open except continued subordination to the authority of some existing state.

This, obviously, has produced a revolutionary change in the structure of the world community. Things have not always been this way. It was only one and a half centuries ago that the leading actors in that community, as we have just seen, were almost exclusively the great multinational and multilingual empires in which so many of the so-called nations were then incorporated. Little over one hundred years ago these empires began to disintegrate. The Russian empire has only been the last to suffer this disintegration. At every stage in this disintegrative process, the question presented itself as to what should be the status of entities thus liberated from their former subordinate position. Previously, it had been the great imperial chanceries that had spoken for them, in the formal sense, in world affairs. If now they were to speak for themselves, in what capacity were they to do so? They varied greatly in their abilities and in their state of preparedness to accept the responsibilities of complete independence. Some, to be sure, became at least for the time being independent monarchies. For the remainder, various expedients had to be found.

The League of Nations, set up in 1919, attempted to meet this problem by its system of mandates, providing a status that was viewed as something less than complete independence but more than complete subordination to any particular sovereign entity. The League's successor, the United Nations, made provision for international trusteeships which, it was thought, might serve the same purpose. But little by little, especially in recent decades, these arrangements for intermediate status have gone by the board; and today the world community may be said to consist exclusively, with only insignificant exceptions, of nominally independent states, members of the United Nations.

Now, the first thing to be noted about these developments is that they have increased enormously the number of countries enjoying the status of independent actors on the world scene, and internationally recognized in that capacity. When the League of Nations was set up, only 29 countries were recognized as members; and the international community could not have embraced many more. When the United

Nations was established, in 1945, there were 51 original members. That number has now grown to 162; and the process of proliferation is by no means complete. Disintegration is still in progress in the area of the former Soviet Union; the same is true of Yugoslavia. Not only that, but there are several instances in which smaller states, not previously generally regarded as "imperial" or "multinational" ones, are now confronted with demands for independence on the part of one or another of their own constituent elements. The Canadians have their Quebecois, the Spaniards their Basques, and the Czechs their Slovaks. Even the Swiss have the restless inhabitants of their Jura Mountains. And even some of those entities that are now clamoring for the status of complete independence in Russia and Yugoslavia have minorities within them that are clamoring for the same thing. The Russian Republic alone has several of them. The Georgians have their Abkhazians and their Ossetians. It is hard to say where, if anywhere, this process of fragmentation is going to stop. As we look into the future, we have to reconcile ourselves to living in an international community composed of around 200 formally independent states, as opposed to the 20 or 30 that would have been recognized in that capacity at the outset of this century.

Now, this has various noteworthy connotations. First of all, it places an inordinate burden upon the protocolary and ceremonial customs of international intercourse. These customs, largely codified at the Congress of Vienna in 1815, were designed for a far smaller number of participants; and a far greater flexibility prevailed in the manner in which these participants interacted with one another on the international scene. The effort to adapt these customs to the huge and highly diverse international community of the present day has produced many strains and no small number of absurdities, both for the United Nations and for the individual participating governments.

But more important still, we have peculiar strains and maladjustments connected with the two outstanding qualities that recognition as an independent state, member of the United Nations, is supposed to carry with it. One of these is the quality of absolute sovereignty. The second is that of total equality.

First, about sovereignty. Sovereignty was originally a quality attached to the person of a great ruler, normally an emperor or someone equivalent. It was his person, not the country or the people over whom he ruled, who was "sovereign." He alone was unlimited in his powers, in the sense that no one else's word could rival his in authority. All of his subjects owed him submission and obedience. It was this that made him sovereign.

In ancient times, and in part down into the modern era, this concept of sovereignty, the supremacy of a single ruler, was often conceived to have universal significance—to be applicable, that is, to all of the known civilized world. The particular ruler in question laid claim to be superior to any other ruler in authority. His supremacy was expected to be acknowledged by anyone else who had any authority over people anywhere. This was the theory that prevailed in a number of the ancient empires. Each bespoke for its sovereign master preeminence over any other form of authority. Representatives of other rulers who appeared at his court were compelled to come before him in the quality of representatives of an inferior power, respectful of his superior and unlimited authority.[5]

In the course of time, these pretensions lost their reality, and it came gradually to be accepted that a ruler, while still being "sovereign," would be sovereign only in the territory traditionally accepted as being under his rule, even if it did not include the entire world. But still, it was he, and not his people or his country, in whom the quality of sovereignty continued to reside. This began to change only with the emergence, in the eighteenth and nineteenth centuries, of non-monarchically governed states, such as the United States, where, there

5. This led to a great deal of angry bickering and playacting, some of it quite absurd, ranging all the way from demands that the visiting envoy enter the presence of the emperor backwards, and then prostrate himself before the imperial person, to the ridiculous shenanigans that took place in the case of Russia as late as the fifteenth century, when a foreign envoy, arriving at the Russian border and being met by an official representing the Russian tsar was told that he, as the representative of an inferior power, must dismount from his horse before the Russian official dismount from his, whereupon each would pretend to be about to dismount in the hope of inducing the other to dismount before him.

being no monarch to whom the quality of sovereignty could be attached, the theory emerged that it was the people themselves who were sovereign, that quality being also enjoyed by their government, as their elected representative. By this time, of course, the universalistic pretensions originally attached to sovereignty had been entirely lost and abandoned. But the quality of complete independence of the sovereign authority, wherever the quality of sovereignty might be said to reside—as an independence that no outside power was at liberty to challenge—remained intact. Theoretically, the sovereign government was supreme on its own recognized territory. There it could do whatever it wanted to do. It could even misgovern its people to its heart's content; this was, theoretically, no one else's business. Attempts by others to remonstrate or protest against acts of a government relating to what went on in its own territory were to be indignantly rejected as "interference in its internal affairs."

A mere glance at the realities of international life will suffice to show that this is not really the way things work today. There are dozens of ways in which actions of a government, even where applicable in the first instance only to its own people and its own territory, affect the interests of other countries. This is true, for example, of its policies in environmental questions; for the planetary environment, as is now widely recognized, is all of one piece, and there are few major internal practices or policies of individual governments in this field the effects of which are not felt, in one way or another, in other countries. It is no less true in the commercial field, where customs duties and subsidies alone can have profound effects on other countries. And it is true particularly in military affairs—in ways that were never present in earlier ages. It is becoming increasingly evident that what countries do about their own defense establishments, in both the designing of them and the deploying of them even in peacetime, can no longer be considered a matter of indifference to their neighbors or to the international community. This involves not only the question, so recently arisen in the case of Iraq, as to how far any country may safely be allowed to go in the creation and cultivation of weapons of mass destruction. Such is now the destructive power even of weapons commonly accepted as conventional that there are points at which the cultivation of them also becomes a legitimate concern of neighbors and others.

The second outstanding quality of membership in the United Nations, as mentioned above, is the principle of *equality* of the sovereign status—a principle on the basis of which each of these present 160-some states is considered to be the exact equal of every other one in point of sovereignty, stature, dignity, uniqueness, or what you will. Here again, we have a principle that differs greatly from that of earlier ages when, as we have seen, there were many gradations of international status and of the way individual peoples might relate to the remainder of the world. One cannot avoid the conclusion that, in creating this theoretical total equality among many nations, the rulers of this century were, whether consciously or otherwise, attempting to transfer to the international community the drastic egalitarianism they considered suitable in determining the rights and positions of the individuals. But just as it is clear that equality of individuals in the face of the law does not preclude the wildest differences among them in other respects; so the theory of total equality among sovereign states in the formal sense cannot and does not change the fact that there are enormous real inequalities among them in many other aspects of national life. None of these find any recognition in the theory of absolute equality of independent nations. So immense, indeed, are these disparities that it is not too much to say that they make a mockery of these lofty terms—"sovereignty" and "equality"—themselves. To suggest that any of the smaller members of the United Nations—or any of the larger ones either, for that matter—possesses under the term "sovereignty" anything akin to the sovereignty once exercised by the emperors of China or Byzantium is to stretch a point beyond all plausibility. And similarly, to pretend that absolute equality exists between one member of the United Nations and another, even in instances (and there is at least one example of this in the UN Assembly) where the economic potential of one particular entity is more than three thousand times that of another one, is to uphold a similar incongruity. The effect of the formal assignment of these qualities of absolute sovereignty and total equality to 160-some political entities of the most wildly varying capacities is to deprive these terms of every real meaning other than what might be called an honorary one—to make of these terms, that is, a designation of courtesy, like the use of "sir" as a common appellation for men, or "madam" for ladies, even where the implications of these designations have nothing to do with the obvious quality of the individual in question.

Were these artificialities the only anomalies now prevailing with respect to the composition and arrangement of the world community, it could be argued that they would be better left to stand as they are—that any attempt to alter them would be likely to invite more complications than it would remove. And there is much to be said for that argument. In most recent instances of the acquisition of the status of sovereign independence by previously subordinate entities, it was precisely the formal status—the trappings of sovereignty: the national flag, the national anthem, the symbolism of the UN seat, and so on—that loomed largest in the eyes of those who had demanded that status. It is now too late to deprive them of these symbols of prestige. But the enormous gap between theory and substance, between symbol and reality, remains. It deserves more attention than it has received, and would deserve it even were it the sole anomaly in the structure of the international community. But it is not.

In addition to the disintegrative tendencies that recently changed, and are continuing to change, the composition of the world community, there are others of a precisely contrary nature. An example of these is the effort of a number of the more advanced European countries to unite in forming the European Community, and to transfer to that supranational entity portions of what has theretofore been regarded as their sovereign authority. And beyond that, even in instances where the disintegrative tendencies in existing states have been most striking, as in the Soviet Union and Yugoslavia, and have been most extensively appeased and accommodated, questions are now arising as to whether some sort of regional center will not still have to be preserved to continue to exercise at least a small portion of the former powers of the former imperial center. Can the various constituent parts of the former Soviet Union, for example, go their respective ways without retaining some sort of a center to handle certain questions—military, financial, environmental, representational, and the like—which exceed the capabilities of smaller political entities? Can Yeltsin's intended commonwealth meet these needs? We stand today in the midst of that uncertainty. And this question, in turn, carries one close to the problems of regional collaboration in general, problems that would probably have arisen at this juncture, in any case, but that intersect at many points with the disintegration of larger political entities and with the many new anomalies this creates. And finally, there are also, integrally connected with all of these questions, the problems concerning the rights and treatment of such minority elements as may remain within sovereign states, even within states that only recently regarded themselves as minorities in larger states but are now receiving, or have received, their independence. If, for example, Yugoslavia is to disintegrate entirely, and if the several parts of it are to emerge as sovereign states, as now seems likely, there will remain, and even with heightened significance, questions of the treatment of the Serbian minority in Croatia and vice versa—questions that are almost insoluble in terms of the present structure of the international community.

The Problem

What we are seeing in all these instances is, as it seems to me, that what were once regarded as internal problems of sovereign states are now becoming in increasing measure international ones as well; whereas the older concepts and modalities of international intercourse, based as they are on meanings of the terms "sovereignty" and "equality" that have lost much of their reality, are simply inadequate to the treatment of the problems all this creates. We have at the moment, in short, in this entire area of the relationship of national to international concerns and authorities, a situation of great confusion and instability which has been, as yet, only dimly recognized, and which will, sooner or later, have to be faced head-on. The task is immense. New modalities and institutions for international collaboration will have to be devised to absorb burdens of authority that the emerging nations are unable to bear, and to accept other burdens that some of the older nations are unwilling to continue to bear alone; to relieve the smaller emerging nations of some burdens of total independence that are too much for them; but also to find places for ethnic minorities in larger countries that will do justice to their own thirst for internal autonomy and international dignity, not to mention some control over their own economic resources, without obliging them to accept at once all the burdens and responsibilities that go with the completely independent status.

To find these new approaches will be an immense task, and a highly complex one, particularly because in no two regions and in no two countries does the problem present itself in precisely the same way. There is, therefore, no universal answer to it. And no one who, like this writer, is attempting to look at the problem in its larger aspects can do more than to suggest certain of the principles that might well be held in mind as one approaches it. Even here it must be pointed out that none of these principles can be of absolute applicability; there will always be the exceptional situations to which, whether entirely or in the main, they will not apply.

First: this is a problem that will, by its very nature, be better faced in the regional context than in the universal one. While the United Nations will have an intimate interest in any attempts to find answers to it, and while that organization could and should contribute wherever it can to the study of the problem, the institutions and procedures of the UN, linked as they are to the rigidities of the present international order, unavoidably incline toward uniformity and universality rather than discrimination of approach and thus are not suitable as vehicles for any significant changes along these lines. If ever there was a problem to the answering of which should be applied the injunction "No uniformities; no broad categories; no sweeping arrangements; each case to be treated on its own merits," it is this.

Second: where the answer is the creation of a new regional organization (as I suspect it will be in most instances), this organization should, on principle, not be centered on the territory, and preferably not even in the capital city, of any great regional power. It is the smaller entity that has the greatest need for such organization; and this need will not be met if there is any formal domination of the grouping, or even any widespread impression of such domination, by any single power overshadowing the others either militarily or economically. To say this is not to hold that the larger power should not belong to, or be in some way associated, with the regional grouping; for its resources and collaboration may be essential to its successful functioning of the association. But the regional association must not become, or appear to be, an agency for great-power authority. A leaf may well be taken, here, from the arrangements of the European Community, based as they are in Brussels and designed to avoid even the appearance of domination by any single power.

These last observations raise, of course, the question as to whether the concerns of any such regional grouping should be confined to the political, economic, and social spheres, or should include military matters as well. Here, again, the answers will depend on the particular circumstances of the situation. But a clear distinction should be kept in mind between intraregional security problems, on the one hand, and universal ones, on the other. These last must, almost of necessity (if only because of the nature of the weapons involved), be left to the great military powers of the entire world, acting in conjunction with the United Nations. But there are important possibilities for regional groupings in assuring the elimination of violence *within* the respective region. While there is always the possibility that conflicts among members of the regional grouping, or with other countries of the region, will assume such dimensions and intensity as to demand outside intervention, it is better on principle that these conflicts be handled, wherever this is possible, within the grouping itself. Neighbors usually have a better understanding of the issues than do people far away. One has an instructive example of this in the interest now being taken by the various European regional organizations in the Serbian-Croatian hostilities. While this interest (probably wisely in this instance) has not carried so far as actual military intervention in the conflict, it has expressed itself in other ways; and in this sense alone it has represented a significant innovation in regional association, with important possibilities for the future.

But the most significant, if also the most difficult, of the functions the regional association might conceivably perform would be to obviate the choice, for the smaller political entity, between continued existence as a subordinate minority community within the political framework of some larger power, on the one hand, and an unreal and almost meaningless status of equal and sovereign independence as a member of the universal UN community, on the other. It may prove easier to break out of the second of these alternatives than out of the first; for it is not inconceivable that the regional association could provide for the small ethnic entity a better means of interaction with the remainder of the world community, and give it a more effective voice in world affairs, than could its mere status as a member of the United Nations. This possibility is a particularly promising one, because these two forms of participation in international life—one the universal, the other the regional—are not mutually exclusive. The one can exist without elimination of the other. And since this would permit the smaller entity to retain, in any case, all the outward trappings and prestige of acknowledged sovereign independence, no one would be asked to suffer any humiliation.

A harder problem presents itself when we turn to the plight of the small ethnic-linguistic minority in the larger state. We have seen that the immediate transition of such an entity from the completely subordinate position in a larger state to the status of complete sovereign independence and membership in the UN is not always the most suitable and effective answer to its needs. A number of the entities now breaking off, for example, from the former Soviet and Yugoslav states will, I venture to predict, learn this to their unhappiness if they are left with a total theoretical independence as their only alternative. Not only this, but for a mother country the abrupt abandonment of its existing sovereign authority over what has been to date a portion of its own territory, and the sudden acquisition in this manner of a new and untried "sovereign" neighbor (or even enclave), can indeed have, or appear to have, humiliating aspects. Whether this difficulty could be eased for either party if the transition, for the unhappy minority, were to be to a status of complete internal autonomy coupled with participation in a regional association, rather than to full sovereign status on a universal basis, is hard to say. It would probably depend on circumstances. But that there should be some intermediacy of status to ease the relationship of the smaller and weaker entity to the remainder of the world community just seems to me to be evident. And if there is any arrangement that could conceivably play a useful role in providing this intermediate status, it would be the regional association.

This, plainly, is a problem to which very little attention has yet been given. Ultimately it will have to be faced. The artificialities of the present order (which can only be increased if we continue to ignore them) are too apparent, and the tensions over the situation of ethnic-linguistic minorities in the larger state are too intense, for either of these situations to be indefinitely ignored. The answer lies, surely, in the creation of a spectrum of potential political statuses larger than that of the national state but smaller than that of a relatively meaningless universality. And where, if not in the principle of regionality, could this intermediate spectrum be found?

Chapter Five

IDEOLOGY

Ideology, a systematic body of beliefs about the structure and working of society that includes a program of practical politics based on a comprehensive theory of human nature and requiring a protracted social struggle to enact.

—*The New Encyclopaedia Britannica*

*A*mong the reproaches that have been leveled against me for failing to make clear my various philosophical views or commitments are those that have centered on the questions of "ideology." These place me in some difficulty, for they bring up the question of what an ideology really is; and this propels me at once into that laborious search for categories and for the meanings of abstract words and concepts which, as it seems to me, attends all philosophical exploration and which is foreign, I am afraid, to my world of thought.

I am not sure that the word "ideology" has ever been authoritatively defined in a manner adequate to this discussion. It is obviously not a religious belief, for the element of irrational faith seems to be lacking.

Equally obviously, it is not a philosophical persuasion, for its preoccupation with contemporary problems places it beyond the range of purely philosophical thought. I might try to define it as a system of secular thought about contemporary politics and social change on a level higher than just the national one, and capable of serving as a guide for public policy. And if this be a fair approximation of what ideology is generally taken to mean in contemporary Western opinion, then it is safe to say that I have no ideology at all.

I have critical reactions to the postulates and assumptions of a number of systems of thought that have, I believe, been regarded as ideological. These reactions have naturally been particularly lively in relation to Marxism, and especially to radical Marxism as manifested in the pronouncements of such men as Lenin and Stalin. These reactions were only natural and, indeed, unavoidable in anyone confronted daily over the course of several years, as was I, by the realities of Stalinist Russia. They were symbolized by the forbidding walls of the mysterious Stalinist Kremlin, visible across the square from my office windows. And because they played a prominent part in the formation of my general views about the problems of the age, they probably deserve a word or two of elucidation.

Marxism

I had at one time the impression that I was a rare bird among those who had taken a long-standing professional interest in Soviet affairs—a rare bird in the sense that I had never gone through what was often called a Marxist period, a period, that is, of fascination with, and enthusiasm for, Marxist doctrine. I had been put off at an early date by a number of the features of that doctrine: by the egregious oversimplifications with which it abounded, by the heartless rejection, and consignment to the outer depths, of entire great categories of mankind (not only the so-called bourgeoisie but all others except the "proletariat"), and, finally, by the shameless polemic exaggerations and distortions by which all this was regularly carried forward, not to mention the appalling cruelties committed in its name.

And these reactions were reinforced, as the years of life in Soviet Russia ran their course, by even more serious questionings. I recall my late friend and colleague Charles Bohlen observing on one occasion, amid the intellectual turmoil of our common confrontation in Moscow with Stalin's communism in the days of the great and terrible purges of the 1930s, that the Communist doctrine, as we then had it before us, had no enduring future, because it had no answer to the phenomenon of death. This was a profound insight; and there was more to it than that. The Marxist outlooks included no recognition that the individual human condition embraced within itself (as was mentioned above, in chapter 2) elements of tragedy (man's mortality was only one) that could not be overcome by even the most drastic manipulations of social environment. To suggest that profound and beneficial changes could be produced in the human condition just by changes in the ownership of industrial enterprises was, I thought, to lead people seriously astray. Men's dilemmas went a great deal farther than that.

Ideology, Today

There were also a few critical reactions on my part to what were often regarded as other major ideological commitments of those pre–World War II days: such things as moderate socialism, liberalism, and conservatism. In general, these movements were so ill defined and confused that it was difficult to come to terms with them intellectually. Nor did my inclinations of that day, highly personal and egotistical as they were, move me greatly to this sort of contemplation. I can recall only a certain detached understanding for the more idealistic tendencies in German social democracy as I observed them from the perspectives of my various Foreign Service posts. Although I was placed on guard by the intolerance even of the moderate socialists for other classes of society than "workers," I recognized that the latter, too, had interests and complaints that deserved respect; and I shared the socialists' repugnance for the stuffy pretensions of much of the bourgeois society of their day. But these were all only the musings of a young man who, if he thought at all about such matters, assumed himself to be totally unengaged in the questions at issue.

It might be noted that these ideologies or pseudo-ideologies of the early decades of this century have today, in any case, largely lost their reality. The extensive breakdown of the class structures of society that played so large a part in their origins has deprived them of much of their meaning. It is now hard to find, in the advanced countries of the West, any such thing as a proletariat in the sense that Marx and others conceived of it. Poor people (and worse than poor) there are indeed in the great city ghettos of this age, but few of them are industrial "workers"; and they bear little resemblance to the "proletariat" of the Marxist image of reality. And the same is true of a real "upper class," as distinct from numbers of momentarily nouveau riche people who have neither the tradition nor the taste to replace the upper classes of previous decades and centuries and who would find it hard to duplicate the culture of those classes, in any case, within the social context of contemporary civilization. What we are confronted with today in practically all Western countries are societies composed very largely of one, vast middle class, uniform in outlook even where it is not uniform in income.

Whether this middle class has anything definable as an ideology is doubtful. Although the study and interpretation of the thought, art, and music of earlier ages proceeds on a very high level among small minorities of the population of the leading Western countries, and although there is a high degree of public exposure of this middle class to popularized versions of the history of culture in the museums, the concert halls, and the television films, it is hard to find among these broad masses any great theoretical interest in public affairs—anything, indeed, beyond the limits of a dreary and unimaginative consumerism, enlivened from time to time by accesses of anxiety in the face of anything that threatens to undermine their standard of living. The fact is that we live, at the moment, in an un-ideological age.

I have had, of course, reactions to many of the intellectual assumptions and commitments of this century, mostly those of the Western world, with which, alone, I have any familiarity. Whether these reactions would be considered to have ideological significance, or whether they would be more properly regarded as aesthetic preferences, is a fair question. I would not be offended if readers assigned them to the latter category. They cannot all be listed here. They arise in the mind daily in a multitude of connections. I might mention only three or four of them that seem closest to what might be regarded as ideological inclinations.

Growth

I react skeptically, for example, to the ideal of economic growth that preoccupies so intensively almost all thought on economic problems in the United States, and a great deal of it, I dare say, in other Western countries as well. Why growth? The assumption that without constant growth a national economy could not be what it was supposed to be—could not, that is, serve the purposes of society that it was meant to serve—seems to me without substantiation. If a given economy adequately serves, at a given time, the needs of the population, provides food and housing and consumer goods in adequate quantities to assure a healthy and comfortable life for all concerned, why should it constantly have to be growing? Would there not be something diseased, something cancerous, something open-ended and unstable, about an economy that had to be constantly growing to be seen as adequate to national needs?

Of course, to the extent that population grows, the economy has to grow with it, since there will obviously be more mouths to feed, more bodies to clothe, more shelters to be provided. But I can think of no place in the Western world or in other regions where population *ought* to be growing. If the preservation of this planet as a suitable habitat for civilization is the overriding imperative of our time, and if population growth is itself the greatest threat we face to the intactness of that habitat, then why should we wish to see further growth of this nature?

And what, after all, is wrong with a physically static society? That *change* is needed—improvement, refinement, whatever you wish to call it—is entirely clear. But "change" is not synonymous with "growth." *Qualitative* growth? Yes, of course; and there is great room for it. That room will not be filled, even with the best of efforts, by our generation or our children's or our grandchildren's or any further generation within the range of useful human speculation. But I fail to see that it is by material expansion alone that qualitative growth will be encouraged or attained. That there will be gaps to be filled here and there in the meeting of material needs is obvious; and when they appear let them be filled. But growth per se, as an aim of all economic policy, why? Where is the end to it—and what?

Automation

I am unable to understand why a society that complains of unemployment should encourage and embrace every conceivable possibility of replacing human labor by mechanical devices. Why the robot in place of the human hand? Because it might be cheaper? A good argument perhaps in many other connections, but in this one—shameful. The aim should be, in a healthy and well-balanced society, to find useful and, if possible, creative work for every mature human being. Must that work invariably represent the cheapest way a certain thing could be done? Are there not other values to be considered? Admitting that not all consumer goods could be produced by handicraft effort, I venture to say that there are instances where they *could* usefully be, at least in greater measure than is the case today, and where it would be better if they were. Is any attention being given to this among those whose efforts guide the development of a modern economy?

Urban versus Rural

Similar questions involve the balance between an agricultural and an urban way of life. This is a vast subject. Countless volumes have been addressed to it; countless others remain to be written. The nature of the problem and the answers to it take different forms in different regions. This is not the place to cut deeply into the subject. I can say only this.

The monstrous expansion of cities and urban regions that has been one of the great social features of this century is simply a horror. The phenomenon is worldwide, but there is little uniformity in the forms it takes. In the less developed countries, these monstrous accumulations of human bodies, vast, dense, and festering, that go by the name of cities—these Cairos and Calcuttas and Mexico Citys and God knows how many more—are essentially the products, the hopeless and frightening products, of overpopulation. Millions of superfluous people crowd into these places, because the already overcrowded countryside seems to have no place for them or because they have the idea that life would be better and easier for them in the urban center. In the advanced countries the tendency takes other forms: notably, the development of great regions of exurbia and suburbia surrounding the city centers, regions having the drawbacks of both city and country and the virtues of neither, while the city centers are abandoned to such of the Third World elements as can crowd into them, and left to serve as the homes of crime, demoralization, misery, and degradation. Meanwhile, particularly in our own country, we stand by to witness the rapid decline of family farming and the reckless raiding and ruining of some of the finest agricultural soil on the world's surface, partly by the developers and partly by forms of industrial farming that exploit and exhaust its fertility, with the result that we export to other parts of the world great quantities of what, in essence, is our topsoil.

Is there no way in which these great disbalances could be corrected? I see only one. It is one that could not be "engineered" or accomplished by the fiat of public authority; it is one that could only be understood and encouraged. It is the movement of as much as possible of the surplus urban population to farming areas, with the view not to these people's becoming family farmers in the old American tradition (for most of them would be incapable of it) but rather to their embracing a life that would combine part-time industrial employment with the cultivation of small tracts of land. This would, in other words, be a way of combining what might be called backyard farming (although on tracts considerably larger than the average backyard) with a relatively undemanding part-time industrial labor. In other words: labor-intensive, not labor-saving, farming. In part, this is already taking place in some regions; but it is doing so without either guidance or encouragement from public authority.

This, in any case, is the nearest I can come to an ideological commitment in the great area of urban versus rural life and employment. But it is better, in my eyes, than a situation in which public authority shrugs its shoulders and says to itself, "Let happen what will to the greatest natural asset that American civilization possesses: namely, its magnificent endowment of fertile, life-giving land. This is none of our concern."

Free Enterprise

And finally, there is the question of free enterprise versus what would in Europe be called *dirigisme,* that is, governmental direction and control of the economic process. Because the Soviet experiment, based on total governmental control, ended disastrously, there has been a tendency, particularly in the United States, to reject the idea of any kind of governmental supervision of the economic process, in the spirit of "Let free enterprise carry us wherever it will; it will be all for the good."

About this, there are two things to be said. First, there are obvious limits, partly of an environmental nature, partly of financial and social ones, beyond which free enterprise should not be permitted to go. This has become evident in a great many contemporary phenomena: among them, the recent savings and loan disaster but also the numerous obviously harmful environmental effects of a wholly unrestrained free-enterprise system. Here the duty of government is not to take charge of, or to try to direct in any way, the workings of that system but simply to make clear the limits within which free enterprise may operate and beyond which it may not.

The second point is that the need for such governmental control obviously varies with the size and importance of the economic enterprise in question. It is in the case of the small retail or personal enterprise—the country general store, the hairdresser's establishment, the cleaner and presser, the small servicing establishment in general—that the need for any governmental laying-down of limits is smallest. It is the great industrial or financial concern for which the limits must be most carefully drawn and enforced.

The task for the governmental policymaker, whether federal or local, is to study the needs, to establish the minimal essential limits, to make these limits absolutely clear, and to enforce them firmly and consistently. And what this boils down to is that neither of these operative factors, the commercial-financial motive or the public interest, must be carried too far and permitted to disbalance the other. The proper balance between the two must be ascertained and observed; and to see that this is done is public authority's business. Whether it is a question of pollution from a smokestack, or of the cutting of a forest, or of the disposal of noxious waste products, it is up to public authority to establish the boundary between the permissible and the impermissible—and this, from the standpoint not of this generation alone but also of those that will come after. Within these limits, God bless private enterprise; and may it prosper!

Well, enough of these aesthetic preferences. They run, almost in their entirety, against the ingrained habits and the conventional wisdom of the age. I have no illusions about the chances for any early understanding or adoption of most of them by those who constitute public authority in this country and elsewhere. There is indeed a question as to whether any democratically governed society such as our own, incapable of demanding of its people sacrifices the reasons for which are not widely visible and compelling, can cope betimes with the strains that overpopulation is placing on the environment. But that is no reason why one may not think about these matters. The historical record, after all, tells us that many impulses that led ultimately to palpable and identifiable results began with ideas that were wholly unacceptable in the climate of opinion of the period of their conception. So let these stand for whatever history wants to do with them, whether this means further consideration, or ridicule, or consignment to oblivion. Such is the normal fate of most products of human contemplation.

Science and Technology

There may, I suppose, be those who will say, upon reading the above, "That is all very well; and it might have done well enough for the beginning of this century, but not for this ending of it. Where have you been during these eighty-eight years of your life? Don't you realize that you have been living in an age of explosive advances in science and technology—advances that are changing our understanding of nature and of ourselves and of the environmental conditions of our lives? Don't you see that these changes render most of what you are talking about irrelevant to the problems we are now beginning to encounter, and that what is required of you is not a set of views that might have fitted well the conditions of the eighteenth century, but rather one that takes account of the immense scientific advances of this age and of the technological innovations they have made possible? Where, in your outdated view of reality, is the place even for the revolutionary changes in communication introduced by the computer? Do such things not invalidate a great deal of what you are saying, or give it at least no more than a historical value, like the works of those earlier thinkers you admire?"

These are fair questions, I am sure. And here, my answers:

I admire immensely the processes and achievements of modern science. I have witnessed with profound and awed respect, albeit necessarily from a great intellectual distance, the labors of the scientists by whom I have been surrounded for forty years in the Institute for Advanced Study. I have been able to sense the greatness in what they, and many of their colleagues worldwide, were doing. I consider their pursuit of the mysteries that fascinate them to be not only a legitimate but a noble occupation for the human mind; and I perceive a certain magnificence in many of the efforts it has inspired, in so far as I can understand anything of them. God forbid that our generation should desist from these efforts or even from the educational programs on which they are based!

The Institute for Advanced Study is unique, or nearly so, in its dedication to the pursuit of pure science, divorced from any considerations of immediate practical applicability. It also takes no part in the tremendous and far-flung efforts of experimental science that are being pursued in so many parts of the world. For both of these other aspects of scientific effort—experimental science and applied science—I also concede, unstintingly, my respectful admiration. This includes particularly the great and epoch-making advances in the exploration of outer space and in the study of the composition of matter of which we read so much in the public prints.

I recognize, in other words, that within the small span of my own lifetime the parameters of our understanding of the physical environment of human life, in both its inward and its outward dimensions, have been greatly and dramatically expanded. And I share without reservation both the worldwide excitement this has aroused and the general admiration for the qualities of mind and imagination that have made it possible.

But I should make it clear that none of this—either my respect for these great scientific efforts or my enthusiasm for their continuation—rests on any belief on my part that they have yet achieved, or even promised for the future, any changes in human life that might affect the ways of looking at things reflected on these pages. For me, as for Alexander Pope and many others, the proper study of mankind has always been man; and until it can be shown to me that the scientific advances of this age have relieved man of some of the moral challenges and dilemmas which press themselves upon him, I must continue to pursue what others are at liberty to regard as my outdated ruminations and reactions.

And technological change? Ah, this is a different thing. It, too, is clearly revolutionary in the speed of its advancement in many areas. Equally clearly, it has produced significant changes in the discipline in our social and personal environment—changes of which we have no choice but to take account. But whether these changes have been beneficial ones, whether they have enriched our lives, whether they have effected any real improvement in the human condition—these are, for me, still open questions; and my answer to most of them is still a skeptical one.

In the case of the computer, for example, I can see that it renders unnecessary certain forms of financial drudgery from which in earlier ages there was no escape. In this respect its utility resembles that of the tractor which relieved the farmer of the endless drudgery of plowing, or the earth mover which made unnecessary so many heavy and exhausting efforts of human or animal muscle. But when the effects of technological innovation are only (as seems to be mainly the case with the computer) to speed the manifold processes of a life that is plainly already proceeding at a pace far too great for the health and comfort of those that live it, or where the purposes of new technology seem only to be to find out how soon and extensively human labor can be replaced by that of the machine or the electronic apparatus, and that in a society already burdened by unemployment, there my interest in it can be no more than casual. Where these are the limits, I see no significant betterment of the conditions of human life or the quality of human beings. So I can only beg leave, while watching these changes with an attentive if skeptical eye, to pursue my more traditional explorations into the problems and challenges of our time.

PART
TWO

Foreword for Part Two

Gentlemen, why in heaven's name this haste? You have
time enough. No enemy threatens you. No volcano will
rise from beneath you. Ages and ages lie before you.
Why sacrifice the present to the future, fancying that
you will be happier when your fields teem with wealth
and your cities with people? In Europe we have cities
wealthier and more populous than yours, and we are not
happy. You dream of your posterity; but your posterity
will look back to yours as the golden age. . . . Why, in
your hurry to subdue and utilize Nature, squander her
splendid gifts? Why hasten the advent of that threaten-
ing day when the vacant spaces on the continent shall all
have been filled, and the poverty or discontent of the
older states shall find no outlet?

—Lord Bryce, *The American Commonwealth* (1888)

*I*n the first part of this treatise, I came as near as I could to reflections
and reactions that might have relevance to the situation of mankind
everywhere. I must now turn to those that pertain specifically, if not
exclusively, to the problems of my own country. And there are a few
words that might well be said by way of preface to these following
chapters, lest their content might lead to other, and unjustified, conclusions.

I am well aware that the United States of this day is very much a
polyglot country, and that within this country people of my particular
native milieu, commonly described by the modern acronym "Wasps,"

are now a minority, and a dwindling minority at that. With the fading from the national memory of many of the aspects of that milieu has gone the currency of many of its values. I, too, have retained only a portion of those values; for no generation retains in toto the values of its predecessors, and least of all do they remain unchanged when the subject has lived extensively in contact with other cultures and outlooks. But some of those values—the bulk of them, probably—have been retained; and these, as they find reflection in this book, will no doubt be widely questioned or challenged.

For all of this, the United States is for me, if only because I was born and reared in it at the outset of this century and served it as faithfully as I could for some twenty-seven years in the American Foreign Service, a country like no other country. One may hope, of course, to have some usefulness even beyond one's country's borders; and that hope I, too, from time to time, have indulged. But there can, for the likes of me, be only one final center of loyalty and concern. Such a center, however strange it now is to me, and I to it, could be only the country into which I was born. The world at large, as a possible center of this sort, would be too broad for these frail shoulders.

Nor do the strangeness of much of the place and the narrow limits of my direct contact with it constitute any total barriers to understanding. There are many aspects of American life that are spread fairly evenly across the country and are not only observable for anyone living anywhere within it but actually press themselves upon his or her consciousness, whether he or she likes it or not. The television screen pours out a never-ending stream of images reflective in one way or another of life across the nation, as do the other great advertising media—images seldom thoughtfully reflective, to be sure, sometimes even designed to mislead, and yet instructive even in their very conceptual shallowness and their obviously ulterior motivations. To live anywhere in this country, in short, is to live in a great deal of it.

Still, the question will arise, at least in some minds, What makes him think that his views on this country would be worth our reading? He is not an expert on it. He has never given special study to its problems. Why should his views have value beyond those of hundreds of other elderly people who, precisely because they recognize similar limitations in themselves, don't write books?

The question is well placed. And my answer to it is only that in writing on this subject, as I am about to do, I am simply trying to respond to the demands of some critics that I try to identify, somewhat more specifically than I have ever done in the past, those of my views and reactions—of my prejudices, if you like—that might be said to be of a philosophical nature. And if, then, there are those who think that this purpose might be served by a sketch of the way this country and its problems look to one who has led such and such a life and has been exposed to such and such influences, then here it is; and this, without apologies for its limitations.

It will be necessary to move swiftly over many of these problems. It will not be possible to do more than to touch very briefly on certain of the questions at issue, and then only from the standpoint of their wider significance. This is not another book about American society in general as it nears the end of the century.

But here these views shall be exposed, as well as I can state them. Some relate to existing physical conditions of American society. Some relate to its habits—habits so deeply ingrained as to approach the status of addictions. Others relate to prevalent attitudes that find their expression in the media and in the utterances of political and other leaders. That some of them will be attractive targets for outraged disagreement, I have no doubt.

I approach the stating of these views with many hesitations. Tocqueville, in undertaking the writing of the second volume of his work on America, said, in a letter to a friend, "It seems to me at this point that I am walking on air, and that I must inevitably fall, headlong and helplessly, into the vulgar, the absurd, or the tedious."[1] At the risk of taking the divine as an example for the ordinary, I must confess to similar

1. The French original: "Ici, il me semble que je suis en l'air, et que je vais dégringoler infailliblement, sans pouvoir m'arrêter, dans le commun, l'absurde, ou l'ennuyeux." Letter of May 26, 1836, to one Bouschitt, as cited in the introduction, by Françoise Mélonio, to the Robert Laffont edition of Tocqueville's major works (Paris, 1986).

anxieties as I confront the writing of the second part of this book. But I
see, as Tocqueville plainly saw, no alternative to the effort.

Precisely because these views will be out of accord with so much of
what passes as the conventional American wisdom of the day, they may
seem to convey a negative and pessimistic view of American society,
even one that challenges its very worth. This being the case, I should
probably preface them with a word or two of explanation.

American politicians never miss a chance to refer to the United
States as "this great country." So insistently do they do this that if their
motives in doing so were less obvious, one might suspect that they were
trying to overcome a certain uncomfortable doubt about this in their
own minds. We could do, it seems to me, with less frequent reassurance
on this point. But they are, of course, right. The United States *is* a great
country—if only in size and populousness and in the significance it has
attained over these past two centuries as a factor in the world community. And the fact that the ways in which it is great are not, to some of
us at least, the ways in which a great many Americans, including
politicians, see its true greatness as lying does not controvert the general
assertion.

For me to try to identify the various elements of the country's
greatness would be, inevitably, to sound pompous and condescending.
We are dealing, here, with something far larger than any one of us—
something of which each of us is only a tiny part, and of which our
judgment can never be more than imperfect. And it would come with
ill grace for any of us, claiming as we do to be a part of the whole, to
list the virtues in which we ourselves, by implication, profess to share.

But beyond that, the country has plenty of faults to balance off
against whatever virtues it could be said collectively to possess; and if it
is indeed great, a signal aspect of its greatness lies surely in its quality as
a vast human battleground on which there is fought out a titanic
contest between not just the virtues and deficiencies of its own life but
many that are shared in high degree by most of the advanced countries
of the world. The outcome of this battle is indeterminate; only one

thing is certain: it will lead to no total victory for one side or the other. For that, human nature and human affairs are too complicated.

In this very indeterminateness—in the limitations of our vision and our power—there lies the same tragic quality that has always marked the great moments of human history. And in this sense America, if a great country, is also a tragic one. But tragedy is a dialectical concept, implying the confrontation between positive and negative phenomena. If the positive aspects of American civilization, as I see them, were not present in a measure at least comparable to the negative ones, even the element of tragedy would be absent, and America would be a very pitiable spectacle indeed. And all I can add, to what I have already said about its greatness, is that this—as a pitiable spectacle—is not at all the way I see it.

Chapter Six

EGALITARIANISM
AND DIVERSITY

The distinction of ranks and *persons* is the firmest basis
of a mixed and limited government. . . . The perfect
equality of men is the point in which the extremes of
democracy and despotism are confounded. . . .
—Edward Gibbon, *The Decline and Fall of the Roman
Empire*

One of the difficulties in writing such a book as this lies in the
problem of classification. Because the effort is addressed to very broad
concepts, vague at the edges and often intertwining and interlocking, it
is hard to find clear divisions between one concept and another. One
can only plunge headlong into this subject matter, hoping that the
reader will himself perceive the interrelationships among the various
headings and topics and will discern something of the broad unity of
philosophical concept that presumably unites them all.

In this spirit, and not knowing any better place to begin in this
exposé of some of my views about my country, I shall select one issue
which, I should suppose, is about as controversial as any that I could

find, and move into it as a starter. For want of a better name, let it be presented as the issue of egalitarianism versus variety.

Tocqueville and Egalité

One cannot speak of egalitarianism without recalling, first, some of the conclusions of the man who gave greater attention to precisely this subject than any other thinker of the modern era: Alexis de Tocqueville. Born in 1805 into an aristocratic French family, Tocqueville, upon visiting the United States in 1831, became fascinated with the contrast between the hierarchically structured society in which he had been born and raised and the highly egalitarian society he found before him in America. This subject dominated his impressions of the United States; and while his great work, *Democracy in America,* the two parts of which appeared with a five-year interval later in the 1830s, referred to democracy in its title, the real subject of the book was equality—equality as observable in America: in the first volume, equality in general, in the second one, in America but elsewhere as well. Actually, he used the two terms "equality" and "democracy" almost interchangeably, because he regarded the equality of status of the members of the citizenry, socially and politically, as *the* outstanding feature of American democracy, overriding all others in importance.

The reason for this absorbing interest in the egalitarian aspects of American society was that Tocqueville was persuaded that this—the triumph of the principle of equality over that of hierarchy and differentiation—was the wave of the future for all of the western European world that he cared about. He saw all of European civilization as tending inexorably in that direction; and while this prospect saddened him, for it implied the demise of all that he had come to love and to respect in the position and the traditions of his own family, he felt very strongly the necessity of studying it, of coming to understand it, and, finally, of coming to some sort of terms with it. He perceived positive as well as negative features in American democracy, and did not fail to recognize the positive ones in his book, as short-term advantages of this form of government; but for the long term he had very serious reservations about it. People, he thought, were more greatly attracted by the principle of equality than by the principle of liberty; and confronted with a choice between the two, as he thought they eventually would be (for he regarded the two as ultimately incompatible), they would choose equality. He described the taste for equality, at one point, as a depraved one, which would impel the weak to try to drag the strong down to their level and would induce them to prefer equality in servitude to liberty in inequality.[1] He thought, too, that equality would lead to an unfortunate centralization of power in the state and that this centralized power would take the form not of any sort of personal tyranny or dictatorship but rather of what he called "an anonymous despotism for which no one person would stand as responsible." "What is to be feared," he wrote, "is not a perverse individual, and not a maddened mob—it is a bureaucratic tyranny that would make possible the weakness of the individual." This tyranny, he envisaged, would not oppress the people in the classical manner but would encourage passivity in them and hold them in submission by pandering to their thirst for the material comforts and for a total social equality.[2]

Looked at from the perspective of more than one hundred and fifty years, these fears of Tocqueville appear somewhat overdrawn, to be sure, but not wholly without validity, at least so far as the United States is concerned. In these intervening years the power of the federal government has indeed gained at the expense of that of the states. The growth of bureaucracy and its role in the governmental process will be noted in the following chapter. And the large proportion of Americans who, while continuing to demand of their government that it assure their material prosperity, fail to exercise their right to vote in the presidential and other elections would stand as a good measure of confirmation for what Tocqueville perceived as their indifference to

1. *De la démocratie en Amérique,* pt. 2, in the Robert Laffont edition of Tocqueville's major works (Paris, 1986), p. 81.
2. Ibid., p. 418. In the French original: "Ce qu'il faut craindre ce n'est pas un individu pervers ou une foule en folie, c'est la tyrannie bureaucratique qui rend désormais possible la faiblesse des individus."

the nature of governmental authority so long as it pandered sufficiently to their material interests. It will be well, therefore, to hold these anxieties of Tocqueville's in mind as we turn to the egalitarian tendencies in the American society of this day and elsewhere.

Egalitarianism and Socialism

These words are being written at a time when the columns of the papers and the television screens are full of what is called the collapse and demise of communism—not only in the USSR and Eastern Europe but in large measure on a world scale. If communism be seen as a governmental system, there is good reason for this. But if it be seen as an ideology—as a form of Marxism—it is only partly true. Radical Marxism of the Leninist variety (which remained, however abused, the theoretical foundation of Soviet society down through the Stalinist period and until the final breakdown in 1991) may have failed as the foundation for a governmental system; but as a theoretical approach to social problems, Marxism in general—or at least a part of it—has deeply influenced the thinking of millions of people worldwide, and this in many instances where these people were not even aware of the source of the influence. And the particular feature of Marxism that has had the widest and deepest effect has been the implicit egalitarianism that has lain, together with the theories of surplus value and exploitation, at the heart of the doctrine.

A striking example of this will be seen, curiously enough, in the Soviet Union itself. Even those of us who saw a good deal of Russian society in the heyday of Soviet power were unaware (at least I was) of the extent to which the regime had instilled, or at least encouraged, among the common people, especially in the countryside, egalitarian tendencies. Where we outsiders saw only a ruthless totalitarian regime oppressing an entire population, the reality was that to a great many in the poorer and more backward ranks of the population the economic misery brought to them by the regime was significantly moderated by its very equality—by the fact that it was shared by the vast majority of the people around them. This equality of misery was in some respects their only solace—the only thing they had to hold on to. And this explains the extreme suspicion and jealousy with which, even in the post-Communist period, they have continued to watch their neighbors to make sure that none of them had contrived to make some money and was living better than they did.[3] It has been particularly depressing to learn to what great extent, even after the collapse of communism, any effort on the part of individual persons in the countryside to better their situation by ventures in free enterprise has been actually resented, opposed, and seen as an effort to take improper advantage of others, by fellow citizens whose own poverty was the product of the Communist system.

In the non-Communist parts of the Western world, it seems to have been primarily the Scandinavian welfare states that have reflected most strongly the egalitarian tendencies prominent in Marxist thinking. This is not unnatural given the extent to which they had their ideological origins in the social-democratic movements, which were essentially Marxist in inspiration. In any case, I can think of no part of the world where society and politics are more deeply penetrated by egalitarian principles than they are in certain, if not all, of the Scandinavian countries.

In the European Marxist versions of egalitarianism, a prominent feature seems always to have been the belief that there could be no social justice until everyone lived in the same personal economic situation as everyone else. To this goal all other factors affecting living standards were to be sacrificed. It did not matter what your priorities were. You might have preferred to earn by hard work, and then to save and skimp in order to attain a way of personal living that seemed to you more comfortable, more tasteful, or in some other way preferable to that of your neighbors. But the fellow who chose to work as little as

---

3. Tocqueville, perceptive man that he was, did not fail to notice this phenomenon: "When inequality is the common law of a society, the most extreme inequalities do not strike the eye at all; but when everything is nearly on one level, the slightest inequalities become offensive. It is for that reason that the thirst for equality always becomes the more insatiable in the degree that the equality is more pronounced." Ibid., p. 522 (the translation is my own).

he could get by with, and not to save at all or to spend his savings at the gaming tables, was as much entitled to this uniform, officially approved style of living as were you. The main thing was that no one should live better than anyone else. Uniformity was an end in itself. If your style of living deviated from it downwards—if, that is, you were poorer than the golden mean, even as the result of shiftlessness—this was nothing discreditable; it was merely a sign that you were unjustly deprived, and deserved greater benefits from the state. To deviate from it upwards, however, or at least to show signs of doing so, was reprehensible. It was a sign that you were depriving someone else of something, and ought not to be tolerated.

By my own observation, and much of it from life in socialist countries, I know of no assumption that has been more widely and totally disproved by actual experience than the assumption that if a few people could be prevented from living well everyone else would live better. I have seen village after village in Russia where the wealthy landlord and his family had been driven out, killed or dispossessed, where the ashes of the ruins of his house stood as mute and tragic evidence of his elimination, but where the prevailing misery could not have been greater than it was. I have, to be sure, seen welfare states where a wide improvement in living standards for the mass of the people indeed went hand in hand with the disappearance of most evidences of ostentatious prosperity on the part of the few. But this had been achieved not so much by the impoverishment of the wealthy as by the prevalent egalitarian social spirit that had caused the latter to conceal the evidences of their prosperity rather than to flaunt it. In itself this was, perhaps, not a bad thing. But it did not prove that the impoverishment of the few was essential to the advancement of living standards among the many.

The plain fact, which I believe will be confirmed by many economists, is that the luxuries of the very rich are of relatively little importance as a factor in the general economy of the modern advanced country. Much of what the rich own must, after all, be invested in ways which, while indeed they are normally profitable to one degree or another for the rich themselves, also benefit, by the very fact of the investment, the general economy. Which is better?—that the rich should themselves invest their surplus income or that the government should take it by taxation, and then, after passing it through the sticky substance of its own bureaucracy, spend it in its own favored ways? The government would claim that it spends it (or what is left of it when the bureaucrats have taken their cut) for the public good. The rich would say that they themselves use it, and invest it, more wisely and economically than the government could. There is much to be said, it seems to me, for the latter view.

To say these things is not to deny that there has been, and no doubt still is here and there in all the European welfare states, such a thing as social injustice. There was far more of it in earlier decades, and particularly in the early stages of the industrial revolution. There is so little of it today in the advanced countries of the West that Marx himself, one suspects, had he been able to observe the industrial economies of this day, would have found his goals very largely achieved, and would have been astonished only by the ways in which this had been brought about, which were not the revolutionary ways he had thought essential to this end. Nevertheless, a certain amount of injustice does exist. Where it does, the state has means of moving against it; and by all means let it do so. But I find, in the liberal treatment of these questions, so much oversimplification, social jealousy, and intellectual posturing that I have no choice but to disassociate myself from it.

Egalitarianism in the United States

When we turn to the United States, we see that here, too, egalitarianism has had profound effects. The first great agency of this tendency has been the American governmental system itself, which is unapologetically and proudly egalitarian. All democratic governments have much of this quality, but in the American government it has particular importance. For while most of the European democratic governments have administrative structures through which laws can be interpreted, and their rigidity modified in the application to the individual citizen, we have, as interpreters of the laws, only the courts; and their interpretive judgments, like the law itself, have only a collective applicability, affecting alike all who come within their purview, and allowing no flexibility in relation to the individual citizen. This system, excluding as it does most administrative discretion and flexibility, gives to the law a position of unique and exclusive importance at the center of government—a situation reflected in the numerousness and prominence of lawyers in our public life and in the enormous amount of interpretative litigation with which our courts are burdened.

Now, because the law consists of great sweeping dicta prescribing the behavior of large numbers of people, and because we are, quite properly, all equal in the eyes of the law, the law constitutes the greatest and most authoritative of all the equalizing influences bearing on our society. And the scope of this equalizing effect is naturally enhanced by the growing centralization of government—by the growth of federal power, that is, in proportion to that of the states. Numbers of issues—such things as abortion, integration, and treatment of social or ethnic minorities—which at the outset of our independent national history would surely have been regarded (if they were seen as concerns for public authority at all) as proper concerns for the state governments, are now the objects of strident demands for treatment at the federal level, whether by legislation or by interpretation by the courts, or even sometimes by constitutional amendment. And every step in that direction, tending as it does to centralize in Washington the control over some of the most intimate details of personal or local life, is a step on the path to that total egalitarianism that loomed so unsettlingly on Tocqueville's intellectual horizon.

But it is not only in the governmental system that such tendencies are present. They are strongly represented in popular attitudes and expectations as well; and here they assume what, in the view of outsiders, must be seen as curious forms. First, there is the attitude toward wealth. Here, in contrast to the situation that seems to prevail in Russia, it has never been regarded as reprehensible to *make* money. To *have* it in large amounts is perhaps more questionable. It means, at least, that you should be more heavily taxed than others are. To have *inherited* it is, however, another matter. Thus George Bush can be seriously charged, by his political opponents, with having been born "with a silver spoon in his mouth," as though it were well established that to have been born to wealthy parents was, at least from the political standpoint, a serious deficiency of character. The politically ambitious person, it may be inferred, should be more careful in the selection of his parents.[4]

It is apparent, from these oddities in American attitudes, that where wealth is resented, the resentment centers not so much on the material comforts and luxuries it affords as on the incidental perquisites—the prestige, the privilege, the enhanced influence—that are seen as accompanying it. It is, in other words, the inequality of status that wealth is supposed to assure, rather than the inequality in wealth or income for its own sake, that arouses the resentment. And this is no doubt a reason why the egalitarian tendencies of the country have centered so sharply on the educational process. The more expensive the educational facilities, from the grade school up, the more they are seen as unjust channels of advancement to privileged status, and are resented accordingly. It matters not greatly whether, in any given instance, the parents skimped and saved and sacrificed in order to make possible the resort to these facilities or even whether the student himself took outside employment to make possible his access to them. Nor was the fact that in most instances they gave superior instruction allowed to stand as a redeeming feature. If such instruction could not be given to everyone, it should, in this view, not be given to anyone.

But it is important to note that the charges and complaints along this line find their expression primarily in liberal intellectual circles and in the press and media rather than among the people who, one might think, were the principal victims of these supposed injustices. It is not so

4. But even here, the matter is complicated. It is not a question of just being born anywhere to such parents. To constitute a serious mark against you, it must have been birth into something called the eastern establishment, where everyone is assumed to be wealthy. Birth to wealthy parents elsewhere in the country is less serious, if indeed serious at all. This curious distinction parallels an oddity of primitive Russian egalitarianism, which accepted the privileges of the party elite, regarded as the normal perquisites of authority, far more easily than it did the minuscule material advantages that might be detectible in the next-door neighbor.

much from the sufferers of poverty as from their intellectual protago-
nists that these complaints come. Much of this may be explained perhaps by the fact that the sufferers have, comparatively speaking, few
possibilities for making their voices heard. But it is among the liberal
intellectual circles that questions of status seem to be of greatest importance; and one cannot evade the occasional suspicion that it is not so
much sympathy for the underdog that inspires much of this critical
enthusiasm as a desire to tear down those who preempt the pinnacles of
status to which they themselves aspire.

Domestic Service

I cannot leave this discussion of the social aspects of American egalitarianism without mentioning the question of domestic service.

Of particular importance here, it seems to me, is the preservation in
some degree of domestic service, as an institution. In the Scandinavian
countries, it has virtually disappeared; and the same situation is being
approached in this country. Here again, it is a question of the golden
mean. Certainly, domestic service was overdone, and the servant class
was often exploited and treated in unworthy ways, in the affluent
Victorian household of a century ago. And then, too, it has not been a
bad thing, in our own age, that many persons of reasonable affluence
have found themselves obliged to perform daily certain of the chores
once consigned to the domestic servant. Some of this has proved to be
usefully distracting and not unbeneficial to health, to humility, and,
ultimately, to the soul.

But this, too, can be carried too far. A society wholly devoid of the
very institution of domestic service is surely in some ways a deprived
society, if only because this situation represents a very poor division of
labor. There are people for whom service in or around the home pretty
well exhausts their capabilities for contributing to the successful functioning of a society. There are others who have different and rarer
capabilities; and it is simply not a rational use of their abilities that they
should spend an inordinate amount of time and energy doing things
that certain others could no doubt do better, and particularly where

these are just about the only things the latter are capable of doing.

There is, in my opinion, no function in human society, which, if truly necessary and useful, is demeaning for anyone. There is none that does not have its dignity, particularly if performed as well as the respective worker can perform it. There is none, for this reason, the performance of which should be looked down on. This goes for domestic service as well as for anything else.

There are those, of course, who do not need domestic service, and there are others who, if they had it, would not know how to use it well. But the only person who should be deprived on principle of the very use of it is the one who would not know how to respect the dignity of the person who performs it, and who would see in the performance of it by someone else a proof of his own superiority. I repeat: the true glory of any useful occupation lies not in the seeming elevation or glamorousness of the position in question but in the integrity and conscientiousness of the effort made to meet the demands of the job. No honest and useful work, however humble, should ever be looked down upon.

I find it hard to picture a great deal of Western culture without the institutions of domestic service that supported it. I can think of none of the great writers of the past, including those who were often strapped for money, who did not have some forms of such assistance. Even the great painters of the Paris *bohème* of the late nineteenth century seem always to have had some sort of a helper who looked after what one French poet called "less details bas et repugnants de l'existence" for them. I cannot, somehow, picture Tocqueville combining his serene meditations with the washing of the pots and pans and the removal of trash from the kitchen premises. That this form of service sometimes involved injustice and exploitation, I admit and regret. That it needed to involve this, I deny. So I regret the passage of the institution.

Segregation

Another of the points at which the spirit of egalitarianism finds its most significant application is the question of segregation versus desegregation. Well aware of the racial overtones that inevitably present themselves in any discussion of this subject—aware, again, that the idea of desegregation has become one of those shibboleths to which American opinion is so prone that anyone who questions one of them finds himself looked at with gasping horror—I still have to express a view of this subject that may not accord with the mainstream of American political and social discourse.

Segregation or its opposite can take many forms and affect many aspects of life. Residential and educational arrangements are only the ones that come most readily to mind when the term is used. There are no doubt others as well. Far be it from me to claim that there are no aspects of American life in which desegregation would have a proper place. But when it comes to these major controversial areas, I would say this:

Forced segregation? Of course not. But neither should there be forced desegregation. People should be allowed to do what comes naturally. There are a great many instances in which people prefer the proximity, the neighborhood, and the social intimacy of people who share their customs, their way of talking, their way of looking at things. This does not mean, and certainly should not mean, that they should not be expected to respect similar feelings on the part of the others. Americans seem to have difficulty recognizing that there can be, and are, differences that have nothing to do with "better" or "worse"—differences that might be called (in the terminology of this day) morally neutral—and are yet greatly worth preserving.

Demands for desegregation are often cast in terms that would allow you to think that this was a matter of principle, the positive value of which we had all accepted, which could tolerate no questioning, and need not even be discussed. We have agreed, one is allowed to conclude, that wherever there is a question of uniformity or of variety, uniformity is always preferable.

But question it I must. Recognizing that a great deal of America is the product of the melting pot, and that most of this has been and remains unavoidable, I see no intrinsic virtue in the melting pot as such. Where differences in customs and life-styles exist, and where there is a possibility of preserving them, I would think it better that they should not be obliterated. The preservation and cultivation of them adds, it seems to me, to the color of life. The aesthetic and spiritual tensions they engender can and should be productive and creative ones. The social tensions that occasionally accompany them are unnecessary and, indeed, regrettable; but they are greatest where the effort is made to obliterate the differences artificially and to force people to ignore them and to try to cultivate an intimacy they do not truly feel.

I have lived in and read about cities in other countries where several cultural and ethnic communities lived peacefully side by side, each in its own part of town, its members mingling, to be sure, with others in the premises and functions of employment, but looking to their own particular communities for the meeting of their social, religious, and educational needs. The Riga of the 1920s, for example, was such a place. Each of these communities had, in this instance, its own schools, newspapers, clubs, theaters, and diversions. So long as they viewed each other with tolerance, and so long as any one of them did not attempt to lord it over the others (as one, regrettably, eventually did) all went well; and there was no reason why it should not have gone on through generations. No melting pot was thought necessary; and indeed, none was ever achieved. Elements of this arrangement of life, though less strictly formalized, can be seen today in New York and in other great American cities.

Obviously, this area of problems is one of great complexity. That there are places and situations where desegregation would be the best answer, I do not doubt. But precisely because of this I am suspicious of all efforts to solve the resultant problems by inflexible national norms. Let the solutions be, by all means, in the first instance responsive to local feelings, local customs, and local needs.

Particularly, in my view, should this apply to primary education. The more this can be democratized at the local level, and the more it can be liberated from the educational bureaucracies of the federal and state governments and even the teachers' unions, the better. That there are professional standards teachers should be expected to meet, and that some minimum standards of professional training might be necessary to assure the meeting of them, I can understand. But the great and essential qualities for teaching at the primary level are surely love of teaching, love of children, and love of subject. No teacher should be without them. No professional training alone can assure them. Let the local community, as embodied in the school district, take into account its own peculiar needs. Let it try to assure that the teachers meet these requirements and that they are adequately paid. Let this apply to the ghetto school as well as to any other. But with this in hand, then, let the school go its way as a neighborhood one. Let the children, if in any way possible, walk to it from their homes, as children always have. And if the school premises are simple and inexpensive, so much the better.

Least of all is there any advantage, visible to me, to be gained from busing children over great distances for the purpose of changing the racial mixture in other schools. Aside from the fact that in most of the larger cities the results of this practice have been exactly the opposite of what they were intended to be (in the sense that the schools ended up no more racially mixed than they were before and, in many instances, far less so), this betrays a serious confusion of priorities. The purpose, function, and dedication of the school is education. And there can be no justification for sacrificing any of this dedication in order to exploit the school (and its children) for what are in reality social, as distinct from educational, needs. Beyond which, we need the preservation and the encouragement of good schools as much as we need the improvement of bad ones. Actually these two needs are not mutually exclusive. But neither of them will be met by attempts to use the schools as instruments for social integration. If the neighborhood school, reflecting, as it should, residential patterns, finds itself accommodating children of racial diversity, fine; and let every child be treated like any other, which is the only way any real teacher would ever treat any of them. But please, no forcing of the mixture for reasons other than educational.

It is the lesson of history, after all, that every attempt at social leveling ends with leveling to the bottom, never to the top. Yet in this case the preservation of the top, I repeat, is as important as the improvement of the bottom. Where we have a good school, let us prize it, value it, encourage it. If it compares well to others, let us be happy that it does. Let others take it as an example and emulate it where they can. The ultimate results will be more beneficial to the educational process than any number of attempts to misuse the school for purposes of social change.

Elitism

The converse of egalitarianism, at least in many minds, would be "elitism." I must confess my amazement at the constant use of this term in a pejorative sense in so much of the public discourse of this country, as though "elitism" were something we had all agreed was reprehensible and abhorrent, so abhorrent, in fact, that anyone who could be plausibly charged with a partiality toward it was thereby stamped as irredeemably wrongheaded and deserving of consignment to outer darkness.

I am unable to understand such a view of the term. The word "elite" is simply a derivative of the word "elect" (*élire*, in French). Its meaning is little different from that of the noun "the elect," signifying those who are chosen or elected. In the United States, to be sure, it is often thought of, and the word used, with relation to some sort of a social elite, with all the negative connotations—undeserved privilege, conceit, snobbishness, disdain for others, and so on—that this term evokes. This, indeed, is what is suggested by the only definition of it given by *Webster's:* "a group or body considered or treated as socially superior." But it is not the original definition. The *Oxford English Dictionary* comes closer to the real meaning of the word when it defines an elite as "the choice part or flower (of society, or of any body or class of persons)." It is in this sense, as I see it, that the term should be used.

And what, pray, is wrong with this? What is implied is not a priggish sort of self-selection, or an assignment of undeserved privilege, but merely the recruitment, out of a general mass of people, of those best qualified to perform certain useful functions of society and the charging of them with attendant responsibility. Whoever rejects the possibil-

EGALITARIANISM AND DIVERSITY

ity of that sort of choice flies in the face of the very principle of
election on which our nation is founded. Surely, these self-righteous
spurners of "elitism" are not recommending that we abandon the very
idea of election—that we choose our public servants by some sort of
lottery, and that the country be governed exclusively by gray medioc-
rity.

The simple fact is that in any great organization—government or
what you will—responsibility has to be borne and the day-to-day
decisions taken not by the mass of those involved but by tiny minorities
of them, and sometimes even individuals, chosen from their midst. This
is not primarily because the judgments of the mass would be necessarily
inferior to those of the "elect" (although one of the reasons for choos-
ing this "elect" ought normally to be the reasoned supposition that they
would have superior qualifications and facilities for making the decisions in question). The primary reason for this sort of selection is the
reality that a large mass of persons cannot, if only for purely physical
and mechanical reasons, be organized in such a way that it could carry
out a regular and systematic program of decision taking. For this, a
smaller body is necessary. And since such a smaller body has to exist,
what is wrong with trying to see to it that it is composed of those to
whom might reasonably be attributed the highest qualifications for the
exercise of this function?

Human beings, after all, may be born equal; and equal they should
unquestionably be in the face of the law. But this is just about the end
of their equality. Beyond this, they vary greatly in the capacity for
being useful to society, or to any group to which they belong. And
when it comes to the selection of small minorities of them to whom
legislative or administrative or judicial responsibility is to be assigned,
there the effort has to be made, at the very least, to find those best
qualified to meet the responsibilities in question. The process of selection may be faulty; it may be dreadfully abused, as indeed it sometimes
is. Human judgment is never perfect; and human institutions are at best
never more than approximations of the ideal. But the effort to select has
to be made. It cannot be avoided. And even those who are most vehe-

ment in their abhorrence of what they call an elite will have to accommodate themselves to this necessity.

The crucial question is not whether such things as elites must exist.
The question concerns only the quality of the elite in question and,
particularly, the standards and institutions by which it is selected. It
does not have to be an elite of privilege, least of all of undeserved
privilege. But we must remember that special responsibility, however
imperfectly it is exercised, often requires special facilities—sometimes
even special conveniences and prerequisites of authority. And superior
position has the right to demand at least outward respect. Respect is
due to the office whether or not the occupant seems fully worthy of it.
All the world, as Shakespeare observed, is a stage; and those who hold
high office (or lower office, too, for that matter) are merely playing
their respective parts in a certain drama, usually as best they can. Outside the office or the public platform or the other outward manifestations of their responsibility—in the intimacies, that is, of home and
family—the selected officials or legislators are, if you will, only human
beings much like the rest of us: beholden to all the silly requirements of
a physical existence, caught in the same turmoil of irrational emotions
and compulsions that assails the rest of us, seldom much more successful
than many others in coping with those imperfections of human nature
to which I invited attention in the first of these chapters. But in the
execution of their office, they represent something greater than themselves; and that something deserves respect.

For these reasons, I can find no patience for those who try to build
themselves up in their self-esteem by denying respect for established
authority and by trying to tear it down: for the students who fancy
they have proved something when they appear in weird and silly cos-
tumes at their own commencement; for the journalists who think they
have shown great cleverness and superiority by ridiculing highly placed
persons for their personal foibles; for the persons who throw eggs at the
limousines of visiting statesmen. Whoever is incapable of respect for
others is usually incapable, whether he recognizes it or not, of respect
for himself. By denying that anyone else could be worthy of respect, he

confesses, unwittingly, his own unworthiness of it.[5]

Such, then, are the thoughts provoked in my own mind by the accusations (some of which I myself have not been spared) of "elitism." Let us by all means have an elite. Let it be an elite of service to others, of conscience, of responsibility, of restraint of all that is unworthy in the self, and of resolve to be to others more than one could ever hope to be to one's self. But in once having this elite, however far it falls short of the ideal, let us respect it and not pretend that we could live without it. Here, I stand unrepentant, in the unabashed pursuit of what others call my elitist tendencies.

Plebiscite versus Representative Government

And if there are forms of elitism the fear of which is overdrawn, there are forms of what might be called its opposite that are not sufficiently feared. And these are the plebiscitary tendencies now making themselves felt in American society.

Our political system was, as the founding fathers conceived it, intended to be outstandingly that of a representative government. The term was often used in contradistinction to the concept of a pure democracy. In a pure democracy laws were to be adopted by decision of the entire community of the citizenry, gathered in public assembly. This, plainly, was something that was feasible only in a very small and intimate community. This explains its usefulness in the institution of the New England town meeting and in the innumerable forms of neighborhood cooperation that exist in small American communities.

Under a representative government, on the other hand—something necessary wherever the size of the self-governing entity surpassed that of the small neighborhood community—laws were to be drawn up and adopted not directly by the public but by a representative legislative body, or bodies, elected by the citizenry for this purpose. With this act

5. I think, here of Burke's stinging reproach to the radicals of the years of the French Revolution: "Respecting your forefathers, you would have been taught to respect yourselves."

of election, the public's active involvement in the legislative process was, for the moment, substantially completed. If citizens did not like what their representative was doing, they had the privilege of publicly criticizing it and, if their criticisms were ineffective, of voting at the next election to put someone else in his place.

While I am not sure that this was ever explicitly stated, it seems to me to have been implicit in this concept that the elected representative was expected, in the exercise of this legislative responsibility, to use his own personal judgment and to arrive at his own decisions. In doing so, he would, of course, also be expected to have in mind what he knew about the sentiments of those who had elected him, but he was not bound to be guided by these alone. He might, after all, have come to question their judgment. He might, in the very exercise of his legislative duties, have learned more about certain of the issues at stake in a bit of proposed legislation than was known to the general body of his constituency. In any case, he would have had the possibility of seeing his views refined by participation in the ordered and structured debate of the legislative chamber. His views must then have enjoyed the presumption of certain qualities above and apart from those of the constituents who had elected him. There was good reason, therefore, why he, once elected, should be guided primarily, in the exercise of his office, by his own knowledge and judgment of the question at hand. This was, of course, the ideal. The classic example for it was given by Burke, as illustrated in his well-known *Letter to the Sheriffs of Bristol*. As a member of the House of Commons, and aware that a position he felt bound in good conscience to take ran counter to the strong feelings of at least a part of his constituency, Burke wrote this letter of some fifty pages to explain to the constituents why he felt as he did about the issue in question and why he proposed to vote accordingly. But then, in order to make it clear that he intended to stand his ground, even if it cost him reelection (which it did), he added the following classic sentence:

> If I were ready, on any call of my own vanity or interest, or to answer any election purpose, to forsake principles . . . which I had formed at a

mature age, on full reflection, and which had been confirmed by long experience, I should forfeit the only thing which makes you pardon so many errors and imperfections in me.

This, I repeat, was the ideal. Normally, and particularly in this country, things have not worked quite that way. Seldom, one must assume, have representatives been prepared to fly as heroically as did Burke in the face of the opinions or prejudices of those who elected them, thus jeopardizing their own chances for reelection. But the ideal remains intact. And it still plays some part in the behavior of the American legislator, if only because he is frequently confronted with the need for decisions on questions with regard to which he has never had the opportunity or even the time to consult the feelings of a majority of his constituents, and is therefore obliged to use his own judgment, or because the issues involved, particularly when it comes to hectic last-moment adjustments of language in specific bills, are too intricate, and too urgent, to be taken in any way before his constituents.

And it is something else again when the electors are asked to express their opinions directly by means of some sort of an officially arranged plebiscite or referendum, or when private polls are taken of their opinions.

The idea of the passage or the repeal of legislation by direct popular vote rather than by regular parliamentary procedures marches under a number of names—plebiscites, public questions on ballots, direct democracy, and citizen legislation among them—but the idea is generally known in this country as "initiative and referendum."[6] In detail, it can take various forms; but provisions allowing for procedures of this general nature already exist, as I understand it, in the constitutions of some twenty-three states, most of them west of the Mississippi. And I have the impression that there is much lively, if not growing, sentiment

6. There are many variations in the meaning given to these terms in the different states; but, in general, "initiative" is taken to mean the initiation and passage of legislation by direct popular vote, whereas "referendum" means the review or removal by such a vote of statutes already passed by a legislative body.

in favor of setting up new such arrangements where they do not already exist, and of exploiting further those that do.[7]

In any case, I mention these tendencies here in order to express my strong aversion to them on principle. I see the idea of initiative and referendum as being in flat contradiction to the principles of representative government that have lain at the heart of our constitutional system from its very foundation.

The idea that legislation should be made or repealed by popular majorities involves, in the first place, the forfeiture of all those advantages of the system of representative government that were mentioned above, especially the presumptive superior knowledge on the part of the legislator of the issue at stake and its background, and the possibility of refinement of decision by means of ordered debate on the legislative floor or in the appropriate committee.

Second, the device of initiative and referendum invites all the evils of single-issue thinking and voting. There are literally no public issues involved in legislation that do not have implications for other issues as well. There are none that have qualities on the merits of which, alone, they can safely be treated. The elected legislator knows this. He cannot deal with any one question entirely in isolation. He is constantly being confronted not just with a single legislative question but with numbers of them. He is obliged to reconcile the position he takes on one question with those he takes on others. He has to balance the pros and cons, and he may never forget that what gratifies one constituent may offend another.

Not so the common citizen, asked to vote on a single public question. This question comes before him in starkest isolation, demanding an answer: yes or no. He is not asked or encouraged to take into

7. In the state of New Jersey, where these lines are being written, the question of an amendment to the state constitution, allowing for the possibility of legislation by initiative and referendum, has been before the legislature for some fifteen years; and the result of the most recent election would seem to presage an early favorable decision. I note, furthermore, that in this most recent election, in California, there were some twenty-eight questions of this nature on the ballot, which I take to be evidence of extensive enthusiasm for this method of legislating.

account the wider implications. Nothing stops him, of course, from taking the trouble to inform himself on these broader implications; and some no doubt do; but there is nothing that constrains them to do it. The more common individual reaction is to give to the questions a relatively casual answer—an answer usually inspired primarily by whatever emotional nerves the question most intimately touches.

The voter-citizen has no choice, furthermore, but to accept the wording of the question as it is flung at him by whoever instituted the poll. He cannot modify it, amend it, or attempt to clarify it. He cannot respond by saying, "Yes, but . . ." or "Provided that. . . ." He is in fact at the mercy of whoever phrased the question. Yet anyone who has any knowledge of the role played by question and answer in public debate knows that the terms of the question often dictate a large part of the answer.

We have, finally, the fact that a decision once taken in this way, if it turns out to have unfortunate consequences, is relatively hard to change. A legislative body, faced with a similar situation affecting any of the laws it has passed, has much greater flexibility in this respect. It may rescind the law, or amend it, or pass another one in its place. For all this, nothing more is required than a simple vote of the body in question. To do any of these things with the decision of a popular referendum is far more difficult. Any change of this nature involves preparatory steps and procedures as cumbersome and protracted as those of the original measure itself. It allows very little flexibility, if any at all, in the recognition and correction of mistakes.

It will be argued that in our federal Congress as it exists today, some of the greatest advantages of the classical concept of formal legislative deliberation have already been forfeited in a number of ways: by the virtual abandonment of ordered and structured debate on the floor of the legislative chamber in favor of intricate political maneuvering in committee meetings; by the abject dependence of many legislators on the sources of their campaign expenditures; and by the penetration of lobbyists into the most intimate recesses of the parliamentary body.

True enough. All these evils exist, and cry out for correction. In certain instances they are even worse than the language used above would suggest. The admission of television cameras into the legislative chamber, in particular, is even worse than the mere abandonment of the use of that chamber for normal deliberation and debate. In the depressing spectacle of the individual legislator haranguing an empty house before the cameras in order to suggest to the folks back home that he is addressing a great legislative body hanging on his every word—in this you have one of the most pathetic examples of the triumph of the contrived image over the reality, a triumph inherent in the very nature of the television medium, and one about which more will be said in another chapter. By this shabby sellout to the television industry, Congress has forfeited a large part of its own dignity and, with it, of the very function with which the founding fathers were concerned to endow it.

It will obviously be very difficult to achieve the correction of these distortions at the federal level. Some may even be already beyond the possibility of correction. To what extent it would be easier to avoid these same evils in smaller parliamentary bodies is impossible to predict. In any case, the proper answer is not, should never be, and in fact cannot be, plebiscitary democracy. The phrase is in itself a contradiction in terms. In the tendencies now running in that direction one has nothing less than the abandonment of faith in the democratically elected individual and the expression of a vain hope that a greater wisdom will be found to lie in the consultation of the faceless collectivity. This implies the loss of the very principle of personal responsibility of the elected representative, on which our governmental system was founded, in favor of an irresponsible and unreal anonymity of power. It leaves an open field to the backstage manipulator and the shameless demagogue. Neither will fail to take advantage of it.

No less symptomatic in this respect is the flood of unofficial public opinion polls recently undertaken (for their own commercial purposes) by the press and the media. No objection can be taken, of course, to this device, except where their results might influence an election already in progress. Such polls can be usefully informative for individual legislators as evidence of public reactions in matters with which they have to deal, so long as it is borne in mind that the polls are, after all, only one of the factors to be considered in the exercise of their legislative offices, and should never be viewed as substitutes for their own independent judgment on matters at stake. The public may, after all, be wrong, in the sense that the polls may reflect serious misapprehensions on the public's part which it is the duty of the legislative representative to expose and to set to rights rather than to accept passively. That is what leadership really ought to mean.

With these exceptions, there is, I repeat, nothing wrong about the sampling of public opinion in this way. But I cannot avoid the impression that the results of such samplings are often served up to the public by the pollster with the innuendo that there is, or ought to be, a certain unchallengeability and finality about them. "You see," the pollsters seem to be saying, "the public has given its verdict. That settles it." Particularly pervasive is this inference when polls are taken of the president's "popularity" at any given moment—of how many approve or do not approve of the way he is momentarily conducting his office—and all of this with the clear suggestion that here, in these undifferentiated and spontaneous reactions of the public, is the supreme and authoritative test of his performance of his presidential office, and the one to which his primary response is due.

It was pointed out above that the ultimate responsibility of government had normally to be borne by minorities, and sometimes even (as in the case of the American president) by individuals. The advantage of the American system has lain in the fact that the method of selection of such minorities or individuals, in the persons of legislative bodies or individual legislators, was regularized and their powers and responsibilities made clear.

What I particularly miss in all these plebiscitary approaches and devices is precisely the element of personal responsibility. This seems, in fact, to be a characteristic feature of all the egalitarian tendencies of the age. One notices that in the Scandinavian countries, where such tendencies find their most striking expression, it is hard to find any instance in which a single person can ever be clearly identified with any significant decision of public policy. Only collectivities appear in the capacity of decision takers; and these, very often, are bureaucracies. Because there is no clear allotment of personal authority, there is no allotment of personal responsibility. And the same anonymity of responsibility marks all the efforts in the United States to solve legislative problems, or to dictate the actions of executive branch officials, by the consultation of popular moods and responses in officially sanctioned initiatives and referenda or by means of the privately conducted opinion poll. Where personal decision lies buried, there, alongside it, lies personal responsibility. Where the role of the individual in public affairs is effaced, there, with it, disappears a good deal of the concept of public affairs that inspired the founding fathers of our republic.

Species and the Individual

I have reserved for mention at the end of this chapter, in view of the profundity of its implications, what I regard as the most significant of Tocqueville's doubts about democratic equality. In the body of the second part of his work, he had already complained of the tendency of the rulers of his age to concentrate on the great masses of their subjects and to neglect the individuals of whom those masses were composed.

> In order to concentrate only upon the people as a whole, one is no longer accustomed to envisaging the individual citizen; in thinking only of the species, one forgets the individual.[8]

And then, again, in the fourth part of his work, in summarizing his final conclusions, he returned, in a different way, to this subject:

> One might say that the rulers of our time seek only to do great things with men. I could wish that they would think a bit more about how to make men great; that they would give less importance to the work and more to the worker; and that they would never forget that a nation

8. *De la démocratie en Amérique,* in the Laffont edition of Tocqueville's major works (Paris, 1986), p. 448 (my translation). In the French original: "... on s'habitue à ne plus envisager les citoyens pour ne considerer que le peuple; on oublie les individus pour ne songer qu'à l'espèce."

cannot long remain strong when each man is personally weak, and that one has not yet found either the social forms or the political combinations to make a nation strong when the citizens who compose it are pusillanimous and soft.[9]

It is true that Tocqueville, in this passage, did not refer specifically to equality or democracy. But he felt that many of the features of the egalitarian-democratic state to which his book was addressed were beginning to pervade European governments across the board, even in the constitutional monarchies. It was this he had in mind when he used, in the second of the above passages, the term "rulers." And the question he was raising was whether the pandering to the material comforts of great masses of people, which he saw as implicit in the egalitarian-democratic society, would not have the effect of depriving the members of the natural elite of that society of the discipline and challenge necessary for the emergence of true greatness among them.

This is not the place to pursue this feature of Tocqueville's thought; but I signal it at this point, because it is, in my own view, one of great profundity. I did not like to leave it unmentioned in a chapter the contents of which took their departure from Tocqueville's views on democracy.

9. "On dirait que les souverains de notre temps ne cherchent qu'à faire avec les hommes des choses grandes. Je voudrais qu'ils songeassent un peu plus à faire de grands hommes; qu'ils attachassent moins de prix à l'oeuvre et plus à l'ouvrier, et qu'ils se souvinssent sans cesse qu'une nation ne peut rester long temps forte quand chaque homme y est individuellement faible, et qu'on n'a point encore trouvé de formes sociales ni de combinaisons politiques qui puissent faire un peuple énergique en le composant de citoyens pusillanimes et mous."

Chapter Seven

DIMENSIONS

... too many of us.
—the author (see below)

The next of the situations in American life which I should like to mention, and the one to which the remainder of this chapter will be devoted, relates primarily to the size and populousness of the country. If I were to be asked by a foreigner what strikes me most about my own people, two points, I think, would come most readily to mind: first, that we are a nation of bad social habits and, second, that there are far too many of us.

Let me stick, at this point, to the second of those assertions. If, as my first ambassadorial chief, Bill Bullitt (see chapter 1), once said, mankind is "a skin disease of the earth," then there is an optimal balance, dependent on the manner of man's life, between the density of human population and the tolerances of nature. This balance, in the case of the United States, would seem to me to have been surpassed when the American population reached, at a very maximum, two hundred million people, and perhaps a good deal less.

There is, of course, no way of measuring exactly the burden that man imposes upon nature. It depends in part on the way man lives. But if one looks only at the rate of depletion of vitally important and nonrenewable natural resources—for example, soil and water—it is evident that American society is rapidly consuming its own natural capital. It is exhausting and depleting the very sources of its own abundance. Much of this could be alleviated by changes in the habits of American society, as it exists today. Water could be more economically used; the use of chemical fertilizers could be curtailed; the destruction of grasslands, forests, and wetlands could be stopped; and so forth. But surely, the present environmental crisis is essentially the reflection of a disbalance between human population—its sheer numbers as well as its way of life—and the resources of the territory on which it resides.[1] The American Indian, as he existed before the white man came, was no doubt sometimes environmentally destructive, too. Even more so, I suspect, were the first white frontiersmen. But there were so few of them that nature could tolerate their destruction. It is this relationship that has changed in the United States, as it has changed in the dreadfully overpopulated countries of Western Europe. And it is this that I have in mind when I say that there are too many of us.

Size and Government

But there is also another sense in which this is true. We are, if territory and population be looked at together, one of the great countries of the world—a monster country, one might say, along with such others as China, India, the recent Soviet Union, and Brazil. And there is a real question as to whether "bigness" in a body politic is not an evil in itself, quite aside from the policies pursued in its name.

There is, in the first place, the question of the effect of size on the

---

1. The *New York Times,* on April 11, 1991, cited the former governor and senator Daniel Evans, who chaired the National Academy of Sciences panel that prepared the report for President Bush on global warming, as saying that population growth was "the biggest single driver of atmospheric pollution."

quality of government. The greater the country, the less the intimacy between rulers and ruled. The more these latter become separated by great bureaucracies and legislative establishments, the more the individual citizen feels isolated from any form of government above the local level. All this tends to the creation of a certain anonymity of federal power. And while this anonymity does not take on in the democracy the Kafkaesque sinisterness that it did under the totalitarian systems (where it was an essential feature of the terror), it still plays its part, contributing to the impression of remoteness and impersonality on the part of government and of insignificance and helplessness on the part of the individual, and thus impairing the very meaning of citizenship. In the times when I have chanced to live in smaller countries, I have envied them the greater intimacy of their political life—the fact that a far greater number of people in government knew one another personally, and that a larger percentage of common people knew at least someone in government. Governmental personalities tended less to be meaningless names to one another and to the constituents, and more to be living, accessible figures. This, to be sure, sometimes favored the intensification of animosities as well as of friendships. But better, I thought, to view with dislike someone you really knew than to fumble in the dark with figures that were no more than remote and inhuman ciphers. It is the anonymous ones that instill the nameless dread, the panic before the menacingly inhuman, the rumbling of the distant drum.

Aside from that, excessive size in a country results unavoidably in a diminished sensitivity of its laws and regulations to the particular needs, traditional, ethnic, cultural, linguistic, and the like, of individual localities and communities. The tendency, in great countries, is to take recourse to sweeping solutions, applying across the board to all elements of the population; and these have the drawbacks of all least common denominators. Particularly is this true in the United States, with its highly legalistic traditions, its dislike (as mentioned in the preceding chapter) of any sort of discriminating administration, its love for dividing people into categories, its fondness for regulating their lives in terms of these categories and treating them accordingly, rather than looking at the needs of individuals or of smaller groups and confronting these on the basis of common sense and reasonable discrimination. One of the unique features of American government is, in comparison with other modern systems, its neglect of intelligent and discriminating administration. It is a system that looks to the legislative branch to pass laws. It looks to the judiciary to interpret these laws. It looks to the executive branch to see that laws are carried out and enforced. But nowhere does it provide for the use of flexible judgment and common sense in their administration. Such questions are left, far more than they ought to be, to the courts, which are obliged to settle, by study of the letter of the law, numbers of matters that ought ideally to be decided on the basis of the merits of the particular problem at issue. But the decisions of the courts, particularly those of the Supreme Court, have themselves a normative character, and allow for little discretion in their application. Rarely, if ever, can the workings of federal laws be adjusted to meet unusual but reasonable requirements of the affected locality or individual.

A good example of this will be found in the current abortion conflict. Both sides seem to assume that this question should be decided by a sweeping national decision, applicable to every woman in the country, regardless of the circumstances of the particular case, as though there were not endless variations in the ways this problem presented itself. The greater a country is, and the more it attempts to solve great social problems from the center by sweeping legislative and judicial norms, the greater the number of inevitable individual harshnesses and injustices, and the less the intimacy between the rulers and the ruled. When I am confronted with the question "What is your position on abortion?" I can only reply, "Whose abortion?" I see no reason why the same rule should apply to tens of millions of women scattered across the land.

And there is a further quality of greatness of size in a country that deserves mention here. One might define it as the hubris of inordinate size. It is a certain lack of modesty in the national self-image of the great state—a feeling that the nation's role in the world must be equivalent to its physical size, with the consequent relative tendency to overweening pretensions and ambitions. I don't mean to say that the great power is always and everywhere imperialistic. There have been times, to be sure, when the United States was very much just that. The turn of the century, the period of the Spanish-American War, was one such time. But there have also been times when little of that sort of thing was observable. The fact remains that, generally speaking, the great country has a vulnerability to dreams of power and glory to which the smaller state is less easily inclined. Such dreams can be, and usually are, benevolent in intent, at least in the minds of their authors. But since the belief that one country can do much good for another country by intervening forcefully in the latter's internal affairs is almost invariably an illusion in the first place, the entertainment of such dreams is usually no more than another example of the proverbial road to hell, paved with good intentions.

Bureaucracy

Mention was made above of the significance of bureaucracy as one of the factors impeding any sort of intimacy in the relationship between the citizen and the governmental establishment. When the distance between the two becomes too great, it is democracy that suffers, bureaucracy that gains. And this mention calls for a few words of explication.

How to determine the number of human hands actually required for the performance of any given governmental function is not as easy a problem as it appears on the surface to be. Most of those who have served for any length of time in a large government office—or in any large organization, for that matter—will readily confirm, I believe, two observations that this writer carried away from his years in the State Department and the Foreign Service.

The first of these is that the growth of bureaucracy is largely self-engendered, in the sense that only a small part of it derives from the real requirements of the function to be served, the greater part being the product of tendencies and pressures arising within the bureaucratic process itself. The bureaucratic apparatus, in other words, grows, like a fungus, from purely internal causes, not connected with any real and legitimate need. Such growth is a form of illness in any large clerical organization and is, as such, not only illogical and unnecessary but at times directly detrimental to the ability of the unit in question to serve the purpose for which it was established. The State Department of the years of his service there often used to appear to this writer as a large, poorly designed, and overelaborate machine, the greater part of the energies of which were consumed in the effort to overcome its own internal frictions, the frictions being, of course, the products of over-staffing and bureaucracy. These last mean: more people involved, more internal correspondence, more staff meetings, more levels of authority, more offices to be consulted before anyone could decide anything. I have sometimes insisted that you could set up an American embassy in the middle of nowhere, with no host government to be accredited to, and its staff would be so preoccupied with its internal problems that within a year they would be complaining of shortage of personnel.

Second, it was clear to me then, on the basis of governmental experience, that there did not yet exist any science that could analyze the causes of this disease or design a cure for it. If any such science has yet been developed, I am unaware of it. The only instances known to me where this tendency to uninhibited self-engendered bureaucratic growth has been successfully halted or reduced have been ones where the methods employed were brutal and surgical ones, usually unjust to many of the persons affected, and usually flowing from causes and motives unrelated to the problem itself. I recall being told by our ambassador to one of the East European Communist countries that when the government of that country, for purely political reasons, forced the curtailment of the size of the American embassy staff from eighty-some to fifteen, it was in his estimation the best thing that had ever happened to them. All went better. The remaining few coped nicely with their assigned duties. The U.S. government, left to itself, would, and could, never have effected this improvement. And a particularly unfortunate result of this absence of any science of organization is that when new units have to be created within the governmental apparatus, the bureaucratically bloated existing unit often comes to be taken as the model, so a certain measure of unhealthy growth is built into the new unit from the very start.[2]

It was, and is, of course, not only the federal government that is affected by these tendencies. They are observable as well in smaller governmental entities, such as state, municipal, and local authorities. They make themselves felt in most large and complex nongovernmental offices—industrial, commercial, educational, and charitable. But for obvious reasons they assume a particularly large place in the governmental apparatus of the great country. This is true not just because the legitimate needs, constituting as they usually do the original point of departure for unhealthy bureaucratic growth, have greater dimensions but also because growth of this sort enlarges personnel requirements not just in an arithmetic relation to the original needs but in a geometric one, so that each increase in the real needs produces an even larger proportionate growth in the bureaucratic superstructure. For this reason, the governmental apparatus of the great country grows around itself a thicker and more formidable bureaucratic coating than does the smaller unit. And this, in turn, enhances the isolation of the individual citizen, whose own personal dimensions suffer no proportionate enlargement, and who finds himself even further repelled by this abnormal protective coating of the government.

This phenomenon of bureaucratic enlargement is particularly dangerous in the democratic society, because as the administrative superstructure grows, so—alas—does the number of persons who have a stake in it and an interest in its perpetuation. If it should indeed prove to be true that the only effective way of combatting such growth is the brutal surgical incision, then the democratic government will be the

---

2. Memory brings up the following. During World War II, when Pan American's flying boats provided the only form of aerial transportation between the United States and Europe, and the Azores offered the only adequate and fully serviceable refueling stop for these planes, the airline maintained a servicing station in the Azores, manned by eleven Americans. When, later, the U.S. Navy decided to establish a small seaplane base there, to fly antisubmarine patrols—a base the dimensions of whose operations could not have been much greater than those of the existing Pan American unit—the Navy, asked to estimate the size of the personnel that would be required, came up with a figure of two thousand.

one least likely to master the problem. Aside from the fact that such an approach would bring injustice to a host of innocent people who are not at fault for being employed where they were not really needed, these people are not without means of self-defense. Their numbers are such that they constitute in themselves an appreciable electoral force, and they would, if their positions were seriously threatened, find considerable support for their cause in Congress—an institution which is, incidentally, not without its own bureaucratic crust, and has no greater awareness than does the rest of the government of the causes of this unhappy condition, or the possible cures.

Thus we are safe in assuming that even if an adequate science of large-scale organization were available, and even if the causes and possible cures for bureaucracy were made evident, the only effective remedial measures would be so uncomfortable for everyone concerned that the tendency would be to regard the treatment as more painful than the disease and to leave well enough, or what appears to be well enough, alone. We must, then, learn to see the governmental apparatus of any country as largely helpless in the throes of this particular sort of elephantiasis, and handicapped, accordingly, in its ability to be to the ordinary citizen all that government, in normal conditions, could and should be. But here again, the severity of this problem grows, and grows exponentially, with the size of the country and the government, so that the government and people of the great power are more heavily burdened by this disease than are those of the smaller entity.

Decentralization

It is under the influence of these views about the disadvantages of "bigness" that I have often diverted myself, and puzzled my friends, by wondering how it would be if our country, while retaining certain of the rudiments of a federal government, were to be decentralized into something like a dozen constituent republics, absorbing not only the powers of the existing states but a considerable part of those of the present federal establishment. I could conceive of something like nine of these republics—let us say, New England; the Middle Atlantic states;

the Middle West; the Northwest (from Wisconsin to the Northwest, and down the Pacific coast to central California); the Southwest (including southern California and Hawaii); Texas (by itself); the Old South; Florida (perhaps including Puerto Rico); and Alaska; plus three great self-governing urban regions, those of New York, Chicago, and Los Angeles—a total of twelve constituent entities. To these entities I would accord a larger part of the present federal powers than one might suspect—large enough, in fact, to make most people gasp.

It would, of course, be pointed out that this would involve many new complexities and not a few inefficiencies. That would indeed be true. The regions thus created would be strikingly varied in character and in the problems they presented for effective government. There would be much room for local innovation and for departure from older national norms. But a case might be made, I think, for the thesis that nothing is more greatly to be feared, in the realm of governmental theory, than the effort to create governmental systems that are logical, uncomplicated, efficient, and vast in scope. That is not the way people themselves are constructed; and a governmental system that strived too hard for these apparent advantages would be bound to do violence to people's deepest needs.

Let me emphasize that what is suggested here is not a change based on ethnic or racial distinctions. Several of these proposed individual republics—New England, the Old South, the Middle West, and the great urban regions—would embrace within their borders a good cross section of the diversity of cultures, traditions, and ethnic and racial colorations now borne by the country as a whole; yet each of them would be marked by certain peculiar cultural and social qualities that would set it off from the others. Ease, flexibility, and intimacy of government, not a quest for racial or ethnic uniformity, would be the purpose of such a reform.

A more serious objection to what I have just suggested is that it is too late: that there are no longer any significant sectional differences in America; that the melting-pot process has gone too far; that modern means of communication, notably television and the cult of screened images generally, are destroying local differences and pressing us all into one mold, forcing upon us a national uniformity, making us increasingly less distinguishable one from another. Beyond which, it will be argued, nothing could resist the leveling effect of the great monopolies, constantly growing with the effects of the recent takeover fever, that dominate our national economy. All the forces of modern free enterprise, we will be told, work in the direction of uniformity—of leveling and equalizing—of the creation of a colorless uniformity of habit, of outlook, and of behavior, before which local and sectional differences in way of life, tradition, and conception have no chance of survival.

Perhaps, perhaps. It would be sad if it were true. But again, perhaps, not all is lost. If sectional differences have indeed been weakened by these forces, they might be reinvigorated, stimulated, and encouraged by the sort of decentralization I have suggested. If traditional and cultural differences are in danger of obliteration, perhaps they could be rescued and sharpened by this very different sort of a framework. Perhaps the interaction among different values, different outlooks, and different goals, which here as elsewhere has served in the past as one of the greatest sources of intellectual and aesthetic fertility, could be allowed once more to fulfill that function.

A pipe dream? Largely, if you will. It is indeed hard to imagine any such changes, bound as they would be to tread painfully on a great many entrenched political interests, having their origin, or even finding any response, in the present American political establishment.

Immigration

I cannot leave this subject of the size and populousness of this country without devoting a few words to the delicate and difficult subject of immigration. Ours is, of course, a country of immigrants. In the pedigree of every non–Native American, other than the first-generation ones, there lies at least one immigrant, often a considerable number of them. We could justly be called an immigrant society.

We have prided ourselves, throughout much of our history, on the welcome we gave to the arriving immigrant, and even on the lack of discrimination we showed in the extension of this welcome. We have gone on the assumption that such were the spaciousness and fertility and the absorbent capacities of this country that there was no limit to either the number or the diversity of ethnic characteristics of the immigrants we could accept. We have gone on the further assumption that such was the universality of the values incorporated into our political system that there could be no immigrant, of whatever culture or race or national tradition, who could not be readily absorbed into our social and political life, could not become infused with understanding for, and confidence in, our political institutions, and could not, consequently, become a useful bearer of the American political tradition. Particularly has the possibility never become apparent to us that in some instances, where the disparity between what these people were leaving behind and what they were coming into was too great, the new arrivals, even in the process of adjusting to our political tradition, might actually change it. One need only look at our great-city ghettos or the cities of Miami and Los Angeles to satisfy oneself that what we are confronted with here are real and extensive cultural changes.

I shall not argue about how justifiable these attitudes proved to be in the past. Perhaps there was more to be said for some of them in the early days of this republic than there would be today. But, in any case, that is water over the dam. We must look at these assumptions in terms of the situation we now have before us.

If there are any grounds for my belief that the country is already overpopulated—overpopulated, above all, from the environmental standpoint—then that would in itself suggest that we should take a new look at the whole problem of immigration. But we also ought to ask ourselves, before we assure ourselves that we could comfortably accommodate further waves of immigration, where, if anywhere, the limits of this complacency are to be found. This is a big world. Billions—rapidly increasing billions—of people live outside our borders. Obviously, a great number of them, being much poorer than they think most of us are, look enviously over those borders and would like, if they could, to come here.

Just as water seeks its own level, so relative prosperity, anywhere in the world, tends to suck in poverty from adjacent regions to the lowest levels of employment. But since poverty is sometimes a habit, sometimes even an established way of life, the more prosperous society, by indulging this tendency, absorbs not only poverty into itself but other cultures in the bargain, and is sometimes quite overcome, in the long run, by what it has tried to absorb. The inhabitants of the onetime Italian cities along the eastern shore of the Adriatic Sea (the scenes of some of Shakespeare's plays) made it a habit, over several centuries, to take their menial servants and their ditchdiggers from the Slavs of the poorer villages in the adjacent mountains. Today, finally, the last of the Italians have left; and the beautiful cities in questions are inhabited entirely by Slavs, who have little relationship to the sort of city and the cultural monuments they have inherited. They have simply displaced the original inhabitants.

Surely there is a lesson in this. The situation has been, or threatens to be, repeated in a number of the advanced countries. It is obviously easier, for the short run, to draw cheap labor from adjacent pools of poverty, such as North Africa or Central America, than to find it among one's own people. And to the millions of such prospective immigrants from poverty to prosperity, there is, rightly or wrongly, no place that looks more attractive than the United States. Given its head, and subject to no restrictions, this pressure will find its termination only when the levels of overpopulation and poverty in the United States are equal to those of the countries from which these people are now so anxious to escape.

There will be those who will say, "Oh, it is our duty to receive as many as possible of these people and to share our prosperity with them, as we have so long been doing." But suppose there are limits to our capacity to absorb. Suppose the effect of such a policy is to create, in the end, conditions within this country no better than those of the places the mass of the immigrants have left: the same poverty, the same distress. What we shall then have accomplished is not to have appreciably improved conditions in the Third World (for even the maximum numbers we could conceivably take would be only a drop from the bucket of the planet's overpopulation) but to make this country itself a part of the Third World (as certain parts of it already are), thus depriving the planet of one of the few great regions that might have continued, as it now does, to be helpful to much of the remainder of the world by its relatively high standard of civilization, by its quality as example, by its ability to shed insight on the problems of the others and to help them find their answers to their own problems.

Actually, the inability of any society to resist immigration, the inability to find other solutions to the problem of employment at the lower, more physical, and menial levels of the economic process, is a serious weakness, and possibly even a fatal one, in any national society. The fully healthy society would find ways to meet those needs out of its own resources. The acceptance of this sort of dependence on labor imported from outside is, for the respective society, the evidence of a lack of will—in a sense, a lack of confidence in itself. And this acceptance, like the weakness of the Romans in allowing themselves to become dependent on the barbarians to fill the ranks of their own armies, can become, if not checked betimes, the beginning of the end.

However one cuts it, the question is not whether there are limits to this country's ability to absorb immigration; the question is only where those limits lie, and how they should be determined and enforced—whether by rational decision at this end or by the ultimate achievement of some sort of a balance of misery between this country and the vast pools of poverty elsewhere that now confront it.

Unfortunately it appears, as things stand today, to lie beyond the vigor, and the capacity for firm decision, of the American political establishment to draw any rational limits to further immigration. This is partly because the U.S. government, while not loath to putting half a million armed troops into the Middle East to expel the armed Iraqis from Kuwait, confesses itself unable to defend its own southwestern border from illegal immigration by large numbers of people armed with nothing more formidable than a strong desire to get across it. But behind this rather strange helplessness there lie, of course, domestic-political pressures or inhibitions that work in the same direction: notably, the thirst for cheap labor among American employers and the tendency of recently immigrated people, now here in such numbers that they are not without political clout, to demand the ongoing admission of others like themselves.

Let me make it clear that I am not objecting, here, to the quality of the people whose continued arrival, as things now stand, is to be anticipated (although I would point out that the conditions in our major urban ghettos would suggest that there might even be limits to our capacity for assimilation). We are already, for better or for worse, very much a polyglot country; and nothing of that is now to be changed. What I have in mind here are sheer numbers. There *is* such a thing as overcrowding. It has its psychic effects as well as its physical ones. There *are* limits to what the environment can stand: the tolerable levels of pollution, the strain on water supplies, and so on. There *are* limits to the desirable magnitude of urbanization; and it is, after all, to the great urban regions that the bulk of these immigrants proceed.

I might point out that these are problems that might more easily be coped with if the United States, as was fancifully suggested above, were to be divided into a relatively small number of constituent republics, and if each of these were to be given control over immigration, at least in the sense of controlling the rights of residence. In that case, it is not inconceivable that certain of the major southern regions where things have already gone too far would themselves become, in effect, linguistically and culturally, Latin-American countries, and would find in that way their own level with relation to the adjacent already Latin-American regions (which might for them, incidentally, not be the worst of solutions).

But since there obviously will be, in the foreseeable future, no such decentralization of the country, these speculations are idle. And the reason why I bring up the subject at all is to emphasize something that gives me considerable uneasiness: and that is the growing evidence (and this, as we shall see, is not the only manifestation of it) that there are grave problems of the American future that are not going to be and probably cannot be, as things stand today, adequately anticipated or confronted at the *national* political level.

This conclusion, if well founded, is an extremely serious one. It says something about the enduring viability of American democracy, as we now know it. But I am reaching, here, ahead of the evidence. There are other situations that would support the same conclusion. These must also be mentioned before the implications of this conclusion are confronted.

Chapter Eight

THE
ADDICTIONS

It is not our affluence, or our plumbing, or our clogged
highways that grip the imagination of others. Rather, it
is the values on which our system is built. These values
imply our adherence not only to liberty and individual
freedom, but also to international peace, law and order,
and constructive social purpose.

—William Fulbright, speaking in the U.S. Senate in
1961

I expressed, in chapter 3, the confidence I share with so many other
Americans in the general form of government established by the American Constitution, and my preference for this form of government,
with the various checks and balances and assurances against distortion
into oppressive rule that it contains, over other forms of government
that do not provide comparable safeguards. To have this confidence and
this preference is not, however, to assume that this form of government
could not be affected by radical changes in the technological and social
environment in which our society is called upon to function; and it is

not to say that to meet these changes successfully would not call for adjustments in existing governmental outlooks and policies. When problems arise in the life of a nation of such seriousness that they seem to jeopardize its very future and to undermine the confidence of a great many of its citizens in the soundness of its political institutions, and when the government confesses itself, explicitly or implicitly, unable to cope successfully with these problems, then one has no choice but to question the adequacy of Western democracy itself, as we know it, for responding successfully to the changing environmental conditions in which it is obliged to exist.

That there are a number of American problems that meet this description seems to me to be beyond question. The list would include such things as environmental deterioration; the decline of educational standards; crime; drug abuse; in general, the dreadful conditions in the urban ghettos; the national budget deficit; the continued inability of our government to meet its financial obligations without massive borrowing at the expense of future generations; the decline of personal savings; and, in general, the excessive dependence on credit to sustain both governmental and personal activity. And beyond these, there are also troublesome societal conditions: attitudes of hopelessness, skepticism, cynicism, and bewilderment, particularly among the youth—that have led many observers to characterize this society (and, I think, not unjustly) as a "sick" one.

Some of these problems have an obvious relation to governmental responsibilities, federal and local, in the sense that their possible solutions are ones that would lie within the traditional competence of public authority to bring about. Others are rooted in social conditions for which public authority has not traditionally been seen as bearing any responsibility. These latter are ones that have their existence in the assumptions, the aspirations, the expectations, and the habits of thought of great portions of the citizenry. It is with them in mind that I ventured, earlier on, to call us a people of bad social habits.

I could not undertake to examine all these problems in detail within the limits of this literary effort. There are some with regard to which I would not be competent to do so, in any case. But I am selecting two of them that stand out, to me, as particularly serious examples of our present helplessness; and I shall venture, again for purposes of illustration, to suggest the sort of measures that might be required for their correction. I do this because I think they are situations that threaten not only American democracy alone but also, in one degree or another, other democratic societies across the globe.

The two problems I have in mind, as examples, are ones that have arisen, first, from the absence of any serious energy and transportation policies on the part of American public authority and, second, from the extensive abandonment by our government of much of the process of public communication, in education as in entertainment, to the good graces of the advertisers, to people, that is, who have no public commitment, educational, intellectual, aesthetic, or otherwise. In both instances, the problems have developed in face of, and largely in consequence of, the indifference of public authority to their development, and its readiness to leave this to the uncontrolled workings of a free-enterprise system.

Transportation

At no time in its entire history does the United States appear to have had anything in the nature of a rational and sustained governmental policy on transportation. The government, with public approval, seems to have been content to leave developments in this field entirely to the chaotic workings of the free-enterprise system, allowing those workings to carry us where they might, regardless of the growing evidence that they were having profound effects on the social and economic conditions of our society.

Thus there was a time, in the 1840s and 1850s, when speculative calculations appeared to favor the building of canals. The result was that great quantities of capital and of backbreaking labor were poured, with the government's blessing, into such enterprises, only to find most of them suddenly and wholly overtaken, a few years later, by the development of the railroads, leaving a great part of the canal investment and its results wasted and abandoned. Society, one way or another, was the loser. The same thing happened little more than half a century later, when what was by then the world's greatest railway network, constructed at vast cost and representing a veritable triumph of American engineering and technology, was sacrificed, with equal abruptness, recklessness, and abandon, to the compelling commercial intrusion of the automobile. In each case not only were enormous capital investments and material values lightheartedly sacrificed, to the ultimate detriment of society as a whole, but the trends of urban development, sensitive as these are to the available means of transportation, were whipsawed mercilessly by these abrupt and profound changes. Government, in each case, remained indifferent.

Nearly seventy years ago, when I was an undergraduate at Princeton, there appeared on that campus a gentleman, whose name and identity I could not possibly now recall, but who left a lasting impression upon me by pointing out, in an evening lecture, that the railway and the automobile exerted diametrically opposite and conflicting disciplines on the development of the urban community—and that this, to the extent that one form of transportation was allowed to exclude or replace the other, was bound to have profound effects on American life.

The railway, this gentleman pointed out, was capable of accepting and disgorging its loads, whether of passengers or freight, only at fixed points. This being the case, it tended to gather together, and to concentrate around its urban terminus and railhead, all activity that was in any way related to movements of freight or passengers into or out of the city. It was in this quality that it had made major and in some ways decisive contributions to the development not only of the great railway metropolises of the Victorian age—particularly of such inland cities as Moscow, Berlin, Paris, and Chicago—but even certain of the great maritime turnover ports, such as London and New York.

The automobile, on the other hand, had precisely the opposite qualities. Incapable, in view of its own cumbersomeness and requirements for space, of accepting or releasing large loads at any concentrated points anywhere, but peculiarly capable of accepting and releasing them at multitudes of unconcentrated points anywhere else, the automobile tended to disintegrate and to explode all that the railway had brought together. It was, in fact, the enemy of the concentrated city. Thus it was destined to destroy the great densely populated urban centers of the nineteenth century, with all the glories of economic and cultural life that had flowed from their very unity and compactness.

This, at any rate, is what one undergraduate recalled gathering from this gentleman's remarks; and the impression has never left him.

Well, there have, of course, been great changes over the intervening decades in the modalities of urban and nonurban life—changes that neither the lecturer in question nor anyone else could at that time have foreseen. These changes have no doubt modified at one point or another the force of the gentleman's observations. But his view of the effects of the automobile on the great Victorian railway metropolis have certainly been mainly substantiated by the intervening decades. And indeed, in some respects these effects have gone beyond what he predicted. For not only have they damaged the center city, but they have exploded with equal violence the suburban settlement which, once connected with the center primarily by the "inter-urban" trolley line, had begun to consolidate its own life as an independent community.

The automobile, in short, has turned out to be, by virtue of its innate and inalterable qualities, the enemy of community generally. Wherever it advances, neighborliness and the sense of community are impaired.

One might have thought that this alone, much of which was surely becoming evident in the 1920s and 1930s, would have sufficed to cause Americans of that day to pause and to ask themselves whether they really wished to junk 99 percent of the great railway system that then existed and to confer upon the automobile and the truck the sort of near monopoly on transportation which (together with their later companion the airplane) they have now achieved. And the wonder as to why this question was never asked is enhanced when it is considered that this, the effect on community, was by no means the only drawback from which the automobile, as an alternative to public transportation, suffered (and continues to suffer).

There is, in the first place, its extreme unsociability. Just as it destroys community in human residence, so it destroys community in travel. Surely there has never been a lonelier means of moving great masses of people about. This writer has found himself obliged to drive, on countless occasions, either alone or accompanied only by his wife, the 150 miles between his regular place of residence and the family farm in southern Pennsylvania. The compulsion to do this has arisen because the nearby Pennsylvania village, once connected with the world around it by a small branch railway line, now has, like countless other such villages, no public transportation of any sort to link it to the outside world. In the course of these hundreds of journeys between the two points in question, six or seven hours' round-trip in each instance, the writer cannot recall that he ever met personally, or communicated with, another person, unless it be the toll collector at the exit point from the turnpike, who sometimes said hello. Time after time, he found himself comparing this lonely and dreary journey with the color and sociability of the English highway of Chaucer's time, as reflected in *The Canterbury Tales,* or with the congenial atmosphere of the railway compartment of the Victorian novel.

Second, there is the automobile's extreme wastefulness. It is wasteful of material, of energy, and of space. The very idea that for the displacement of one or two human bodies on their daily comings and goings there should be required something upwards of a ton of metal, the power of something like a hundred horses, and some ninety square feet of paved highway, is in itself an absurdity of the first order. The railway is in all these respects far more economical. All this is well known to public authority; and it is at this point that the lack of a national transportation policy transects the similar lack of a policy in the field of energy. And because the automobile is more wasteful, it is also more expensive—to the individual owner and to the economy at large.

Third, the automobile is, as everyone knows, a major polluter. So, no doubt, was the steam locomotive, but in a different way, and in far less volume. The source of energy for the electrically driven train also involves pollution; but it involves far less of it than do the many automobiles required to replace it; and even this pollution could surely be further curtailed by other expedients.

Fourth, the automobile, insofar as it replaces walking for the displacement of human bodies over short distances, is a distinctly unhealthy innovation. Walking, the experts tell us, is the most useful and readily accessible form of exercise available to the average human being. In an earlier age, adult people walked for a great many of their comings and goings. They walked to and from church, the trolley stop, the corner emporium, the houses of friends. Today, most of these movements are performed, expensively, awkwardly, and at the cost of considerable nervous strain, in the automobile. The vast majority of children, similarly, once walked to and from school. Today they sit, passive, bored, and inactive, in the family car or the school bus. And at the slightest sign of inclement winter weather, the schools have to be closed, because His Majesty, the automobile, dislikes snow and ice. In the pre-automobile age, this, at least in my native city of Milwaukee, was unheard of. I find it hard to believe that these changes have constituted "progress."

We have, again, the almost immeasurable boon that the automobile has been to crime and to juvenile delinquency. This scarcely needs elaboration. In the pre-automobile age, the criminal had a limited potential radius of escape. Even within the town where he committed his crime, he had to walk or to take a streetcar to distance himself from the scene of it, in either of which cases he could easily be observed by others, and not just his head and neck but his full head-to-foot appearance. To get out of town he had to pass through the bottlenecks of the railway station, the ticket window, the waiting room, the platform. Today, conveniently anonymous at the wheel of his car, he can within an hour's time be forty or fifty miles away, in any direction, from the scene of his crime, and buried among a mass of many thousands of other vehicles and poorly visible drivers. And as for juvenile delinquency: any parent can confirm that the varieties of mischief and of self-destructive (sometimes tragic) behavior open to the youngster who can escape from parental observation and control in the family car are far greater than those that were open to the teenager of earlier decades who, to call on his girl, had to walk down the street and sit with her in the family swing on the front porch or escort her, walking, to the movie.

And finally, the automobile suffers from the fact that, enticing as are its services to the able-bodied, it leaves essentially unserved whole great categories of persons—the very young, the very old, the sick, the poor, and the handicapped—who for one reason or another cannot safely and successfully place themselves at the wheel of a car, but who, so long as the automobile retains its monopoly, have no way of getting around unless they can persuade someone else to drive them. The railway, on the contrary, was capable of accommodating, and normally did, all such people.

It is not the intention to argue, with these observations, that there is no proper place for the automotive vehicle in American life. Of course, there is such a place; and it is a prominent one. For fire prevention and control, for police and medical services, for the lonely country dweller, living far from everywhere, for taxi services, and for the movement and delivery of freight within major urban areas and between neighboring ones, it would obviously be silly to reject the advantages the motor vehicle offers. But beyond these and other necessities, there is no reason why that vehicle should be allowed to retain the virtually total monopoly of transportation that it has now generally achieved. There is a large area within which public ground transportation, given even a fraction of the public and private financial support that for many years has been poured out to the automobile, the truck, and the airplane, could provide a healthier, cheaper, more comfortable, socially preferable, and environmentally less destructive manner of moving persons and goods around. It should, surely, be the task of public authority to determine what should be considered the proper balance among these various modes of transportation, and then to see how pressure could best be brought to bear to steer development in the desirable direction.

It would be wrong to suppose that any adjustment of that sort could be carried through in any short space of time. It has taken seven or eight decades to bring about the present, unhealthy dependence upon the automobile; it would presumably take nothing less than several further decades to reduce it to its proper place in modern American life. This would be true if only for the fact that the personal financial and other interests of millions of people would be affected. Even more important would be the psychological adjustment this would imply. But every useful process has to have a beginning; and in this instance the beginning is far overdue.

The power of the automobile, as a revolutionizing factor in the life of practically every country, worldwide, has been extraordinary. Let no one underestimate it. There appears to have been no place in the world that has been able fully to withstand it. The automobile's apparent liberating effect: the feeling of enhanced power it conveys to the person at the wheel; the sense of personal freedom it allows; the ability it promises for instantaneous changes of plans, for escaping from awkward places or situations and for seeking out preferable ones, for expanding the scope of one's activities, and for avoiding the delays of movement to or from the railway station or the trolley stop: all these contribute mightily to the illusion of freedom that this vehicle embodies and constitute enticements few can withstand if the possibility of acquisition presents itself. The fact that much of this sense of freedom is illusory, that the automobile's needs often demand the waste of much time as well as the saving of it, that its expense and its mechanical requirements often simply add to the strains of an already overcomplicated and nervously exhausting modern life, and that it bears the various social disadvantages listed above: all this retires before the force of its attraction. Small wonder, in these circumstances, that countless millions of people, devoid of any public or social restraints, have placed the apparent personal advantages of driving an automobile ahead of the less easily perceived social disadvantages, and have thrown themselves into a dependence on this vehicle that has assumed the dimensions of an extremely serious and not readily curable mass addiction. It will not be easy to wean them from it.

The task of public authority, in promoting any adjustment of this nature, will be all the harder for the fact that it will have to involve the employment of both the carrot and the stick. Any attempt to reduce the ubiquity of the automobile will be self-defeating unless attractive alternatives are provided in public transportation. On the other hand, no improvements in public transportation will be effective unless serious disincentives are created to the use of the automobile. Because the automobile is now coming up against its own inherent limits in a number of our great cities, where traffic congestion and the cost of parking space are beginning to inhibit its use, certain of these disincentives are already coming into existence. But such self-imposing limits will have little beneficial effect—they will, in fact, only promote the further disintegration and decay of the city centers—unless they are balanced with compensatory improvements and expansions of public transportation. And this last will not occur without the determined and enthusiastic involvement of public authority.

It is plain that the federal government has traditionally viewed the providing of freight and passenger movement within the country as a field of activity to be left for exploitation by private enterprise. The assumption seems to have been that so lucrative was this field of activity that private enterprise could be counted on to assure that the needs of all communities and of all classes of society would at all times be met by the private entrepreneur.

If the experience of many decades proves anything at all, it is that these expectations were quite unrealistic and have not been satisfied. Instead, we have today a situation where thousands of smaller communities have been left without any public transportation at all, where the movement of freight has been largely abandoned to the expensive, destructive, and heavily polluting trucking industry, where the long-distance movement of persons has been left almost exclusively to the automobile or to the inordinately and, for the poor, almost prohibitively expensive device of the airplane, and where the only fast and reasonably priced public passenger service over even a moderate distance—the rail service between New York and Washington—is one that recent administrations have made no secret of their desire to destroy if they can.

The only hopeful approach to the correction of these conditions would require the recognition by public authority, at long last, that the assurance of reasonably priced public transportation facilities, serving not just the rich but the poor and not just the great urban area but the small community as well, is a proper responsibility of public authority, no less than are those other facilities, such as the sewage system and other public health arrangements, that are commonly and traditionally recognized as such.

The Advertiser

I had thought of adding a few words on the subject of television, and not so much on its evils, which are widely recognized, but rather on the extreme difficulty of the problems it presents. But then it became evident that television was actually only a part of a much larger problem—that of the growing substitution of the visual image and spoken voice for the printed word; and that this, in turn, was only a part of a problem larger still: namely, the extensive domination of almost every kind of public communication by the advertisers. In the light of all this, I see no choice but to treat all these problems under a single heading; and I apologize in advance for whatever confusing of ideas this may involve.

Let us start with some words about the advertising industry and its role, generally, in public communication throughout the country.

The advertisers provide, or so one must suppose, the main and (many would say) indispensable source of financial support for practically every form of public communication in the United States, with the partial exception of the book and the publicly funded radio and television. Is there anything wrong with this? Whence, if not from the advertisers, could this support possibly come? The question is a reasonable one. And there would seem to be no answer to it. As things stand today, without advertising presumably very little of the communications industry would survive.

In part, this would not be a bad thing. We would live very well without a good part of what this industry produces: without the drugstore trash, the comic books, the video games, the pornographic filth, and their equivalents on the screen and over the air. The continued prevalence of this unsavory stream owes itself to the insistence of the advertisers on reaching every part of the public whose pocketbooks can conceivably be tapped, however unattractive or pernicious the means this seems to necessitate. But there is, of course, another great part of the produce of the communications industry that is quite beneficial, if not essential, to the advance of the cultural and intellectual life of the country; and for this, too, as things now stand, the advertiser's support seems indispensable.

Is this bad? Is the advertiser's influence reprehensible?

The advertisers are not bad people—not worse than the rest of us. I have nothing against them personally. We cannot blame them for the nature of their motivation. We all have to live. They do what is profitable for them to do, and what is permitted. I must absolve them, too, of any tendency to influence the partisan-political inclinations of the public they reach. They have normally no interest in appealing to that public in a partisan way when to do so might be to alienate one part of it while it gratifies another. If there are any objections that can reasonably be raised to the sort of influence they exert, these probably center on two points. The first is the intense consumerism they stimulate—the subtle suggestion pervading so much of their effort, and repeated endless times, that people's problems could be solved, and a happy life assured, just by their buying this or that. The advertisers' efforts tend to inculcate, in other words, false values, because it lies in their interests to do so. And the second of the two points relates to the peculiar sort of blandness they inflict on those—the publishers, the editors, the producers—who are dependent upon their support.

Where the influence of the advertisers makes itself most prominently felt is surely in the pressure they exert on their clients, particularly those in the publishing world, to achieve at all costs greater popularity and wider circulation. This, of course, is a motivation the editors have anyway; it is in their own interest. But the fear of losing the advertising if they fail to make progress in this direction intensifies the motivation; and the results are often achieved at the expense of quality. This puts a premium, in particular, on entertainment rather than on serious content—again a premium to which the editors would be sensitive even without the advertiser, but one which is simply intensified by the pressure the advertiser brings to bear. One can see the effects of this in almost all forms of periodical publishing and screened communication.

Another significant consequence of the interests of both advertiser and client is the curtailment of the period of time that the attention of the reader or the viewer is demanded for any particular item. Not only are there the frequent interruptions of screened material by insertion of the advertisements themselves, but there is also the tendency to shorten all offerings lest the attention of the viewer or the reader or the listener be lost by the tedium of being asked to concentrate on anything longer. The result is the markedly staccato nature of a great deal of what is served up to the public on screen or printed page or over the airwaves. Attention is constantly being abruptly yanked from one thought or image to a wholly different one.

In the cases of movie and television, this effect is inherent, anyway, in the very nature of the media, the images of which flick instantaneously on and off the screen. And some of this is also inherent in the newspaper, with its wide variety of small news items. But the rule seems to be that never, if this can be avoided, must the attention of the viewer-reader-listener be drawn to any single image or thought for more than two or three minutes, and never must he or she be asked or encouraged to undertake the effort to stop and analyze the interrelationship of any of these images or thoughts. It is hard to escape the conclusion that this, well meant as it may be, constitutes a massive abuse of the capacity for concentrated thought on the part of countless millions of people.

Nor is this all. Most of the material, journalistic or literary, with which the advertiser is impelled to associate himself is material which would normally be credited in the eyes of the reader-listener-viewer with a certain underlying integrity, in the sense, at least, of an absence of any specific ulterior motive in its authorship and presentation. It normally is what it purports to be. Let me refer to this as the "legitimate" material.

The same is not true of the advertising. It would be going too far to label it as "untruth." Most advertisements contain some elements of truth. But the advertiser has no commitment to the truth as such. Advertisements could be best defined as "not necessarily truth, and largely something else."

Now, the difficulty comes in with the immediate proximity to each other, on the screen or on the printed page, of these two kinds of communication—one kind, let us say, intended or pretended truth, the other, not necessarily even that. It is clear that the public, well aware of the difference between the two, dislikes being confronted with pure advertising, devoid of any legitimate material.[1] The advertiser, therefore, finds himself obliged to accept some admixture of legitimate material as a companion and a lure for whatever he himself has to offer. But he also finds it in his interests to reduce the legitimate material to a minimum in order to make more room for the advertising. A glance at the *New York Times* for the day on which this passage is being written reveals that of the thirty-five pages of the prestigious first section of that estimable journal, thirteen are devoted exclusively to advertising, whereas on each of a further seven pages a single column of legitimate material, occupying only a small part of the page, is squeezed in among the advertisers' far more strident demands for attention. A majority of the pages of that section, in other words, consist overwhelmingly of advertising material; and most of the remaining ones partly so. Thus the naive reader looking for news in what is ostensibly, by its own definition, a *news*-paper comes away with decidedly the smaller pickings; the advertisers had the greater ones. A similar situation would be found to exist, I am sure, in a high proportion of newspapers across the country.

The advertiser would like, of course, wherever he can, to borrow some of the legitimacy of the nonadvertising material by the very intimacy of the physical association of the one with the other on the page or on the screen. Who has not seen, for example, on the television screen, the use of such things as policemen's uniforms, doctors' gowns, nurses' uniforms, and even priests' robes, with a view to attracting to

1. I am reminded of the Berlin nightclubs in the wide-open days of the Weimar Republic. The proprietors discovered that the public, salacious as was its curiosity, did not like the dancers entirely naked. A fig leaf made all the difference.

the advertisement something of the credibility these garbs are generally taken to imply? Who has not heard, in the advertising of drugs, the claim that "doctors say"—an obvious and cynical attempt to exploit for commercial purposes the public's confidence in the medical profession. The most egregious of these subterfuges is the frequent use of children's figures and voices, introduced in the obvious calculation that people will think that "kids don't lie"—in reality, a shameful abuse of the innocence and dignity of the child. And something of the same can be occasionally found on the printed page, where what is in reality advertising is sometimes made to resemble one form or another of the legitimate material carried by the organ in question.

Again, it may be asked, Does this matter? People are not easily fooled. Even children become adept at spotting advertising where they see it and arriving at their own assessment of the credence it deserves.

True. And yet it is hard, once again, to avoid the impression that this systematic association of "truth" with "not necessarily truth" on the same pages and the same screens, together with the obvious effort to confuse the two, does not constitute another abuse of the human intelligence. Aside from which, it represents an egregious abuse of the public's confidence in the professional groups—the doctors, the clergy, the police, and the like—whose names and figures the advertisers appropriate to their own uses. This is particularly regrettable, because the abuse of confidence ultimately ends with the denial of it; and the public's confidence in precisely those professions is essential to the very strength and health of society.

The Junk Mail

Before we leave the subject of advertising, there is one more aspect of this question that should be mentioned; and it is one that concerns the U.S. Postal Service.

Mention was made above of the tendency of the advertisers to appropriate to themselves the dominant place in whatever medium admits their involvement, crowding the legitimate material into a smaller space and reserving the larger one for their effusions. We have a curious illustration of this proclivity, by analogy, in the use the advertising industry makes of the Postal Service.

As we all know, the common citizen, desirous of dispatching an ordinary private letter, is now asked to pay twenty-nine cents. The dispatcher of a piece of "junk mail," and in the first instance advertising matter, pays roughly one-half the price of "first-class" mail for his missive. The result, as millions of us are daily reminded, is that our mailman arrives overburdened, and we find ourselves deluged with great masses of material we have never asked for and do not want, most of which we throw away unlooked at, thus passing the problem along to the trash collectors, and adding our little bit to the national problem of waste disposal, not to mention the wild and environmentally pernicious wastage of paper this involves.

What reason can there be for this monstrous distortion of burdens? The Postal Service was intended to be one of the ordinary amenities and conveniences that the government owed to the common citizen; and, in strange contrast to public transportation, it has normally been so regarded by our government. Surely, the normal needs of the individual citizen should have been given first priority, and not only should the desire of others to exploit this great distribution system for commercial purposes have received second priority, but these others should have been asked, since they expected to profit by the exercise, to make the higher payment. Clearly, it is the ordinary citizen who should be asked to pay the lesser junk-mail rate and the junk-mail patron who should pay the first-class rate. One might note in this connection that aside from the motives that lie behind its dispatch, the junk mail is the bulkier, the heavier, and the harder to handle of the two categories, and ought logically to bear the proportionately higher costs, anyway.

One can assume only that this is another instance in which what is "not necessarily truth" is given the higher priority in the eyes of the government over the legitimate needs of the populace because there is more money to be made by private enterprise in the distribution of it, and because the people who make that money are better organized to bring political pressure to bear upon Congress than is the common citizen, who sees no choice but to submit, with a sense of resigned helplessness, to whatever Washington decrees.

Television

This is perhaps the point at which something should be said about the device which is both a favorite outlet for the advertisers and the most intimate occupant and companion of the American home: the television set. Of all the questionable habits of the American people, this device ranks only with the automobile in its power as an addiction. And like the automobile, it disguises its domination under a promise of liberation.

To say this is not to deny that there is a legitimate place for this device in the home. For the old, the helpless, the house bound, the ill, and the weary, it can, depending on their needs and its content, be a blessing. Even for those who suffer none of these handicaps, it can, used sparingly and with discrimination, render useful and unique service. There could be no question of its complete removal from the home; nor is anyone suggesting it.

Yet it, too, has serious drawbacks. Like the automobile, it is essentially antisocial. Occasionally, to be sure, it can stimulate discussion in the home; but more often it replaces it. The greatest disadvantage of the viewing of it is the passivity this involves and enforces. The viewer, at his best, is the passive witness, the unengaged observer. He receives; he is not asked to give, is in fact precluded from doing so. He is devoid of responsibility. None of his own muscles, mental or physical, are exercised; none of them are drawn upon. The screen diverts but does not demand. And this deficiency is enhanced by the peculiarly druglike, almost narcotic, soporific power it exerts. It draws and holds attention, even when its offerings are of the most trivial, banal, and useless. We all know this. Once the screen is illuminated, few can deny it their gaze. Scenes and images which, appearing before us in real life, would scarcely invite more than a bored flick of the eye, rivet attention when they appear on the screen. In this sense the television box could be said to inflict upon the viewer something even a bit worse than passivity and mere inactivity; a sort of induced flaccidity—a species of unhealthy withdrawal from active participation in anything at all.

In the case of many adults, this could be said not to matter very much. Many of them, it could be argued, have neither the imagination nor the incentive to make very good use of their leisure time in any event. If they were not watching television, they might, it will be said, be doing something worse.

But it is another thing in the case of the children. It is not that what is purveyed to them on the screen is always directly harmful, intentionally or otherwise. Some of it even tries to be helpful. The evil lies rather in the forfeiture of what the child might otherwise be doing if he or she were not watching television.

A child, in contrast to the resigned, nondeveloping adult, has little time to waste. It is at a stage of life when it *can* develop, and should be developing. Time must be allowed for school, for homework, for meals, and for play. But play, if it is to contribute to the development of the child, must be active, physically or otherwise, not passive. It must be play that requires the active participation of the child, develops muscles, exercises the mind and the imagination, strengthens and enriches. Without this, real growth will not take place. Not only is it essential that precisely this kind of play should have a part in the child's day; but this, childhood and adolescence, is the only stage of life when it can occur. And this means that when school and meals and homework have taken their due, there is, even in the best of circumstances, little time for other things. How much of this precious time, then, can the child afford to waste on a form of diversion that is passive, physically enervating, and contributes nothing to the growth of mind or body or emotional capacity, if only for the simple reason that it exercises none of these faculties?

Let me emphasize again, the evil of television for the child viewer lies not so much (leaving the advertising aside) in what it gives to him directly, for much of this is harmless pap, if not particularly edifying. The evil lies in what it deprives the child of: the sacrifice of what the child might be doing if it were not sitting, passively and uselessly, before the screen.

Television is, of course, not the only offender in this respect. Its deficiencies are ones that it shares, in one degree or another, with the radio, the rock-and-roll cassette player, the movie, even the passive watching of sport in the open. But television bears a special responsibility because of its inviting nature and because of its very convenience and ready accessibility in the home. There it stands, the television set, ready to be flicked on with the touch of a finger, ready to divert the child that doesn't want to do its homework, ready to relieve the harried, overworked mother of the burden of facing up, at that moment, to the question of what to do with the idle, bored child.

Particularly unfortunate, here, is the extent to which the screen takes the place of reading—and thinking. I am speaking here of all forms of the screen: the movie as well as the box. Reading, in contrast to sitting before the screen, is not a purely passive exercise. The child, particularly the one who reads a book dealing with real life, has nothing before it but the hieroglyphics of the printed page. Imagination must do the rest; and imagination is called upon to do it. Not so the television screen. Here everything is spelled out for the viewer, visually, in motion, and in all three dimensions. No effort of imagination is called upon for its enjoyment.

And as for thinking, here the question is one of language. The capacity for effective speech is, again, something that comes only through the exercise of it. Listening can be stimulating; it can in some instances invite imitation. But it is not enough. We all know the relative linguistic incoherence of the present younger generation. Very few of today's young people can express a single thought clearly, firmly, correctly, and coherently. Nor can they write that way. Few teachers would deny, I think, that a depressingly high percentage of students go through both high school and college without acquiring the ability to produce, through their own pens or mouths, a single paragraph of straightforward, lucid English prose.

Much of this, presumably, can be laid to the deficiencies of the schools. But another great part of it comes, surely, from the failure to acquire, or the abandonment of, the habit of reading. And who is to say how much of this, in turn, is the product of the enticing, obliging, competitive presence of the television set in the home or in the student's room, demanding nothing, providing everything, calling for no effort, linguistic or otherwise, on the part of the spoiled and lazy youngster? It has sometimes seemed to me that the child who has never had the experience of finding itself left to itself on a rainy day in a room with nothing greatly interesting but a filled bookcase, with the rain streaking down the window, with no television set, and with nothing to do but to pick up a book and read, is truly deprived.

And the deprivation goes farther than just denial of the stimulus of reading. For language is the discipline and structure of thought. It is a question whether without clarity of language, there could really be any such thing as concentrated, persistent, and sustained thought.

Here, again, the television set comes in, and not the television set alone but all the other commercialized media as well. For it is, as I said above, the custom of the media to purvey whatever it is they have to purvey in disconnected, staccato bursts or images, never inviting the viewer's or listener's attention to any one thought or proposition for more than a few moments, never asking, or allowing time, for any comparison or analysis of contrasting or seemingly conflicting thoughts, and thus not only *not* stimulating and developing the capacity for sustained and thoughtful attention to any subject but positively debauching it. The press does this; so does television; so do the movies.

In part, of course, this tendency is connected with the cult of the visual image in the place of thought: the image as captured for the fragment of a second on the photographer's lens; or the moving image similarly captured, but again only briefly and fleetingly, on the motion picture or television screen. And how much of the attention of old and young is appealed to in this present civilization—outstandingly in the commercial media but in others as well—by the supposed presentation of reality in images of just this sort! This writer could not count the times—they must have run into the hundreds—when he has himself been appealed to, and often in the name of "education," to appear as a performer before one or the other of the photographic media with a view to stating all over again, usually in the form of an interview, this or that disjointed fragment of something he has already written.

Now, isolated images of this sort, like well-selected photographs in a book, can, and sometimes do, serve to make vivid one or the other of the elements in a sequence of sustained thought. In that sense they can, though they rarely do, constitute a minor enrichment of the thought process. But they cannot substitute for thought itself. A mental world dominated by fragmentary images of this nature can hardly be a thoughtful one.

The human mind—intelligence, judgment, the capacity for critical and logical thought—will not be developed without challenge. It will not be developed by passive diversion. It will not be developed by a steady diet of light entertainment. It will not be developed without a schooled sense of language, and exercise in its use. It will be not developed, in short, without trial and discipline. "I cannot praise," wrote Milton, "a fugitive and cloistered virtue, unexercised and unbreathed, that never sallies out and sees her adversary, but slinks out of the race, where that immortal garland is to be run for, not without dust and heat."[2]

The public of a great country that lets a large portion of its leisure time be wasted by steady exposure to media that provide none of this challenge is depriving itself in the most serious way of something that will be vitally needed if it is to retain its competitive importance in the world. There are other parts of the world where want, poverty, or the cruelty of social pressure is producing a more serious and relentless discipline of both mind and body; and this difference, if not corrected, must someday make itself felt in the "dust and heat" of international life.

2. From the *Areopagitica*.

Conclusions

These two devices, the automobile and television, are only examples of what appear to me to be collective bad habits—addictions, if you will, of American life. What do we see about ourselves on the basis of these examples?

We see that great masses of people, left to themselves and allowed to pursue their private pleasures and interests as the spirit of the day moves them, will spoil themselves if the requisite facilities for doing so are available to them. And the commercial interests—the advertisers and the others—will eagerly provide those facilities, because this involves consumer spending and they make money out of it.

The politicians, left to *themselves,* and anxious to say only what they think people and the special interests that support them want to hear, will be the last to try to halt this process. Their main concern will be not to oppose it but to exploit it.

The only visible corrective to this sad situation would be leadership—the readiness, that is, of some thoughtful person or persons in high position to look long and carefully at the above-mentioned questions and similar ones, and to say, publicly, persuasively, and persistently, what needs to be said about them, even if this has to be done to the jeopardy of such further electoral prospects as confront them.

This is not the problem of America alone. Other democracies all face it to one degree or another. But in most of the others, it is less serious than in the United States. This is so for various reasons; but among them there is the fact that as a rule the European political parties at least profess to have ideological commitments that oblige them to confront the larger questions of social development, whereas the American parties, being almost totally unideological and quite devoid of such commitments, are not so constrained.

One can contemplate only with sadness and apprehension the prospect of the American federal government intervening in problems of the habits of daily life among the citizenry. Certainly, it would be better if this could be avoided. Yet whenever public authority, here as elsewhere, has stood passively by and permitted technological innovations to be thus recklessly and uncritically appropriated into people's lives without concern for their social effects, it has assumed, whether or not it meant to, a measure of responsibility (and who else is to do it?), it will draw a cloud—is already drawing such a cloud—over its own adequacy as a form of government for a great people in the modern age.

Chapter Nine

FOREIGN POLICY, NONMILITARY

I do not say that we ought to prefer the happiness of one particular society to the happiness of mankind; but I say that, by exerting ourselves to promote the happiness of the society with which we are most nearly connected, and with which we are best acquainted, we shall do more to promote the happiness of mankind than by busying ourselves about matters which we do not understand and cannot efficiently control.

—Thomas Macaulay, speaking in the House of Commons in 1845

Introduction

The passing of the Cold War, in presenting us a world which appears to be devoid of anything that could be seen as a major great-power enemy of this country, also obviously presents us with a problem for which few of us are prepared. One has to go back to the 1920s to find anything that could be even remotely regarded as a precedent for it;

and even then, conditions have changed so greatly since that time that the precedent would be of very little relevance.

What presents itself, in this situation, is a demand for nothing less than a redesigning of the entire great pattern of America's interaction with the rest of the world. To treat this whole subject in a graceful and coherent form within the limits of a single chapter in a book of this nature would surpass the capacity of this writer. He can only attempt, as a starter, to sketch out what he feels should be the main thrust and balance of American policy in the remaining years of the century, and then to give at least a partial elucidation of this concept by commenting on several significant aspects of the problem, without attempting to bring all of these individual comments into one, comprehensive statement.

The Parochial Interests

Anyone who sets out to design or to conduct the foreign policy of a great country has to be clear as to the interests that policy is supposed to serve. Only if the image of these interests is clear in his mind can the policy he evolves have coherence and usefulness.

Those who conduct American foreign policy have two sets of interests to bear in mind. First, there are the parochial interests of the country itself, in the most narrow and traditional sense of that term. Second, there are the interests that engage this country as a participant in the affairs of the international community as a whole. Both of these sets of interests deserve our respect and attention. But it is those of our own country, in the narrower sense, that lie closest to our hearts; and they demand our first consideration.

There is nothing wrong about this allotment of priorities. It is not the dictate of a national selfishness or disregard for others. This particular territory and these particular people, ourselves, are all that we, as a national state, have control over. The management of our society, and this in a creditable way, is for us an unavoidable responsibility as well as a privilege. Unless we meet this responsibility, no one else will; for there is none who could. And unless we meet it creditably, there will be very little that we can do for others—very little that we can do even to serve global interests. The first requirement for a successful participation by the United States in the confrontation with international environmental problems, for instance, will be success in coping even halfway creditably with the similar problems within its own territory.

But there is another reason, too, why the service to our own national interest is more than just selfishness. Our society serves, for better or for worse, as an example for much of the rest of the world. The life of no other people is so widely and closely observed, scrutinized, and sometimes imitated. So true is this that it is not too much to say that the American people have it in their power, given the requisite will and imagination, to set for the rest of the world a unique example of the way a modern, advanced society could be shaped in order to meet successfully the emerging tests of the modern and the future age.

The example, in any case, is going to be there, whether favorable or otherwise, and whether we like it or not. Our handling of our own problems is going to be carefully watched by others, no matter what we do. But if the example is only one of failure—of the evasion of challenge, of the inability to cope with our own major problems—this will be for others, aside from the loss of respect for us, a source of discouragement, a state of mind which can have far-reaching consequences, and for which we will bear a measure of responsibility. It is because no country can hope to be, over the long run, much more to others than it is to itself that we have a moral duty to put our own house in order, if we are to take our proper part in the affairs of the rest of the world.

But beyond the above, and as background for all that follows in this chapter, I should make it clear that I am wholly and emphatically rejecting any and all messianic concepts of America's role in the world: rejecting, that is, the image of ourselves as teachers and redeemers to the rest of humanity, rejecting the illusions of unique and superior virtue on our part, the prattle about Manifest Destiny or the "American Century"—all those visions that have so richly commended themselves to Americans of all generations since, and even before, the foundation of our country. We are, for the love of God, only human beings, the descendants of human beings, the bearers, like our ancestors, of all the usual human frailties. Divine hands, as I suggested in chapter 2, may occasionally reach down to support us in our struggles, as individuals, with our divided nature; but no divine hand has ever reached down to make us, as a national community, anything more than what we are, or to elevate us in that capacity over the remainder of mankind. We have great military power—yes; but there is, as Reinhold Niebuhr so brilliantly and persuasively argued, no power, individual or collective, without some associated guilt. And if there were any qualities that lie within our ability to cultivate that might set us off from the rest of the world, these would be the virtues of modesty and humility; and of these we have never exhibited any exceptional abundance. The discussion that follows is predicated on the rejection of such illusions.

We saw, in the preceding chapters, some examples of the failures and unsolved problems of our society. There are others that could have been mentioned. Until these inadequacies have been overcome, the task of overcoming them will have to have first claim on our resources. Comprehensive programs of reform in several areas of our life will have to be devised, put in motion, and carried through. Until this is done, we will not know what resources we can spare for foreign policy; and those we find it imperative to continue to devote to that purpose will have to be cut to the bone. What we should want, in these circumstances, is the minimum, not the maximum, of external involvement.

All of this seems to me to call for a very modest and restrained foreign policy, directed to the curtailment of external undertakings and involvements wherever this is in any way possible, and to the avoidance of any assumption of new ones. This means a policy far less pretentious in word and deed than the ones we have been following in recent years. It means, in particular, a rejection of the tempting but fatuous assumption that we can find, in our relations with other countries or other parts of the world, relief from the painful domestic confrontation with ourselves.

There will no doubt be those who will be quick to label what has just been suggested as a policy of isolationism. The term is not very meaningful; but if it means what I think it does, I could only wish that something of that sort were possible; for most foreign involvements are burdens we should be happy to be without. But unfortunately, as will be seen shortly, whatever possibilities may exist for the curtailment of our external commitments and obligations, there will always be a goodly number that cannot be eliminated—not, at least, in any short space of time—and of which we must acquit ourselves as best we can.

The reason given above—namely, the priority of our domestic concerns—is not the only reason for the modest and restrained policy suggested above. There are others that will, I hope, become apparent from some of the detailed comments that are to follow.

The Global Interests

I have said that in addition to these parochial American interests which we have no choice but to respect, there are interests of the entire world community that also require our consideration.

First, there are the multilateral bodies to which we belong and in the activities in which we participate. Outstanding among these, of course, is the United Nations. The disappearance of the Cold War, with the extreme bipolarity and other distortions that accompanied it, should bring an enhancement rather than a reduction of the importance of the UN as a factor, generally, in world affairs. But beyond that, to the extent that we can resign some of our responsibilities, particularly in peacekeeping matters, to the UN (which is probably where some of them belong anyway), it can ease the shift toward a less ambitious and more self-effacing American policy. This will not mean divesting ourselves of all responsibility for the treatment of the problems in question; it will mean only that our efforts, instead of being unilateral, will be exercised through the UN, in multilateral bodies.

And there is one other aspect of UN affairs in the pursuit of which the U.S. government will have every reason to take an active part. The receding into the distant past of World War II, coupled with the disappearance of the Russian empire and the breakup of Yugoslavia,

FOREIGN POLICY, NONMILITARY

has already raised basic questions for the United Nations, particularly with regard to the future composition of the Security Council. In whatever direction one looks for the solution to these questions, one will find oneself coming up against a problem to which reference was made in chapter 4: the problem, that is, of finding a place for the smaller ethnic entity that is too restless to remain comfortably within the sovereign framework of a larger state but is not fully qualified or prepared to assume all the responsibilities of a total independence and equality of sovereign status as a member of the United Nations. In any efforts it may make to redesign the composition of the Security Council and to revise the structure of the international community, the United Nations should be able to call upon the most enthusiastic and creative collaboration that the U.S. government is capable of giving to it.

There will be other multilateral forums, either beyond those under the UN or only tenuously connected with a UN patronage, which can also serve as channels for American diplomacy in this coming period. Where they are available, they should be used. This writer was never partial to the use of multilateral channels for Cold War diplomacy; but for a country anxious to remove itself from the limelight and to give priority to its domestic challenges, the use of multilateral rather than unilateral approaches to world problems has much to commend it.

Beyond this, there are of course the serious formal and long-term commitments this country has already assumed. These, particularly its military alliances, may be subject to eventual modification or termination; but for the short term they are there and must be respected. There are numerous other contractual arrangements, particularly foreign and military assistance programs, most of which, as will be seen below, ought probably to be terminated as soon as possible; but that does not mean that the termination need be rude or abrupt. It should merely not be unduly delayed—and particularly not in the many instances where our interest in the programs in question is primarily of internal motivation, either by domestic-political pressures or by the parochial interests of individual governmental offices or private bodies.

There is also the interest our government has traditionally taken in the foreign economic activities of American business, and the extent to which it is at this time involved, multilaterally and unilaterally, in efforts to liberalize world trade and especially to encourage and support American exports. These involvements will surely continue; and it is not the purpose of this writer to urge any diminution of them within the framework of a more modest and restrained foreign policy. But the involvement of private interests in this entire field of activity is so overwhelming, and so seldom has the part our government has taken in these matters had anything to do with calculations of the national interest, as compared with private ones, that there is little place for the mention of it in a discussion such as this one. Suffice it to note here that our government's involvements with international bodies such as the General Agreement on Tariffs and Trade (GATT), the World Bank, and the International Monetary Fund, not to mention its unilateral exchanges and involvements with individual governments in matters of international trade policy, must be expected, however they may relate to the national interest, to continue essentially unabated in the years that lie ahead, and thus to make a mockery of any charges or suspicions of a total "isolationism."

Finally, there is the entire area of the global environmental problem. Here, too, of course, the form of American involvement will have to be primarily multilateral—through participation, that is, in the work of the United Nations Environmental Program, and of other multilateral undertakings concerned with environmental matters. More will be said about this in the ensuing comments. But it should be noted here, and emphasized, that this is one aspect of foreign policy where the American interest is no smaller, and no less urgent, than in the need for domestic reform. And the priorities should be adjusted correspondingly.

The Governmental Machinery

The value of any policy purporting to reflect the national interests of the United States cannot be greater than the ability of the U.S. government to carry it out. And that will depend, in turn, on the extent to which the policymaker is free to address himself to that particular problem—the extent, that is, to which his field of vision and his energies are not preempted by competing undertakings in which the national interest is not a factor at all.

First of all, let us note the manner in which our government is at present set up for the conduct of foreign policy. In recent decades, the power to make foreign policy decisions has been scattered all over the vast panorama of Washingtonian bureaucracy. The process is theoretically under the ultimate control of the president, in the sense that anytime he decides to put in his word, that word is the controlling one. But the president is a very busy man. The time he has to devote to this sort of thing is limited. It was pointed out in an earlier chapter of this disquisition that under the American system of government, but not under many others, the president has to be both chief of state and prime minister, not to mention his responsibilities in party leadership. This puts great strain on him. The number of decisions, great and small, that enter daily into the conduct of American foreign policy are multitudinous. The State Department alone, we are told, receives, and is obliged to respond to, more than seven hundred telegrams a day. The president cannot possibly occupy himself personally with more than the tiniest fraction of such demands. The vast majority have to be delegated.

In recent years, this process of delegation has occurred in such a way that the power to take the necessary decisions has been fragmented, and is, as I say, farmed out all over the governmental pasture. In addition to the Department of State, the National Security Council, the Pentagon, the CIA, the Treasury, the Department of Commerce, and no end of legislators, legislative committees, and staffs all have their fingers in this pie. Parochial bureaucratic outlooks, interests, and competitive aspirations clash at every point. The result is, for obvious reasons, a very messy business. In this confusion, such a thing as a clear, firm, and prompt decision—and particularly one where all the relevant aspects of national interest are brought together, calmly weighed, and collectively taken into account—is rare indeed. It would do little good to have, here or there, at one place or another in the Washington scene, clear concepts of long-term national interest, so long as the power to make decisions remains thus fragmentized. As things now stand, many of the decisions taken are the results of long, labored, and tortuous compromises among endless numbers of individuals and committees, each of whom or of which has a different idea of the interests to be served. The result, not surprisingly, is everything else than a coherent, concise, thoughtfully formed, or clearly articulated foreign policy.

This writer has long had a vision of the most desirable means of correction of this deplorable situation—a vision that conforms, as he sees it, to the intentions of the founding fathers, but is most unlikely to be widely shared in the nation's capital today. He considers that the president needs to have at his side, for the immediate conduct of all aspects of the country's external relations, a deputy, whose powers in this field would be comparable to those of the normal European prime minister, and that this should be none other than the secretary of state himself. Subordinate to the authority only of the president himself in this broad field of activity (and by "this field of activity" I mean, literally, *all* aspects of official external American policy, political, military, commercial, or other), the secretary of state should be empowered to exercise not merely the direction over the operations of his own department but a general supervision over those of any and all other offices of the executive branch in the country's external relationships.

This suggestion should not be taken too dramatically. What is intended is not to create a line of authority for the secretary of state over the heads of other departments. What is envisaged is only that he should be, for the range of problems indicated above, primus inter pares among his cabinet colleagues, that actions in this field should not be undertaken by other departments and agencies of the government without his knowledge and consent, and that he should have adequate opportunity, in case of disagreement, to lay his position and that of his department before the president.[1]

---

1. I might interject at this point that if any of our numerous students or commentators on American government and politics want an interesting subject for exploration, they might do worse than to inquire into the reasons why so many of the presidents of this century (Woodrow Wilson, Franklin Roosevelt, Richard Nixon, Jimmy Carter, Ronald

I mentioned, above, the National Security Council. Should it be retained at all? Not, I would hope, in its present form. It has been developed, in recent years, into something like a duplicate State Department. Presidents, for some reason, seem to have found this politically convenient. No other reason for it is visible. It adds, of course, importantly, to the cumbersomeness and the confusion of the entire foreign affairs bureaucracy.

The original concept of the National Security Council was, as I understood it at the time of its founding, a sound one. It envisaged the occasional coming together of a small group of the president's senior foreign affairs advisers, to help him in his confrontation with questions of particular urgency and gravity. For this, there was required a secretary, with a small secretariat, to keep record of the meetings and to assure the follow-up of decisions. A council so conceived and so charged with competence need not have been an operative body; least of all need it have been a duplicate Department of State. But it could, if chaired (as it ought normally to be in the president's absence) by the secretary of state, have been a suitable locus for treatment of the more important problems of coordination of foreign policy within the government.

Plainly, of course, there would always likewise be Congress to be taken into account. It, too, has its constitutional place in the designing of foreign policy. Decisions taken in the executive branch will always have to be compromised with the views and wishes of individual legislators and congressional committees. But here is where politics comes in. Here, the president and the secretary of state, both political figures, are the ones whose responsibility it is to make the unavoidable decisions as to the extent to which congressional views and wishes, very often the

---

Reagan, and George Bush) have conspicuously disregarded their secretaries of state when it came to the more important questions of foreign policy, and have tended to conduct policy in such matters directly out of the White House, often through the agency of unofficial persons or security advisers (Colonel House, Harry Hopkins, Henry Kissinger, Zbiginew Brzezinski, Admiral Poindexter, Robert McFarlane, and Brent Scowcroft), either neglecting their secretaries of state or assigning them to tasks of partial or subordinate importance.

reflection of lobbyist pressures, should be deferred to, compromised with, or defied in the designing of foreign policy.

In the days of my directorship at the State Department's Policy Planning Staff, I was sometimes urged to take into account, in our recommendations to the secretary of state, the domestic-political aspects of the recommendation in question. "Should you not warn the secretary," it would be asked of me, "of the domestic-political problems this recommendation would present, and make suggestions as to how they might be met?" I resisted firmly all such pressures. Our duty, I insisted, was to tell the president and the secretary what, in our view, was in the national interest. It was their duty, if they accepted the force of our recommendations, to see how far these could be reconciled with domestic-political realities. This was a duty that they were far better fitted to perform than were we. And if we did not give them, as a starter, a view of the national interest in its pure form, as we saw it, no one else would, and they would not be able to judge its importance relative to the domestic-political pressures by which they were confronted.

Somewhere along the line there ought today to be, as there was then, someone charged with defining and holding before the eyes of both president and secretary of state the interests of the country as a whole, as distinct from those of individual groups or bodies of its citizenry. That being the case, there ought also to be, in regular and close contact with the secretary of state, a subordinate whose position would not be affected by changes of presidential administration and whose experience and memories could serve to remind both secretary and president of the lessons learned, and the precedents established, by previous administrations. For these purposes, I would suggest, the secretary of state ought to have, to assist him in his tasks, a permanent under secretary of distinctly nonpolitical coloration, either a highly experienced diplomatic official or someone from private life long versed in the ways of international life. And this official, in turn, should have under his authority two deputy under secretaries: one for such international travel (of the sort now too often performed by the secretary of state himself) as could not be avoided, another for the administrative concerns of the

Department of State and the Foreign Service (both of which organizations, one might hope, would gradually be greatly reduced in size). Flanked by these senior assistants, the secretary of state, himself avoiding like the plague, let us hope, all forms of official foreign travel, would normally be found sitting in dignity in his office on the seventh floor of the State Department, receiving as few visitors as possible, leaving to the permanent under secretary and his other subordinates the daily burden of contacts with members of the Washington diplomatic corps and with the various international bodies, and giving his attention to *all* the major problems of America's external relations across the globe—not, as is at present the case, only to a single one of them, and for long periods on end. There would, under such an arrangement, be none of the hectic shuttle diplomacy, conducted in person by the secretary of state, that has marked American practice for the past two or three decades.

As for the *real* Department of State (and not this imagined one): this, and the Foreign Service it controls, is in a dreadful state: vastly overstaffed, poorly organized internally, so overelaborate and cumbersome that it becomes practically useless as an alert and responsive channel for presidential decisions. Its chief officer, the secretary of state, is sloughed off, suffocated by a cloud of competitors from other quarters of the government, and given only partial and limited peripheral tasks in a field of activity where he was supposed to be the president's first assistant and alter ego.

And down that same slippery slope has gone the Foreign Service, to the brave beginnings of which, in the 1920s, this writer was once an immediate witness and of which he was a beneficiary. Victim for over sixty years to ignorance, indifference, domestic politics, and envy in many quarters, what was once supposed to be a well-selected, well-educated, well-trained, well-disciplined, and devoted corps of career civil servants, men and women, schooled to the service of the nation in a particular field and all held to the same competitive standards in selection and promotion, the Foreign Service has been steadily kicked around by official Washington until what remains of it today, to be sure, is a considerable band of faithful individuals, serving with intelligence and devotion at foreign posts not *because of* the way the government has treated them but *in spite of* it. These, however, are buried among masses of other individuals, who have undergone no such process of selection and who share little of this sense of commitment. The American diplomatic missions abroad, the premises of which were originally supposed to have been the offices of the various agents of the Department of State, diplomatic and consular, are now packed with outsiders, the children of other and more influential departments of the government, to a point where the members of the Foreign Service find themselves, like once the unhappy wife and son of Homer's Ulysses, barely tolerated guests in their own home, and in some instances almost squeezed out of it. It speaks for a portion of American youth that it produces people able and willing to carry on under such conditions.

This, I suppose, is all that could be expected of a government that knows and cares as little as does our own about the traditional institutions of diplomacy and the needs they imply. The way that governments interact at the diplomatic level is a rather esoteric subject, fully to be mastered only by a certain amount of firsthand experience. But in the long run, the instrumentalities for the projection of our diplomacy are bound to be the reflection of the level of enlightenment brought to the shaping of them by masses of people, not only short-term political appointees, legislators, and civil servants but journalists and media personalities as well, few of whom have had such experience or attach any great value to it. In these circumstances, the spectacle our Foreign Service now presents—of a considerable number of able and devoted people working, side by side with thousands of less able ones, in rather overblown and absurd organizational complexes, most of them nominally American embassies—will long remain the object of wonderment and amusement on the part of the foreign statesmen who come in contact with it, but of despair on the part of the few Americans who once learned, and can still remember, the original purposes the institutions of diplomacy were supposed to serve, and the reasons why they were so designed.

The Domestic Lobbies

The limitations of our governmental institutions for policy-making are not restricted, however, to the habits and organizational confusions of the executive branch. There is also the effect on policy-making of domestic political considerations and pressures. It is to the power of these pressures that we owe the fact that what American policy has too often reflected has not been the national interest but something quite different: the parochial interests of minorities—lobbies, factions, or special pressure groups of one kind or another—to the influence of which both branches of the government, legislative and executive, have shown themselves to be extensively responsive. Anyone who has ever served in a policy-making position in the State Department or at one of its missions abroad knows how frequently this source of pressure has been the determinant of governmental action, and how unfortunate have often been the consequences of this abuse of the policy-making function. So numerous and conspicuous have been the instances of this sort of thing that illustrations would seem superfluous. The China lobby, the Israel lobby, the sugar lobby, and dozens of others that could be mentioned: they have all been there to twist the arms of American politicians whenever the interests of their particular clientele appear to be at stake. And who can blame them? If blame is to be assigned for such efforts and for the effects they have had on American policy, it is not the lobbyists themselves who deserve it; their motivations are understandable enough. It is rather the statesmen who have yielded to them even when they knew that the national interests would have warranted a firmer resistance.

The temptations to yield to this sort of abuse are, of course, for both branches of the government, great; and it would be too much to expect that this yielding could ever be completely avoided. Such is the nature of our political system. But it is important to recognize that to the extent that this tendency cannot be controlled and reversed, American foreign policy will never be fully under control. In every instance where special interest is allowed to prevail in a given aspect of American foreign policy, it is the national interest that comes out that much shorter, if only because the area in which the national interest could find reflection in the final product of policy is thereby curtailed. And anyone who undertakes to comment on the real and major long-term interests of the country as a whole, as I am about to do, has to ask his listeners to remember that whatever merit his comments may have will be restricted to that narrow area in which policymakers might still feel free to think in terms of the national interest rather than the interests of particular pressure groups or lobbies.

The Real Alliances

Another limitation on the freedom of our government to act in formulating its foreign policy will be found in the commitments into which our government has already entered—or allowed people to feel that it has entered. These are of two kinds: the formal military alliances and the others.

Let us take first the alliances. There are two of these: the North Atlantic Treaty and the Security Treaty with Japan. Both represent commitments of great seriousness. So long as they endure, they demand our faithful recognition and observance. But both, if they are to be related to their original purposes, have been profoundly affected by the disappearance of the Soviet Union as a major military power; and both require reexamination in the light of that development.

We have, in the case of Japan, the Security Treaty of September 8, 1951, with the many supporting agreements concluded in later years. It is on the provisions of that treaty that the stationing of American forces on Japanese territory and the American use of certain military facilities in Japan are based. The basic engagement was negotiated at the time of the Korean War and was retained in the ensuing years in the light of the official assumption by both parties that the Soviet Union was a threat to the security of both parties—a threat calling for, and justifying, their close collaboration in the military field. The question that now arises is whether that assumption still holds and whether this kind of collaboration is still justified.

From the standpoint of American security, Japan occupies in the Pacific region a position analogous in certain respects to that of the British Isles in the Atlantic region. In both instances, the United States has a definite interest in seeing that the respective archipelagoes do not become victim to aggression or intimidation by any of their great continental neighbors, and that there is preserved a relationship with their governments that is based on the recognition of a community of strategic interests.

These lines are being written at a time when Japanese-American relations are strained over economic-commercial issues and when the Japanese authorities cannot be expected to view this country with the same feelings of confidence, or of need for American protection, that prevailed in 1951. Nevertheless, the United States remains, even in Japanese eyes, a major military and naval power; and the advantages, to both powers, of a collaborative relationship between them in questions of the military security of the Pacific region are so great that they deserve recognition even in the absence of any very encouraging political relationship.

Most of the original rationale for the existence of the present defense arrangements was obviously lost with the ending of the Cold War. (Something of it, we should remember, will continue to exist as long as the problem of the effort of the North Korean regime to develop nuclear weapons is not solved.) Whether the Japanese government would like to see these military arrangements continued unchanged, the layman has no means of knowing. If it does not, there is no apparent reason for their retention in their present form, and we should welcome their abandonment or modification. But if any suggestions from our side for their abandonment would be regarded by the Japanese as a hostile political gesture, incompatible with a desire on our part to maintain the present collaborative attitude on Pacific problems in general, then the alliance would probably better be retained in some form until and unless the situation changes.

A somewhat similar situation prevails with respect to NATO. Here again, and particularly with respect to the security problems of the European continent, NATO has certainly lost much of its original rationale. It is the view of this writer that the time has passed when there was a necessity for the stationing of American forces on the European continent; and more will be said about that in the next chapter. But there are certain questions about the place of Europe, generally, in the spectrum of American interests over this coming period which deserve a word or two of comment at this point.

It is true that the focus on Europe that predominated in American opinion and policy from the time of the foundation of the republic down into the first half of this century is now being relatively weakened by changes in the ethnic and national composition of the American populace and by the growing importance for this country of Latin America and the Far East. And this might well be seen, along with the disappearance of the "Soviet threat," as reason for the abandonment of the NATO tie.

But things are not quite that simple. The British Isles and parts (particularly the northwestern part) of the European mainland are still the source of a major portion of our cultural and political heritage. To say that the peoples of that region are our "friends" would be misleading. Friendship between peoples and countries is not the same thing as friendship between individuals. The best we can hope for from other peoples is that they should be aware of having a stake in our survival as a great power and of the value to themselves of a relationship of mutual confidence with us. This has been the basis for the relationship of most of the European peoples with us over the past century. It is in our interests that it should continue.

But beyond that we must recognize that the British and the peoples of continental Western Europe emerged from the experiences of the two world wars with a strong sense of insecurity, founded in a distrust of their own ability to assure their security or even their postwar recovery exclusively by their own efforts and without American help. It was this that led some of them to press us, at the beginning of the year 1948, to enter into a military alliance with them. The impression that there really was a Soviet threat had something to do with it, of course, as did their lingering fear of the Germany in their midst; but behind that, and more important still, lay their own lack of confidence in themselves, bred of the bitter memories of the two great wars and the realization that without American support they could scarcely have ended either of those wars without jeopardy of their political independence and security. Something of this insecurity and of this sense of dependence on the United States has endured to the present day, despite the complete recovery of their economies and the extensive revival (particularly in France and Germany) of their military strength. It has not been fully relieved even by what has recently happened in Eastern Europe and in the Soviet Union. The idea of facing a world, however changed, without the assured support of the United States still arouses among the peoples of Western Europe feelings of uncertainty and insecurity.

It is undesirable that these, our most reliable European friends, should be thrown unnecessarily into the apprehensive frame of mind that would flow from a complete and sudden abandonment by us of our contractual ties with that region. That the reasons for this sensitivity on their part are largely subjective and not fully rational does not render them less important.

Beyond that, we must remember that NATO, while designed mainly as a military pact, was not entirely that; it had, in the minds of its founders, nonmilitary purposes as well as military ones. Whether it will continue to be needed for these nonmilitary purposes has not yet been clarified, but it is not impossible. The alliance has begun to take an interest in the broader question of the reconstruction of the security structure of the European continent in the wake of the Soviet collapse, and in the promotion of the movement of European unification. It remains to be seen how far this involvement on NATO's part will go, or what significance it will have, but precisely because of this uncertainty, the present is no moment for any final decisions about the future of the alliance. The best we can do, as we watch the unfolding of these great readjustments in European affairs, is to bear in mind the fundamental considerations that should underlie our relationship with that great region, and to be alert for opportunities to play a helpful role without violence to any of these deeper principles.

The two relationships of alliance continue to stand, then, despite the disappearance of most of their original rationale, as claims on the attention of our policymakers and of the resources we have to devote to our external relations. There is, surely, a lesson in this. The lesson is that far-reaching involvements with other countries, if allowed to endure for long periods of time, have a habit of surviving the situations that gave rise to them in the first place. Their very existence creates new situations, which their creators could never have envisaged. Thus any effort to put an end to them, however logical and natural this may appear in the light of the fading of their original purposes, becomes a new political action, the desirability of which has to be judged against the changing realities of a new day.

The Implied Alliances

Beyond these two formal alliances, the terms of which exist in writing and have had the ratification of the U.S. Senate as provided by the Constitution, there are a number of special relationships with countries of lesser size and military power which are all too frequently referred to as "allies" but in regard to which the use of that term stands on shaky ground. How many of these there are, I would hesitate to say. Outstanding examples would be Egypt, Greece, Turkey, Israel, the Philippines, South Korea, Pakistan, and others whose qualification for this dubious distinction seems to even be more ephemeral. In a number of instances, the use of the term "ally" with regard to these countries seems to rest on little more than the fact that for long periods of time, originally for Cold War reasons or in deference to long-standing Middle Eastern commitments, we have been devoting large sums of money to the maintenance and the strengthening of their armed force establishments—have been doing this, in fact, for so long and with such prodigal generosity that it seems to have become a habit, so that its withdrawal, like many other benefits long accorded, would be regarded as a signal offense.

It is not my intention to deal, in this book, with the current relations of our government with specific other governments. So I shall not go into the justification for this beneficence on our part in individual cases.

Some of these handouts appear to be essentially rental payments for territory or facilities made available to American armed forces. I can only say that since most of these relationships, too, like the two alliances mentioned above, have origins that are now being increasingly questioned, I should think they all deserve some reexamination in the light of present conditions. But I would like to take this opportunity to register my objections to the use of the term "alliance" to describe them. I am not aware that any of them have been defined as "alliances," as such, in treaties properly negotiated and ratified by the Senate of the United States. This sloppy and careless use of the language simply sows confusion of understanding.

The Third World

Beyond the great-power allies and those other countries just mentioned (let us call them, for want of a better name, the "favorites") with whom we have special relations, there lie approximately 150 other "sovereign" entities, members of the United Nations, which are objects of our attention and with which, with rare exceptions, we maintain at least formal diplomatic relations. The majority of these are the beneficiaries of one or several of our many aid programs, military and civilian; and our involvements with them consist very largely of arrangements for one-sided assistance.

Within the framework of these aid programs, some fourteen billion dollars would appear to be leaving our treasury annually, to end up, in one way or another, in the hands of foreign regimes. Over half of the "programs" are ones for military assistance; the remainder, the civilian ones, come under the heading of International Development and Humanitarian Assistance.

Although there is a sizable portion of this largess that could, in my opinion, be well omitted, I do not mean to suggest that all of it should be. A portion of it—something like two billion dollars—seems to be routed through multilateral organizations; and for this, if only for public relations reasons, there would seem to be good reason. Another four billion would appear to be going mainly to the "favorites," in the form of grants, largely for military purposes. The rationale for these, as we have seen, would seem to lie largely in the power of Cold War habits, as yet not fully overcome, or in the support they are seen as offering to our involvements in the Middle East. The remainder, some seven or eight billion dollars, directed principally to smaller countries, may seem negligible in monetary terms compared with the remainder of our budgetary outlays; but for a government confronting our deficits it is a not inconsiderable figure. And this financial aspect of our aid programs is not the only, or even the principal reason, for the doubts I have to express about them.

The first of these doubts have to do with the sheer numbers and complexity of the administrative effort involved at the Washington end. If I interpret correctly the governmental figures for the fiscal year 1990, some eighty-four countries were then benefiting from American economic aid, and ninety, largely but not entirely the same ones, from our military assistance programs. One shudders to think of the number and complexity of the various written agreements these programs must have involved; for the aid took various forms and categories, and there must have been multiple agreements with many individual countries. To get any idea of this vast and confusing network of engagements would be a task of research requiring many days not just of individual effort but of staff effort as well for its completion. And this task would be multiplied severalfold if it were extended to include an examination of the uses the respective recipient governments made of this aid.

What legislator, one wonders, could possibly dispose over the amount of leisure time it would take to survey all these programs? Or what common taxpayer, either, for that matter? I find it hard to believe that there is any single person or office, even in the State Department, where all this information is conveniently available, its content critically surveyed at frequent intervals, and the results of such oversight effectively fed into the formulation of national policy. To figure out what we are really doing, and to what results it is all leading: this would be the policymaker's nightmare and the bureaucrat's heaven. The question presents itself, Is there not something badly wrong, and even dangerous, when the operations and obligations of public authority in a given field attain so great a profusion and complexity that they escape the normal possibilities for official, not to mention private, oversight?

Even more problematical is the question of the motivation for all these "programs." The government's official professions along this line sound very inspiring. We are going to "alleviate suffering," to "promote sound economic policies," to "promote the growth of market-oriented economies through budgetary support," to "provide expert advice to foreign governments," and so on. And, oh yes, we are going to "support the emergence of democracies as well."

But is there anyone in Washington, it may be asked, who ever stacks these noble aims up against the results actually achieved? I cannot recall any of these aid agreements ever being canceled because it failed to reveal any great usefulness in any of these respects. Indeed, the wide spread of them (military aid programs, for example, for all but seven of the fifty African countries, and for twenty-two out of the twenty-four Latin-American countries) would suggest that these benefits are distributed sweepingly, by categories, and that little or no attention is paid to the results, or lack of results, in individual instances. Some eighty-seven countries are, we are given to understand, benefiting from aid programs under the title of Military Education and Training. We are presumably teaching the soldiers of these countries how to use weapons; and I have no doubt that in many instances we are supplying them, directly or indirectly, with the weapons we are teaching them to use. But against whom are these weapons conceivably to be employed? Forty-three of these recipient governments, for example, are African ones. They are not greatly involved in intercontinental conflicts. It is hard to imagine against whom they could use these weapons, and the training we are supposedly giving them, if not against their neighbors or, in civil conflict, against themselves. Is it *our* business to prepare them for that?

Taking, again, just the African continent as an example: this sort of thing has been going on for years. And what do we see when we look at that continent today? On every hand, egregious overpopulation, and its unchecked proliferation; disease, particularly AIDS; exhaustion of resources; destruction of environment (the slaughtering of the rain forests and the growing of the Sahara). And democracy? In three or four cases, yes—perhaps; but in how many others—chaotic conditions, deterioration of civilization, civil disintegration. I am not saying that these latter phenomena are the *results* of our many involvements; but it is hard to see that the latter have had any noticeable effect in preventing or impeding them, or show any promise of having such an effect in future. And is it not apparent that in the face of these powerful trends our aid efforts are puny, and beside the point? Similar questions could be raised about programs in other continents as well. Africa is simply a particularly dramatic example.

However one views it, the evidence seems to me to be overwhelming that the great bulk of our aid programs are essentially self-engendered, in the sense that they have very little to do with the *real* needs of the countries to which they are addressed, but reflect very well a variety of motivations on the part of those in Washington who have authorized the programs. These would include the gratification Americans derive from picturing themselves as the teachers of others in matters of democracy and economic progress; the tendencies toward bureaucratic empire building in Washington; the incurable tendency of Americans to do everything by uniform categories rather then by careful and discriminate attention to the requirements of the individual case; the interests of official intelligence gathering (in the case of the military programs); residual Cold War reactions; cloying involvement with individual foreign leaders or regimes; and, finally, sheer bureaucratic inertia and habit—the feeling that when something has been going on for a long time, why change it?

These motivations are not all discreditable. Some are attributable to the general feeling that when one country is rich (or is usually so described), it ought to try to be helpful to those that are poor. This, surely, is a commendable reaction, testifying to the generosity of spirit of those who experience it. But does it not also reflect a serious underestimation of the depth of the problem, an overestimation of the importance and effectiveness of our response, and a lack of concern for the real results of our efforts to give aid, as compared with the comfort we derive from seeing ourselves as the giver of it?

Multilateral Diplomacy

Most of these observations have pertained primarily to bilateral relations with other countries. It remains to say a word about the multilateral ones. These take place in both the global and the regional contexts, the global ones being largely the concern of the United Nations.

Whenever the initiative for undertakings by the UN comes from us, there will be, of course, no question of our support and participation. But even when the initiative comes from others, there are two reasons why, unless we have strong reasons of principle for not doing so, we should not deny it either of those responses. There is, first, the need of the United Nations, as an institution, for our moral support. It is, as I have already said, the only symbol of the community of fate that links all the branches of the human family. It would be an immense loss—a loss to civilization generally—were that ideal to be neglected or abandoned, and this particularly at a time when the unity of the ecological structure of the planet and the demands that unity creates for the coordinating of national environmental programs are becoming increasingly evident to people everywhere.

But beyond that, for a country that wishes to present a low profile in the time that lies ahead, as this country has every reason to wish to do, collaboration with other countries in international undertakings under UN auspices, and particularly in ones flowing from initiatives other than our own, holds many advantages. It is needed not so much as a protection for others (for American initiatives for multilateral enterprises are more apt to be naive than sinister) as it is for ourselves, relieving us, as it does, of responsibilities we ought not now to be assuming, restraining us from those flights into political and verbal posturing to which many of us seem to be inclined. Not the self-trumpeting leader in great moral causes but the modest, willing worker together with others in the vineyard of international collaboration: that is the image of itself that America should wish to project to others, but primarily to itself, as the twenty-first century, so replete with uncertainties and dangers, begins to impose itself upon us.

As for multilateral collaboration at the regional level: I have already pointed out that there are many problems that, one might suppose, could be more easily and effectively treated in regional international bodies than in global ones. I can perceive no conflict between the regional and the global areas of multilateral collaboration. I am sure that the respective bodies of the United Nations will be only too happy to encourage, if not to sponsor, efforts of this nature at the regional level, wherever these promise success in bringing the various parties together and achieving significant results.

But regional organization and collaboration must take its departure, as it does in the European Community, from the nature and the needs of the respective region; and in no two cases will these be alike. North America, for example, presents particular problems in this respect, owing to the predominant geographical and economic position of the United States and the great cultural differences that divide its neighbors to north and south. It is, in fact, hard to think of any region that lends itself more poorly to intimate regional collaboration in a number of fields. Here, admittedly, one will have to feel one's way.

But the United States has every reason to cultivate with particular care and thoughtfulness its relations with these neighbors, and especially with Canada and Mexico. And where wider possibilities for collaboration on a regional basis present themselves, let us give them every support and encouragement, ourselves treading very lightly, doing all in our power to disarm the inevitable suspicion that we are attempting to dominate the process and exploit it to our own, selfish advantage.

Such thoughts about the prospects for regional organization here in North America are one thing. Thoughts about such organization in other continents or regions are another. For the most part, these latter are matters we understand poorly and in which we have no reason to interfere or to judge.

An exception to what has just been said is Europe. There is no apparent reason why we should belong to any regional European association. There *are*, however, reasons why we should take a special interest in any tendencies toward such association in Europe and should give them our encouragement and support.

It is true that this country becomes, with every day that passes, less European in the composition of its population and in the relative importance of Europe among its various interests and concerns. Nevertheless, its governmental tradition and its political culture generally have been largely derived from that side of the ocean, particularly, though not exclusively, from the British Isles. And the close relationship between the security of Western Europe and that of this country has not only been recognized in two great wars but has been sealed, in a sense, by those many Americans who laid down their lives in the service of it.

For these reasons the European continent is, for us, more than just another continent among continents. Whether there is still need for a NATO at a period where there is no significant threat to the security of Western Europe from any outside quarter is, as has already been pointed out, a reasonable question. Our interest in Europe's security will remain whether there is a visible threat or not. This does not oblige us to be a member of any European regional association. It does give us reason to hope for the continued vitality and prosperity of the civilization of that part of the world, and to be the great and good friend of any efforts by the Europeans to promote this by collective effort. The Europeans, as mentioned above, are our good friends as are the inhabitants of no other continent—not because they love us (words of that sort are misplaced when one is talking about great peoples) but because they recognize both the common traditions that unite us and the importance of our attitudes and our disposition for their own security. This is the nearest one can come to friendship in the relations between peoples. That being the case, we have reason to value the dispositions we encounter on that side of the water. And that, too, should be recognized as one of the guiding principles of American policy.

Human Rights

This brings us to the questions of "human rights." Let us first glance at the extent of our involvement in this cause. The Department of State, as I understand it, in addition to harboring the Bureau of Human Rights and Humanitarian Affairs headed by an assistant secretary of state, now has a "human rights officer" attached to the normally already redundant staff of every American diplomatic mission anywhere. One part of the duties of these particular officials is said to be the preparation of an annual report on the human rights record, so called, of the host country. The department, for its part, maintains in Washington a "human rights reports team," to read and ponder such reports and to prepare a consolidated report for Congress. It does all this, to be sure, not solely of its own volition; these procedures are now, at least in part, required by law. But what is under consideration here is not the involvement of the Department of State alone but of our government as a whole in the question at issue. And thus extravagantly do we, like a stern schoolmaster clothed in the mantle of perfect virtue, sit in judgments over all other governments, looking sharply down the nose of each of them to see whether its handling of its domestic affairs meets with our approval.

That these commitments constitute one more limitation on our freedom of action in foreign affairs—one more instance in which we have committed ourselves in advance to behave in a given way in a wide category of instances, none of which can be specifically foreseen—is beyond doubt. And is this justified?

I spoke of this matter, in its purely international aspects, in chapter 4. At the risk of a certain repetition, let me now look at it from the standpoint of American foreign policy.

Let us recall, first of all, that the manner in which regimes customarily treat their subjects, worldwide, is largely a matter of tradition, habit, and popular concepts of what is right and what is wrong. All these are subject to change, to be sure, over long periods of time, but seldom, if the results are to be lasting, can the change be abrupt.

It is the habit of a great many regimes, across the surface of the globe, to deal harshly with those of their nationals who have opposed their positions of power, or who are suspected of doing so. In most instances, their opponents, if the shoe were on the other foot, would behave in much the same way. The incentives to such behavior are never-ending; and unless the national traditions and political habits sternly rule them out, they will normally be yielded to. The pressures of outside opinion may occasionally cause the respective regime to go a bit easier for a time in this respect; but unless these pressures are supported by the inherited political culture of the place, and particularly by the existence and tradition of democratic self-government, such gestures of moderation are not apt to be lasting.

The pressure of outside opinion about human rights sustained over long periods of time, can indeed produce beneficial changes in both attitudes and institutions. The role of private opinion in this direction, when applied in support of gradual change, is important and should be welcomed. Whether governments, and the U.S. government in particular, should be involved in exerting such pressures is more dubious. In this respect, governments have to take the world pretty much as they find it. Their task—at least, the task of the U.S. government, as I perceive it—is to conduct its own relations with other governments in a manner conducive to a minimum of bilateral friction and to the maximum of usefulness to world peace and stability. This will be most effective if the sound old principle on noninterference in the other's domestic affairs is respected—if the lines of responsibility, in other words, are clearly recognized. This includes the responsibility of each regime for the governing of its own people. Each of them has, alone, the power to shape the situation in this respect. It must be, from the standpoint of morality, the judge of its own behavior. Outside pressure, particularly from another government, is seldom helpful, and may be counterproductive.

For a foreign government to exert such pressure, in circumstances impossible to foresee, for an indefinite time into the future, strikes me as in all respects a questionable procedure; and I cannot but regret the lengths to which we have shown ourselves prepared to go, and the leadership we have even taken internationally in promoting, on the governmental level, the cause of "human rights."

The die is now cast. Formal obligations have been entered into. The practice has found sanction in American public opinion. So be it. But I would ask it to be noted that this is one more instance, like several others mentioned in this chapter, where indulgence of the desire to appear virtuous in our own eyes has placed limitations on the area in which we would have the flexibility to act usefully in more significant areas of international life.

Morality and Foreign Policy

Just forty years ago, in a series of lectures at the University of Chicago which later found publication in book form, I casually mentioned moralistic preaching to others, along with an excessive legalism, as one of the more regrettable features of American policy in the earlier decades of this century. This had, as it turned out, the unintended effect of landing me in a good deal of controversy. The controversy usually took the form of allegations that I had advocated for this country a cynical and amoral policy, devoted to the cultivation of America's military power and devoid of respect for the noble national ideals of which America foreign policy ought to be the reflection.

I have, on numerous occasions, endeavored to set to rights what I felt to be the misunderstandings involved in such charges. In particular, I addressed to this subject an entire article, published in the quarterly *Foreign Affairs* (Winter 1985–86). But I plainly did my job poorly, for very few readers professed themselves satisfied with the answers.

I stressed, in the article just mentioned, the fact that government, although constitutionally charged with the conduct of foreign policy, was an agent and not a principal, and that the area in which a government was at liberty to be guided by moral convictions was not identical with that in which the individual had his existence and arrived at his decisions. I also confessed, in that article, my regret that I in earlier years had had a part, although a very small one, in setting up within our government facilities for the conduct of secret operations. I expressed, as the more mature judgment of later years, the view that all forms of foreign policy that involved secrecy and concealment were neither in keeping with the American tradition nor did they fit naturally with the established modalities for the conduct of American foreign policy.

Were I writing such an article today, I would go even further and add that the involvement of our government in the acquisition of secret intelligence, by espionage and other unavowed processes, while perhaps occasionally unavoidable, has had ascribed to it a degree of importance far greater than it deserves. This judgment has rested on my long-standing belief that well over nine-tenths of all that our government needs to know about life beyond our borders, even in military matters, can be better and more safely obtained by the scholarly scrutiny of information already available to us in legitimate ways than by the most elaborate efforts of espionage, secrecy, and concealment. I make these points in order to emphasize that I am concerned to distance myself from all aspects of American policy that cannot be openly and honestly avowed.

One should not conclude from these observations that I am advocating the sort of open diplomacy that Woodrow Wilson talked about so many years ago, during and after World War I. I regard it as a matter of course that all covenants formally arrived at with other governments should be made publicly known and duly recorded in the publications of the United Nations. But I feel very strongly that the privacy of negotiations looking up to the conclusion of such covenants must be protected. The results of negotiation, in other words, must be made public, but the soundings, contacts, discussions, and negotiations leading up to such agreements must be covered by the right of privacy; and it is up to the government to protect that privacy, even in the face of the often obtrusive and insistent demands of the press and the media.

Beyond these observations, I am disinclined to resume the rather fruitless discussion of the relationship between morality and foreign policy with which I have had so little luck in the past. So I shall now content myself simply with an effort to state the principles by which I would like to see us and our government guided in these respects.

I would like to see this government conduct itself at all times in world affairs as befits a country of its size and importance. This, as I see it, would mean

- that it would show patience, generosity, and a uniformly accommodating spirit in dealing with small countries and small matters;
- that it would observe reasonableness, consistency, and steady adherence to principle in dealings with large countries and large matters;
- that it would observe in all official exchanges with other governments a high tone of dignity, courtesy, and moderation of expression;
- that, while always bearing in mind that its first duty is to the national interest, it would never lose sight of the principle that the greatest service this country could render to the rest of the world would be to put its own house in order and to make of American civilization an example of decency, humanity, and societal success from which others could derive whatever they might find useful to their own purposes.

If this be seen as immorality, let those who see it that way make the most of it.

Conclusions

In the behavior in recent decades of the American political establishment in matters of foreign policy, I see reflected a number of persistent motivations, most of them illustrated in what has been said in this chapter. I see, thus reflected, remnants of the astigmatism and the corruption of understanding the marked the Cold War period. I see the impulse to cater to the demands and desiderata of powerful special domestic-political interests. I see a great deal (some of it contradictory) of what I think of as diplomacy before the flattering mirror: the desire to appear as the gracious and high-minded lady bountiful (the many aid programs), as the thrilling military adventurer—the knight in shining armor, rushing to the aid of the threatened and the downtrodden (Vietnam, Panama, the Persian Gulf War)—and as the unbending champion of democracy and human rights. I see the addiction to established habit, and the ponderous inertia, of entrenched bureaucracies. And in all of this I see the never-ending compulsion of successive administrations to present themselves, for the popularity polls, in postures that feed the

American public's favorite wish-images of itself. All this I see. What I do not see is any marked concern for the national interest in the narrow sense, on the one hand, or for the wider interests of the threatened planet, on the other.

The reader may recall the observation made in chapter 3 to the effect that every political regime, in all places and all times, speaks with two voices: one for the interests of its people as a whole, the other for its own interests as one of the contenders in the inevitable domestic-political competition. And it strikes me that in the behavior of the American political establishment, as noted above, there is a decided, and undue, predominance of the second of those two voices. I am not arguing that it should not be heard at all. I know that this distortion of priorities is one of the prices we pay for the advantages of our form of government. I have no doubt that most of our politicians, confronted with this reproach, would say, "Don't you realize that in order to have the ability to act in the national interest, we first have to gain power; and that to gain that power requires precisely the sort of compromises and pretensions that you are professing to deplore?" But to this I would have to reply, "Yes, within limits. But I don't see any great difference in your behavior before and after an election. One electoral test successfully surmounted, you at once begin thinking of the next one; and the domestic-political considerations again crowd out the interests of the nation as a whole."

Still, I see this situation as the fault not so much of the individuals who command, at one time or another, the seats of power but rather of the political system that installs them in those positions. Is there not, I wonder, some serious structural defect that puts so great a premium on one sort of political motivation, and so little on the other?

Chapter Ten

FOREIGN POLICY,
MILITARY

Not until statesmen had at last perceived the nature of
the forces that had emerged in France, and had grasped
that new political conditions now obtained in Europe,
could they foresee the broad effect all this would have
on war; and only in that way could they appreciate the
scale of the means that would have to be employed, and
how best to apply them.

—Clausewitz, on the military consequences
of the French Revolution

*T*he effort to evolve a sound theory of military strategy and to relate
it to the other concerns of the national state has been, I believe, a
difficult problem for most great countries; but it is hard to believe that
any country has ever been farther from finding satisfactory solutions to
it than our own. This is a field in which we have no established and
authoritative doctrine to guide us. Our own experience, where it might
have held lessons, had seldom been thoughtfully studied; nor would it,
even when carefully looked at, have had more than a limited relevance

to the problems that face us today. The American Civil War, though as great an encounter in terms of the manpower and firepower involved as had ever taken place to that time, was, after all, a civil conflict, many aspects of which would not have been characteristic for great international wars. The various writings of Admiral Alfred T. Mahan deeply influenced American thinking, particularly professional naval thinking, about the uses of sea power, as these presented themselves at the outset of this century; but they had relatively little to tell us about land power—how it was to be used in war, how to be maintained in peacetime, and how to be fitted into national policy in times of both peace and war. There were available to us, of course, the works of the great European thinkers on military theory and strategy, particularly Clausewitz and Jomini;[1] and scraps of their writings have no doubt long been studied at the various American armed-forces colleges; but it would be too much to say that those writings made any significant impression on the political establishment in Washington from which so many of the decisions affecting such matters had to flow. Beyond all of which, it is a question how much of this earlier thinking, even if carefully studied, would be relevant to the situation that now lies before us. Military theory, after all, has always had to reflect the technological and political realities of the time; and these have changed tremendously with the effects of the two great European wars of this century. A reservation, to be sure, must be noted here in the case of Clausewitz, many of whose observations on the dynamics of conflict and on the interactions of political and military interests in war have retained their relevance and validity over the entire 160-odd years since they were written; but if they have entered perceptibly into American thinking on the relationship between military and political policy, this has been, as a rule, only in a highly simplified form.

---

1. Carl Philipp Gottfried von Clausewitz, (1780–1831), the well-known Prussian general, writer on military subjects, and military theoretician. Antoine Henri, baron de Jomini, (1779–1869), the prominent military figure and writer, of Swiss origin, founder of the Imperial Russian Military Academy.

The Nuclear Fixation

Before we can look usefully at the challenges with which this present situation confronts us, we must dispose of, or at least relegate to its proper place, the hugely confusing and misleading factor that has dominated American strategic thinking ever since the Second World War—namely, the nuclear weapon, with its companions in the other weapons of mass destruction. For so bizarre and distorted has been, from the beginning, the structure of thought addressed to the place of the nuclear weapon in American theory and strategy that only with it out of the way can we turn in any rational manner to the situation we now have before us.

Actually, it did not take the advent of Gorbachev and the end of the Cold War to discredit most of that body of thought. It was evident as early as 1950 (and this writer tried in vain at that time to persuade his superiors in government to recognize this) that any American policy based on the first use of this form of weaponry—any policy, that is, that envisaged its uses for purposes other than deterrence and built our entire defense establishment around it—would lead to much confusion and would have suicidal implications. The nuclear weapon was, in fact, from the start an essentially useless weapon, useless at least for any rational purpose. And if there was ever any doubt of this, the development of what McGeorge Bundy has called "the tradition of the non-use of these weapons since 1945," a tradition to which we were brought by relentless confrontation with reality over the years, has disposed of it. But none of this sufficed to dull the obdurate enthusiasm of British, French, and American strategists for the weapon itself. And thus we had arrived, by the first year of the 1990s, at the nightmarish situation where more than fifty thousand nuclear warheads were in world arsenals, and 97 percent of them in the arsenals of the Soviet Union and the United States. Obviously, it would never have been possible to use more than a very small fraction of these weapons in combat without creating, in addition to the millions of directly caused casualties, a worldwide environmental catastrophe. The mere existence in human hands of those huge accumulations of nuclear explosives, incapable as they were of serving any coherent military purpose, was thus a danger to civilization in general, and an unnecessary one.

It had become apparent, even before the Gorbachev era, that the motives for this great buildup on the NATO side, while formally given as the necessity of deterring the Russians from launching some sort of an attack on the West, were in actuality largely subjective. If there was any doubt about this in the earlier years, the development of NATO doctrine during the years of Gorbachev's predominance disposed of it. For it was only grudgingly and slowly that the military establishments of the NATO nuclear powers showed themselves willing to take account of the new situation that had obviously been created by the drastic changes in Russia.

Plainly, to the immense relief of many of us, President Bush's initiative of September 1991 and the response it produced from the Soviet side, constituted a first great step in the liquidation of this dreadful situation.[2] There is reason to hope that the process thus hopefully begun will not stop at that point. But the addiction in question—the unreal hopes and expectations attached to nuclear weaponry—dies hard. There is still no withdrawal on the American side from the pernicious adherence to the principle of first use. There is still no readiness to contemplate a complete and comprehensive test ban. One still hears talk about "modernizing" (that dreadful euphemism) our strategic weapons.

Our objective for the coming period ought obviously to be: first, the halting of the proliferation of nuclear weaponry; second, reduction of both Soviet and American arsenals to the minimum necessary to balance the greatest of the other arsenals; then heavy pressure for the further reduction of all these arsenals, with a view to the ultimate total elimination of this form of weaponry worldwide. Only when all that

---

2. President Bush, in this initiative, announced several important unilateral cuts in American weaponry and proposed negotiations for mutual reductions of multiple warheads on certain types of nuclear weapons.

has occurred will we, and the rest of the world, be able to design defense policies directed to the realities of a postnuclear world. But a prerequisite for any real advance in those directions will be, of course, the abandonment by the U.S. government of the principle of first use, as well as any idea that it could expect the smaller powers to part with such of the weapons as they have while the United States and its European nuclear allies retain indefinitely their own.

The War of Annihilation

It is not too early to consider what, in the case of the United States, defense policies for a nonnuclear world might be. But precisely because the world with which we would then be dealing would be a nonnuclear one, it will not be useless effort to take account of certain of the great misconceptions that prevailed in American strategic thinking in the period immediately preceding the nuclear era, a period that included the two great wars of this century. These were distortions prevalent primarily in the military mind, always given to extremism when it came to the relation between military and political objectives; but they were readily appropriated into militaristic civilian thinking as well.

The first of these misconceptions related to twin concepts of total war—war of annihilation, that is—and unconditional surrender. It is not unnatural that military leaders, once involved in leading forces in combat, should make it their aim to achieve the complete destruction of the enemy's forces, and should be reluctant to entertain any ideas, such as political objectives, that might run counter to this purpose. There is, in military thinking, a certain absolutist quality that strongly resists anything that tends to obscure or to impair this purity of motive and action. This rests on the outwardly plausible thesis that the first and only thing to be thought of so long as the war is in progress is the desirability of reducing to zero the recalcitrance of the enemy—of making him entirely subservient to one's own will—the theory being that when this has been accomplished all political objectives can be easily attained. ("Let us begin by beating them; after that it will be easy," said the French general de Boisdeffre to his Russian counterpart, in negotiating the Franco-Russian alliance of 1894.)

This thesis was accepted, in both wars, by civilian as well as military leaders. It obviously commended itself to Franklin Roosevelt, in whose mind it was no doubt supported by the reflection that any preoccupation with political objectives, as distinct from the purely military ones, during the war would be controversial and divisive in the domestic-political sense. But it was a view that pervaded all official thinking in Washington during the Second World War. How many times were those of us who pressed for a clarification of our political objectives in those years put in our place by the refrain "In wartime, my boy, we don't take our eye off the ball"—the ball, being, of course, the undeviating pursuit of total military victory.

There were, however, two flaws in this so clear and outwardly persuasive way of looking at things. First, the experience of many previous wars made it evident that the manner in which one conducted a war, and the unfolding of events on the battlefield, affected the political situation in ways that had not been foreseen when the war was undertaken. Every day of the fighting produced changes—in the relations among allies, in the attitudes of populations affected by the war, in geographical and economic realities—that affected political objectives. Among other things, it became evident in the two world wars that the very costs of the struggle might begin to exceed all that the war had been meant to achieve. A particularly striking example of this was the First World War, where either side could have terminated the hostilities in 1916 by accepting the maximum stated peace terms of the other side, and still have been better off than they were by continuing the war, as they did, for another two years. The costs of the continuation of the struggle in blood and in resources, in other words, could begin to exceed all that one could hope to achieve by even the greatest formal military victory.

It also became apparent, in that as in other wars, that the continuation of the fighting might be serving the purposes of others, be they allies or neutrals, the achievement of whose purposes would be scarcely better, if at all, than the objectives which the enemy was pursuing. An example of this could be seen in the final months of the Second World War, when it became evident, to some of us at least, that what our Soviet allies were setting out to do in the areas of Eastern Europe they were in process of conquering would not be greatly preferable to what would have occurred had these regions been left in custody of the Germans.

Unconditional Surrender

A logical concomitant of the concept of the war of annihilation, and a concept that greatly commended itself to the American leadership in both world wars, was that of "unconditional surrender." With this device, the enemy, now deprived of his ability to resist, was also to be deprived of any part in the shaping of the postwar situation. The victor, in addition to being now all-powerful, was also considered to be both all-virtuous and all-wise. He, it was inferred, would know exactly what to do with the conquered country and with all other post-hostilities problems. He would need no help from the defeated enemy in making this determination. That enemy, supposedly hopelessly benighted and wrong-minded, was to be totally excluded from participation in the fashioning of the regime of peace under which he, and his people, would now be obliged to live.

This was the concept under which the British and the French (not, fortunately, the Americans) brought the First World War to an end. In World War II Roosevelt (much to Churchill's unhappiness) unilaterally proclaimed it as an Allied principle at the close of the Casablanca Conference in January 1943. It had, of course, and particularly in Franklin Roosevelt's eyes, the advantage of avoiding, so long as hostilities were in progress, all necessity of coming to terms with one's own allies on the question of what it was that one was fighting for and what the peace was supposed to look like, and thus of preserving at least the outward façade of solidarity in the Allied camp while the guns were still speaking.

Obviously, this way of ending a war was closely connected with the question as to whether it was the regime or the people of the enemy country against which one conceived oneself to be fighting. If it was primarily the regime that was viewed as the enemy, then it was at least logical that one should be reluctant to negotiate a compromise peace with a regime the unseating of which was one's principal war aim. During the Second World War no one in any of the Allied countries (and this, quite understandably) wanted to conclude a compromise peace that would leave Adolf Hitler at the helm in a defeated Germany. This was in itself no reason why one should not have been willing to discuss the prospective postwar situation with anti-Nazi Germans whose aim was to overthrow Hitler and who had plausible prospects for replacing him if they succeeded. But here, too, Western statesmen found themselves paralyzed by confusion and lack of agreement about who it was that they *would* like to see at the head of things in a defeated Germany in place of the Nazis. Yet the ban on discussion of political objectives while the war was on precluded any discussion of these matters among the Allies until after the final surrender of the enemy. And this brings up another of the questions about the suitability of unconditional surrender as a way of ending wars; for if one had not come to complete agreement with allies, before the war ended, about what it was that one was fighting for, an unconditional surrender was bound to raise all these awkward and divisive questions abruptly and in the most acute manner when hostilities ceased.

By and large, it must be said, there are many drawbacks to unconditional surrender as a way of ending a war. In excluding the regime of the defeated country from any significant participation in the drawing up of the post-hostilities regime, it also absolves them of all responsibility, while saddling the victors with total responsibility, for what is to come. But it also assumes that it is both desirable and possible to exclude an entire population from participation in the designing of its own future. While this can perhaps be done for a short time, it cannot be done for very long. And the results of these two great wars, ostensibly ended by unconditional surrender, afford a startling demonstration of this reality. In less than two decades after the end of World War I, Germany, nominally the defeated party, was again the greatest military power in Europe. Within two or three decades after the ending of the

Second World War, Germany and Japan, the two defeated powers, were the most prosperous and economically powerful countries in their respective regions. All these reflections stand as a warning against moving into future wars without taking into account the experiences of the two great European wars of this century and of their consequences.

Destruction for Its Own Sake

Another serious misconception that has influenced American military policy in the past, particularly but not exclusively in connection with nuclear weaponry, has been the belief that the value of a weapon was directly proportionate to its destructive power. This had much to do with the attractiveness of the idea of bombing targets, particularly urban targets, from the air—a predilection which has fascinated military strategists ever since the zeppelin raids of World War I, which enjoyed its heyday in World War II, and which dominated military thinking in the subsequent nuclear period. The military mind has tended to be obsessed with the concept of destruction—sheer destruction, destruction for its own sake—as the central aim of warfare. This has been understandable. You "destroy" the enemy's positions, his lines of communication and supply, and the military industry from which he obtains his weapons. You also destroy as many of his military personnel as you can. And you do all this, if possible, from the air—but in any case, with the least possible destruction of your own military resources. What better? Is not the "body count" the really decisive count? And does this not all contribute to your sole wartime objective, which is the destruction of your enemy's entire military capability and the subjection of his will to your own? I can recall more than one instance of military men saying during the war that their task was simply to "kill Germans."

All this is understandable. It is all a part of the concept of *la guerre à outrance*—the "war of annihilation." But there is something about it that gives me the deepest uneasiness. It is not only that the factor of discrimination—the capacity of individual types of weaponry to be used in a discriminating way—is underestimated. But it is also related to the question of the purpose of warfare. The purpose should be, it

seems to me, not just to work maximum destruction on the chosen
enemy but rather to produce a useful effect on his understanding and
his disposition—to convert him, if there seems to be no other way of
doing it, to a more useful and more acceptable frame of mind than that
which forced you to resort to arms against him in the first place, and to
do this with the minimum, not the maximum, of destruction. (It was
Clausewitz, after all, who maintained that the amount of the military
effort put forward should be determined by the political, not the purely
military, goals to be achieved.)

We all live in the same world; and if the aim of warfare is not to be
genocide (and who, in the Western world, would conceive it to be
that?), then it must be the purpose, in any military conflict, not so much
to "destroy" the enemy militarily as to change his frame of mind—to
convert that frame of mind, the one that led you to fight him, into one
more useful to the cause of world peace and more compatible with the
ideal of human progress. That it should have required, in the given case,
military effort to produce this effect on the enemy is sad and regrettable; but the fact that it *has* required it is no reason for regarding him as
lost to this world for all time and for resorting to methods of warfare
which, while perhaps reducing him to a total desperation, seem irrelevant to, or perhaps even subversive of, the task of changing his mind. It
is this, I suppose, that I had in mind when I wrote in my diary, upon
once contemplating the vast areas of civilian destruction in Hamburg,
where, in the Second World War, seventy thousand civilians had been
killed by Allied bombings in three days, that

> if the Western world was really going to make valid the pretense of a
> higher moral departure point—of greater sympathy and understanding
> for the human being as God made him, as expressed not only in himself
> but in the things he had wrought and cared about—then it had to learn
> to fight its wars morally as well as militarily, or not fight them at all; for
> moral principles were a part of its strength. Shorn of this strength, it was
> no longer itself; its victories were not real victories. . . . The military
> would stamp this as naive; they would say that war is war, that when
> you're in it, you fight with everything you have or go down in defeat.

But if that is the case, then there rests upon western civilization, bitter as this may be, the obligation to be militarily stronger than its adversaries by a margin sufficient to enable it to dispense with those means which can stave off defeat only at the cost of undermining victory.[3]

Well, these are just some of the thoughts, rising out of our earlier military experiences, which, as it seemed to me, might usefully be borne in mind as we move to the question of what our national theory and strategy of warfare might best be in what we must hope will be the nonnuclear age of the near future.

Alliances and Special Relations

The first thing to bear in mind, as we contemplate our military future, is the sort of war we do *not* have to plan for; and that is a great war among great powers. The experiences of this past century have made that plain. In the light of modern military technology, no all-out war among great industrial powers (and that means all the great powers of this day) can now be other than suicidal, regardless of the formal theoretical outcome in terms of what are called victory and defeat. If war of this sort cannot be ruled out, civilization will be. And what, then, could be the purpose of such a war, or the purpose of preparing for it?

Does this mean that now, in the apparent absence of any great-power adversary, this country has no need to maintain any significant military establishment—any establishment, that is, appropriate to its size and its weight in world affairs? The answer is obvious: not at all. And this, for several reasons.

First of all, there are the existing commitments, primarily those that relate to the United Nations and to the other parties of the alliances of which we are a member. These commitments all imply the maintenance of *some* sort of a military establishment on our part. What sort of an establishment is another question; but the answer to that question is certainly not no establishment at all.

3. *Memoirs, 1925–1950* (Boston: Little, Brown, 1967), p. 437.

We have, in the first place, our formal alliances with Japan and with the other members of the NATO community. Mention was made in the last chapter of some of the political aspects of these engagements. But their military aspects were the primary reasons for their conclusion in the first place, and, diminished as those military aspects now are, they are by no means trivial.

Insofar as concerns the security arrangement with Japan, it is worth remembering that while such threat to Japanese security as may have been seen to be coming from the Russian side has been largely removed, now and for the foreseeable future, uncertain situations still prevail in Korea and in China. Until there is greater clarity about both these situations, it would be premature to attempt to define the future military relationship of Japan to the United States. For this reason no hasty decisions—and, above all, no unilateral ones—should be taken with relation to the existing military arrangements.

With respect to NATO a somewhat different situation prevails. In 1948, and over the entire subsequent period, this writer had a view of the most desirable long-term relationship of the United States to European defense that was different from the one that found acceptance on either side of the water. It was his view that the United States, while cordially accepting the status of a great and good friend of European security, should not itself be a member of any organization set up by European governments to promote and assure that security. There would seem, in his view, to be even more reason for this restriction in the coming period than there was in 1948. For this reason he would hope that in the search for a new European security structure designed to meet the changed situation prevailing in the light of the Soviet breakdown, the accent would be put on a European organization of which the United States was *not* a member. These thoughts lead in the direction of the Western European Union, an organization set up in 1948 to include only the Low Countries, France, and England, but now expanded to include Germany, Italy, Portugal, Spain, and the UK. This organization bears a recognized but still somewhat cloudy status as an arrangement contributory to the purposes of NATO; but it differs from the latter outstandingly in its failure to include Canada and the

United States. It appears to the writer that the development of this organization into the nucleus of a future European security structure would be more responsive to the realities of the future American relationship to European defense than would be the retention of NATO for that purpose. But it is not to be expected that the opposition to this view will be much less intense today than it was in 1948; and in any case the situation in Europe, with the emergence of new countries along its eastern borders, is still too uncertain to provide a basis for a final and long-term decision.

It is also the view of the writer (and in this he is likely to find more support than in the position just described) that the time for the stationing of American forces on European soil has passed, and that the ones now stationed there should be withdrawn, by agreement with the European countries affected, as soon as this can conveniently be done. Such a move, we should note, would not mean the end of the NATO Treaty, or even any significant adjustment of its present language. It would therefore not prejudice the study and eventual solution of the long-term problem discussed above.

If, however, NATO should be retained as a military pact, and if this country were to continue to be an active member of it, I would hope that ways might be found to give to it much less the aspect of an alliance aimed against any single other country, and more that of an expression of enduring interest in the security and prosperity of all European countries than is now the case.

The Third World

A third source of the requirement for American armed forces in the coming period is the state of affairs in regions other than the European and East Asian ones. Here, we are confronted with many uncertainties, and not a few dangers. There are several countries (Iran, Iraq, and Libya are presumably only the most conspicuous of them) where we are regarded, at least by the prevailing regimes, with outright, sometimes burning, in any case unconcealed hostility. There are other places where we encounter the envy and jealousy of people of whom the least we can say is that they are unaware of having any stake in our prosperity or security. What forms this hostility will take in the future, we cannot know; but we certainly cannot exclude the possibility that problems may arise in those parts of the world that will engage our interests and our security and will demand from us, whether unilaterally or in league with other powers, some sort of a military response.

Just what this will mean in terms of the kinds and quantities of the forces we will require is something that no individual in the position of this writer could possibly estimate in any detail. In early 1947, at a time when the nuclear weapon was not yet fully installed in the position of preeminence that it was destined soon thereafter to assume, I, in speaking before the National Defense Committee of the U.S. Chamber of Commerce, attempted to face up to what seemed to me then to be the prospect of a world (and a nonnuclear world) without any great external enemy; and gave my best estimate of the sort of armed establishment I thought we might require. Conceding the need for the maintenance at all times of adequate mobilization facilities for hostilities on a larger scale, I thought that what we needed to maintain in normal times, and maintain in a state of reasonable readiness, was "a certain minimum number and balance of ground force divisions of full fighting strength, modern, well-trained, well-equipped, and prepared for action on extremely short notice." Similarly, in the case of the Navy, while again stressing the reserve facilities necessary for its expansion in times of more serious crisis, I urged the regular maintenance of a naval force "which could support in the combat sense and logistically any emergency armed effort this country might be called upon to put forward, and which could show the flag creditably on the high seas and in the ports of the world." I expressed the view that it was more important that these forces in being should be alert and modern than that they be large. Similar sentiments were expressed with regard to the Air Force.

Some of this, it seems to me, might still have some relevance to the situation we must expect to face in the postnuclear era. Much of what I had in mind, particularly in regard to the land forces, could be supplied by the Marine Corps (an entity which I personally regard, and not just from the military standpoint, as one of America's finest institutions). The Army would have to come up with the remainder. And so far as the backup reserve forces and facilities are concerned, I still feel, as I did and said on the occasion just referred to, that we have every reason, and even reasons going far beyond those usually cited in just this connection, to create and maintain a comprehensive national service corps for all young people in this country, one of the varieties of participation being, on a voluntary basis, service in one or the other of the armed forces.

Military Planning

All of the above has been put forward on the hypothesis that the views presented in the foregoing chapter, about the sort of foreign policy the United States might now wish to have, would be acceptable as a basis for the design of our military posture. This would mean, as the reader will recall, an essentially defensive policy, designed to give this country the time and the peace to address itself intensively to the solution of some of its great domestic problems.

There is, however, one note of caution, relating to the military aspects of this policy, which ought to be sounded before this discussion is complete. This relates to military planning and preparations.

This writer, in his study of the diplomatic history of the final years of the nineteenth century, was struck by the realization of how extensively the outbreak of the First World War was determined by the military planning and preparations that had long preceded it. This was true even where this planning and these preparations were not initiated with any idea that the war they envisaged was inevitable—simply with the idea that it was possible. Yet it was the planning and preparation themselves that advanced very materially the inevitability of the conflict in question.

Of these two activities—planning and preparation—it is, of course, the latter that is of the greater importance in heightening the tensions that lead to war. But the planning is important, too. When, in a given military establishment, the idea of a possible war with a specific power is laid down as a basic framework for military planning, the months and years that follow see the emergence of many thousands of documents, and the holding of a comparable number of planning conferences, in which the presumed adversary figures as "the enemy." Gradually but inevitably, as this long planning process runs its course, what was first considered a hypothesis insensibly becomes a probability, and finally attains, in the minds of those who conduct it, the status of an inevitability. When this happens, people find that they are planning and preparing not for a possible conflict but for one which they regard as unavoidable and inevitable, the occurrence of which is now only a matter of time. From that point on, their behavior, and the behavior of the whole governmental apparatus in which they are embraced, attains the quality of an airplane which, in its takeoff, has passed the point of no return. From that point on, any diplomatic effort to avoid the war becomes inexcusable in military eyes, because it throws doubt and confusion over preparations for what they regard as an inevitable encounter.

In the early 1890s the Russian military command for the entire southern portion of the empire became convinced that war with England over the control of the Turkish Straits was inevitable (which, as the future was to show, it was not). In the light of that persuasion, the officers of that command made, on their own initiative, elaborate plans for a military-naval descent on the Turkish coast near the Bosporus. So completely were they persuaded of the inevitability of such a conflict that they came within a hair's breath of proceeding with the implementation of these plans before soberer heads in Petersburg found out about it and managed to stop them. Had they gone ahead with this implementation, they would almost certainly have provoked a wholly unnecessary war with England. Such were the dangers unleashed by the impression, which had been allowed to implant itself in many Russian military minds (and in not a few civilian ones), that war with England was an inevitability.

In 1913, not long after he had assumed the presidential office, Woodrow Wilson was alarmed and at first indignant to learn of various sorts of military planning then being conducted, under the auspices of the General Staff, at the War College. His apprehensions were later allayed, and the planning was allowed to continue, albeit (to use the words of the historian who related the episode) in a form "camouflaged and . . . handicapped by the President's attitude."[4]

The president's anxieties were no doubt exaggerated. But there was a grain of reality in them. Pursued far enough and long enough, this planning process, like many others, might well have engendered attitudes that would have given it the quality of an important determinant of events, rather than just a precaution in the face of certain possibilities, as which it was no doubt originally conceived.

These are my reasons for considering that in the designing of a new military posture to replace the one that has endured for some forty years, our government would do well to avoid any sort of planning based on hypothetical conflict with a specific country. To many excellent military minds this may seem strange. The writer recalls spending an entire long evening with one of the most distinguished of the country's military figures, discussing the question as to whether it was possible, even theoretically, to shape, train, and equip any great military establishment without, as a basis for this process, naming some other power as the most likely adversary, to the hypothetical conflict with which all planning should be directed.

It remains my view that to do this last is not only possible but desirable and that, in designing America's military posture for the future, one should avoid designating any particular country as the one to which plans are directed. One can, of course, have his imagination in this respect; and military planners will not be able to avoid its urgings. But it will be better if plans can be held to the envisaging of a variety of possible conflicts without identifying any specific country as the specific target. We may expect to have troubles enough in this world even in the best of circumstances without putting flesh on the creations of our own imagination.

4. Richard D. Challener, *Admirals, Generals, and American Foreign Policy* (Princeton: Princeton University Press, 1973), p. 365.

Ulterior Considerations

Let me revert to the thoughts put forward at the beginning of this chapter. It is small wonder that a democratic political system, where government consists of the dynamic interaction of thousands of rapidly changing civil servants and elected officials, should have difficulty in evolving a consistent and coherent doctrine to guide it in a governmental function so full of ironies, dilemmas, and apparent contradictions as is the maintenance in peacetime of a national defense establishment. How is one to rationalize the training of men for military combat when the professed hope is that the skills for which they are trained will never be put to the ultimate test of combat itself, and when the theory is that the better they are trained the less likelihood there will be that what they were trained for will ever actually take place? How does one maintain morale in a form of training that one hopes will never be put to serious use? And, as if all this were not enough, how does one accomplish this when advances in military technology are making it evident that the use of modern weapons in warfare among highly industrialized and technologically developed states can never be other than suicidal, and when the destructive power of certain of these weapons, notably the nuclear ones, has become so appalling that they have suicidal aspects for the user even when used against a helpless victim and are met with no retaliation? The dilemmas introduced by the cultivation of such weapons have alone sufficed to sow an almost hopeless confusion in all traditional doctrines of military strategy and the forms of training they call for.

But still, there can be and will no doubt continue to be, in addition to the great and nuclear wars that have become senseless, smaller and nonnuclear ones that have not lost, or at least will not be seen to have lost, all rationale. And for the possibility that one or another of these should touch in some serious way the vital interests of the United States, the maintenance of *some* armed forces, and well trained and equipped ones at that, cannot be avoided. One must also bear in mind, as this writer sees it, the advantages of military discipline and training as formative influences on character. Whoever has never learned to accept orders without the loss of his own dignity, or to give them without impairing the dignity of the one to whom they are given, is unlikely to be very successful in the control of himself. And where such qualities can be better inculcated than in military training at its best, this writer does not know. In addition to which there is, in the best sense, the truly useful democratizing effect of men and women being thrown, at least for a time, into the company of others of their own age group, drawn from all ranks of society and all stages of education. Beyond that there is the fact that in this age of sophisticated military technology many forms of training for men and women in uniform are ones that can be turned to useful employment in civilian life. For all these reasons, proper military training, and the development of a suitable military establishment generally, is not only a political necessity but can play a useful and constructive role in the development of a society.

One could wish that ways could be found for the employment of armed services for purposes more constructive and inspiring than just training for the combat they must hope never to have to conduct. It has been suggested, for example, that the Navy could lend its help in peacetime to civilian efforts, national or international, to restore and preserve the healthfulness and productive abundance of the world oceans. Other possibilities, too, will present themselves. But there are also dangers in the employment of armed personnel, particularly of the ground forces, for purposes (other than emergency actions) foreign to their main dedication. Here, too, doctrines and traditions, more helpful than any yet established, will have to be created.

It is among the various uncertainties and contradictions mentioned above that American policymakers will have to wend their way in the years ahead. It will be helpful if the various war colleges, and particularly the National Defense University, will give such problems their serious attention. But there will also be the necessity of educating the political establishment, the public, and the media in whatever, in the way of doctrine, is worked out. Here, too, rapid progress must not be expected. Much time will have to pass, and a great deal will have to be achieved in constructive thinking and public debate, before the United States will have anything in the way of a thoughtful and nationally accepted defense doctrine.

Chapter Eleven

WHAT IS
TO BE DONE?

. . . the advantage, even the necessity, of having somewhere in the state a person beyond the competition for
office, who is entitled to be heard in any matter on
which he may think it his duty to speak; who has the
right to warn, to encourage, and therefore, to be consulted by, the agents of authority.

G. M. Young,
Victorian England: Portrait of an Age

The Problem

It should be clear, even from what little was said above about our
national problems, that there are a number of these problems with
which the political system of the country has not been coping successfully, and where there is little reason to hope, as things stand today, that
it will cope more successfully in the future. There is no need to attempt
to draw up at this point an exhaustive list of these problems. They
include social, educational, financial, technological, cultural, and, in a
sense, even spiritual ones. And if one looks for a single characteristic

that explains the difficulty the country's political establishment has in confronting them, one will find it, I believe, in the fact that they are all long-term problems rather that short-term ones.

That the elected officials and legislative bodies of the country have difficulty in confronting such problems is neither surprising nor really discreditable. The legislators are all beholden, and rightly so, to the constituencies that have elected them. These constituencies normally have limited and highly parochial interests which the legislator is asked to reflect; and they have a right to see these interests represented by the one they have elected. Actually, the latter has normally been obliged to cater to these aspirations anyway, in his appeal for electoral support, and is thus extensively committed to them before he even takes office.

These same reflections apply no less, of course, to those occupants of executive authority who, like presidents and governors, owe their positions to electoral decision. But for all major participants in the governing establishment, elected or appointed, there is one great and immediate hindrance to participation in a careful and systematic study of national problems in their long-term aspects; and this is the fact that these persons are simply too busy. Anyone who has ever been responsibly involved in government at a senior level (or in business, either, for that matter) knows that both of the devices commonly employed to reduce the burdens on the senior executive or legislator—the increase of the supporting bureaucracy and the development of high-speed electronic communication—have the ironic effect of increasing those burdens rather than reducing them. The result is that both the member of Congress and the executive official now finds his in-basket filling up daily with demands on his attention far beyond his ability to cope with personally. The last thing he could think of would be to stand aside and devote days and weeks to the study of any of the major pressing, and unsolved long-term national problems, and, above all, to give to this effort the peace of mind and the undisturbed concentration necessary to its success.

If, then, the active political establishment remains thus limited in its capacities for making the sort of contribution I have just been discussing, is there no place where we can look for this sort of help? There is indeed such a place; for the country is by no means poor in human resources that are not subject to these limitations. There are numbers of men and women in private life whose situations and capacities would permit them to make such a contribution if the will to call upon them were there, and if the necessary institutional facilities were available.

These persons fall, roughly speaking, into two categories. The first consists of those who in the past have rendered services of a high order in public life but are now in official retirement. They normally bear with them all the experience and knowledge acquired in their earlier official service, but seldom—in many instances, never—are they called upon, at least not from the government's side, to make use of it. Whatever else there might be to question in the argumentation of this volume, one fact stands out in the mind of its writer as incontrovertible: namely, that there could be no country that makes less use of the accumulated experience of those who have served it—none that is more frivolously neglectful and improvident of these assets—than the United States of America. The principle by which our government appears to have been guided for many years and decades in the past is that among the qualifications for public office, experience counts for precisely nothing—that for the great majority of executive positions anyone whose qualifications meet the political requirements of the moment will obviously be preferable to anyone else who may have had rich experience in the respective field but whose political qualifications fail to meet that test. The result is that the country is replete with people—ex-presidents, ex-cabinet members, ex-governors, former distinguished legislators or jurists, retired diplomats, and many others—whose entire treasure of accumulated experience is simply allowed to rot away, unused.

The second category embraces those many persons who have never served in governmental office at all but who, often in places far removed from Washington and the other great urban centers, have won the admiration and high respect of their fellow citizens for contributions to our national life in other capacities: as business leaders, scholars, academic administrators, scientists, publicists, journalists, and media personalities, or in other ways. Among people of this sort will be found a fund of experience, of integrity, of judgment, of insight, and of devotion to the public interest that could well be made use of at the national level but is simply not so used. Many of these people, owing often to their own modesty, are well known only locally, but have qualities that deserve wider recognition. They represent in their entirety a national asset we have no excuse for failing to tap.

It will no doubt be argued that members of both these categories are today not lacking in opportunities for making available to the public and to the government whatever fruits of experience they have to offer: that they are at liberty, whenever they can and desire, to write articles or give speeches that command one degree or another of public attention. It will also be argued that presidents and governors have many times made use of ad hoc commissions, manned entirely or primarily by private citizens of this sort, for the study of specific problems of governmental policy, in the hope or assumption that their conclusions might serve as guidance for those who have the governmental responsibility.

All this is true; but it is far from being fully responsive to the need at hand. For obvious reasons, articles and speeches by the common citizen, no matter how eminent, seldom reach more than a very limited spectrum of listeners or readers. The press and the media seldom cite them in their news columns or programs, and, when they do, then only in miniscule fragments, usually taken out of context. And as for the ad hoc commissions: of these there have indeed been a very considerable number. Some of them have done distinguished and highly valuable work. But their effect on public opinion and governmental policy has seldom been commensurate with the value of the contribution. The reason for their appointment, in the first place, has too often been the desire of a president or a governor to deflect from himself responsibility for a decision demanded of him which he finds it politically awkward to make. The appointment of a commission buys time, permits him to take advantage of the brevity of memory that marks both the media and the public, and commits him to very little. The customary course of events is that the commission assembles, studies the problem in good faith, and renders its report. It is then duly thanked. The report is made available to the press, which devotes at best a single, little-read column to its conclusions. It is then consigned to the secretarial service of the legislative body most directly involved, which prints the text of it in the *Congressional Record* or some other suitable publication; after which, failing the vigorous protest of some legislator, it is reverently laid to rest in the archives and passes from human memory. The members of the commission that produced it, meanwhile, have long since gone apart, never—in many instances—to meet again. There is thus no follow-up. The greatest positive result of the exercise is that the respective president or governor who originally ordered the report is at least partially relieved, as he hoped he would be, of the charge that he "did nothing about it."

To have any serious effect on governmental policy and action, a commission or other body giving this sort of outside advisory assistance to government would have to have a number of characteristics that the ad hoc commission simply does not have: among them, greater permanency, a wider spectrum of responsibility, an ability to relate recommendations in one field to those in another, and, above all, a general prestige that would lend to its findings and conclusions weight and endurance in the public eye and would compel serious attention to them on the part of governmental policymakers, executive and legislative.

The Answer, in Principle

It is these considerations that lead to my belief that the federal government requires, for the fulfillment of the responsibilities that now rest upon it, the presence at its side of a permanent, nonpolitical advisory body—one that permits the tapping of the greatest sources of wisdom and experience that the private citizenry of the country can provide. It also seems evident that the meeting of this need would require an institutional innovation of a wholly unusual nature, quite devoid of precedent in the national experience. In the inquiry as to what such a body might look like, how it could be selected, and how it would operate, it will be best to start by identifying some of the basic requirements to which, as conceived here, it would have to respond. The following would seem essential:

1. Membership would have to be drawn exclusively from persons outside the active government establishment, devoid not only of any existing official position but of any current political connections or ambitions that could influence their independence of judgment.

2. The body would have to be purely advisory to the constitutionally established governmental institutions, executive and legislative. In no way should it preempt, infringe upon, or attempt to substitute for any of the constitutional powers and responsibilities of those bodies.

3. The body would require, on the other hand, governmental sanction. It would have to be established by governmental initiative, as a response to a governmental decision having both executive and legislative approval. There is no apparent reason why this decision should require a constitutional amendment. An act of Congress, with presidential approval, should suffice.

4. Membership in this body would have to be by presidential appointment. Nothing less than this would give to the body the solidity, authority, and prestige necessary to the function it would be asked to fulfill. Procedures would have to be devised, however, to assure that such appointments were strictly nonpolitical and were exclusively from among persons responding to the requirements mentioned in paragraph 1, above.

5. The body would have to have, as an institution, a permanent financial basis of an endowment nature—a basis that would relieve it of any and all dependence on annual governmental appropriations. Otherwise it would be drawn into the regular federal budgetary process and become just one more football on the field of American politics.

6. It would have to be understood, finally, that this institution would, unless otherwise requested by the president, occupy itself only with long-term questions of public policy, avoiding matters of current contention, restricting itself to the identification of the preferable principles and directions of action, and refraining from involvement, either by prior suggestion or by ex post facto comment, with the implementation of the judgments it might offer.

These requirements seem, to this writer, to be fundamental to the implementation of the general idea that this discussion is intended to bring forward. Were any of them to be ignored, the entire reasoning of what is suggested here would no longer stand.

With these essentials in mind, let us see what an entity designed to serve these purposes might look like in greater detail. But may I, before approaching this task, be allowed a word or two of explanation.

It would be silly and presumptuous to suppose that any one person, working in isolation and not in interaction with others, could just toss off the design for an institution of this nature and expect it to be accepted in its entirety as a serious and finished proposal. Anything of this novelty and importance would have to be the product of many minds, not of a single one, and would have to be refined by long consideration, prolonged public discussion, and extensive political compromise.

Yet I know of no other way of bringing out the full spectrum of considerations and requirements that would have to be faced, if the need for such a body were to be conceded, than by setting up something in the nature of a model for this purpose, as I now propose to do. Let me emphasize that this is only one model out of many others that could, I am sure, be suggested. That it represents my own best suggestion by no means precludes the possibility, or even probability, that there might be a number of better ones, or improvements upon this one. But this will, if it serves no other purpose, stand as an example, at least, of the problems one would meet if one were to proceed along this path.

A Council of State

The entity in question would have to have, first of all, a name. Just what that name would be is perhaps not important; but a name must be given, at this point, if only as a handle for discussion. Others who have struggled with the same question have suggested a "Council of Elders." This is, of course, a possibility. It would certainly be desirable, if not essential, that the members of such a body have the dignity of ripe age

WHAT IS TO BE DONE?

and experience. On the other hand, the use of the term "elders" might appear to reflect the assumptions that youth precludes wisdom and that age assures it, neither of which assumptions could be farther from the truth. To avoid confusion on this point, I would prefer to see this imagined body called the "State Council" or, better still, the "Council of State." This latter designation will have to serve, in any case, for purposes of illustration in the remainder of this discussion.

The Council of State, in the model I am creating, would be a permanent body. It would have its seat in Washington—not, preferably, in a regular governmental building, but not far from Capitol Hill. Its members—persons of high distinction, the desirable qualities of whom will be discussed shortly—might number the same as those of the present Supreme Court—namely, nine. Anything larger than that would invite fragmentation of effort: overspecialization, division into committees and subcommittees, formalization of internal discussions—bureaucracy, in short. And that would be fatal.

Staff there would, of course, have to be for each of the members; but these staffs, too, should be small, making up in quality of personnel for severe restrictions on their numbers. Bureaucracy, after all, may develop among staff as well as among principals; and it is essential, in the case at hand, that bureaucracy be avoided.

The Council would have full freedom of choice as to the subjects to which it would address itself. These might be ones flowing from its own initiative, or they might be ones accepted for examination in response to requests from the president or from one or both of the houses of Congress. The only restrictions here would be that these problems should be ones national in their scope and of major long-term importance for the fortunes of the nation. The perspective from which they would then be examined would have to be that of the national interest in its entirety, not the interests of any particular geographical or social segment of the nation. Short-term problems, particularly controversial ones under current political scrutiny and debate, should be ruled out from the start.

It would also have to be understood that in examining such subjects as it chose for consideration, and in reaching its conclusions, the Council would not attempt to address itself to such domestic-political complications as any particular solution might present. The Council's task would be confined to telling the country, including the politicians, what ought to be done in the long-term interests of American society. It would then be the responsibility of the politicians, as practitioners of what has been called "the art of the possible," to see what might be politically possible in the way of the implementation of these judgments, assuming that they wanted to implement them at all.

It would have to be assumed that the subjects thus taken under advisement by the Council would be ones demanding careful and deliberate study before judgments could be arrived at. This process, with relation to any single subject, might be a matter of some weeks, or months, or even years. Presumably, if only for this reason, it would be advisable that no more than two or three subjects, and preferably only one, be held under advisement at one time.

Members of the Council would be entitled to draw, for informational and research purposes, on the Legislative Reference Service of the Library of Congress and perhaps on the facilities of other departments and agencies of the government as well. They would also have the privilege of inviting and hearing, but not of subpoenaing, or of placing under oath, witnesses, official or otherwise. They would be not only entitled but indeed expected to preserve complete privacy of internal discussion before arriving at a given judgment; but their findings, once completed, would, in addition to being formally laid before the president and Congress, be made public in their entirety. These findings, as noted above, would not have mandatory quality for either branch of the government; they would be considered as advisory to both. Their value, if accepted, would be to serve as guidelines for governmental action, not as recommendations for specific measures. And there is no reason why these opinions should not serve similarly as guidance for state and local authorities as well as for private public-interest bodies across the country, to the extent all these latter were prepared to accept them as such.

It would be essential, I think, that the Council neither solicit, nor hold in its files, nor take official cognizance of classified information of any sort. If its findings were to be made public, the evidence on the basis of which those findings were arrived at should be ones to which the public also had unrestricted access. But it might be hoped that the Council's judgments, given the prestige they ought to command, would come to take a prominent place in the national literature on the subjects in questions, and would thus, regardless of their immediate significance for governmental action, come to have a certain pedagogical value for American opinion at large.

Membership on the Council

The most difficult problem to be faced in the establishment of such a body would be that of the manner in which its members should be selected and appointed. That it should be the president who makes the final appointment seems, as already noted, an inescapable conclusion. Only this could give to its members the personal prestige and moral authority they would need if their efforts were to be useful. If that prestige and authority could not be assured, it would be better to drop the whole idea and to have no such council at all.

But that the president should have the sole power to appoint to membership on the Council of State does not mean that the circle of persons from which such appointments might be drawn should be unlimited. It is essential, actually, that it not be; for were the president at liberty to appoint just anyone at all, his choices could not fail to be influenced by his own political considerations or obligations. Some means would have to be found, therefore, of defining and establishing a limited category of persons—a panel, in other words—from among the members of which, and from them alone, the presidential appointments might be made. And it is essential that the composition of this panel be of such a nature that appointments from it not lend themselves to political exploitation.

This situation is, of course, not without precedent. There are other instances, as well, where eligibility for appointment is limited by common sense or by tradition, if not by statute. A president, for example, could scarcely appoint to the Supreme Court a person wholly devoid

WHAT IS TO BE DONE?

of training or experience in the law. But since, in the case of a Council of State, there would be no single professional background to serve as the criterion for eligibility, a different set of criteria would presumably have to be laid down.

It might be useful, before confronting the question as to how this could be done, to ask ourselves what personal qualities would be required for useful service on such a body.

The candidate would have to be, first of all, a person of high distinction, sectionally if not nationally, who had earned that distinction by an outstanding career in any of the major professions. He could, for example, be a physician, a jurist, a scholar, an educator, a clergyman, a high military figure, or a diplomat in retirement. Even a distinguished earlier political career would be no disqualification (it might, in fact, be exceptionally useful); but it would have to be a career that was clearly and finally terminated, and well in the past. It would have to be a primary and inalterable rule that no one could be considered eligible for this panel who at the time held any political or other governmental office, who was actively involved in the national or state political process, or who was prominently engaged in the leadership or management of any political party. Had there been any such involvement at an earlier date, there would have to be a plausible presumption that there was now no intention to resume it, and no apparent likelihood that it would be resumed.

Beyond these qualifications of experience, a likely candidate would have to be widely known and respected, at least in the section of the country where he or she resides, for the highest qualities of personal integrity and character, for common sense and maturity of judgment, and for a wide spectrum of interests, cultural as well as social. Beyond which a strong measure of modesty and the absence of any fondness for deliberate popularity seeking should weigh heavily in his or her favor.

That people of these qualities can be found scattered across this country, and found in an abundance at least sufficient to the purpose at hand, few would deny. One of the greatest deficiencies of American public life is surely, as was noted above, the failure of the political process to tap and to bring to the surface the formidable resources of human excellence that the country actually harbors. The problem before us here would be to devise suitable ways of finding such people and of creating for them a framework of identification and formal status that would permit them to constitute a panel from which, and from which alone, a president could make appointments to the Council of State.

The establishment of such a panel would admittedly be a novel undertaking, outside the American tradition. Were it not so, something of this nature would presumably long since have been created. There may be good reasons why it was not created in the past. But it is hard to see how the creation of something of this sort can now be avoided if the country wishes to cope, in a bolder and more imaginative way than the regular political process appears to permit, with the long-term problems that are beginning to confront it.

The Panel

What is involved, then, in the case of the proposed panel, is not an *organization* but merely a formally composed list of persons of a certain level and quality of distinction. One might hope that selection to this panel would come to be considered the highest form of distinction that could be conferred on any ordinary American citizen not serving in elected or other governmental office. The bearers of it would have, as among themselves, no organizational cohesion. They would not normally meet or take decision as a body. They would have no chairman or collective spokesman. Indeed, they would have no collective identity. They would comprise, in their collective capacity, nothing more than a list—but a very exceptional list—of names: names of great distinction, from which alone a president could make appointments to a Council of State.

A second question to be thought of, before one turns to the question as to how such a list is to be composed, is that of the number of persons of which it should consist. Too small a list would be unduly confining for a president. Too large a one would water down the importance of the distinction and would frustrate a president by confronting him with too many names with which he was unfamiliar. A manageable and serviceable number would seem to be something around one hundred: a number, that is, that could accommodate people drawn from all parts of the country but small enough to preserve the quality of the distinction conferred.

With all this in mind, and assuming that the above be accepted as generally reasonable suppositions, we still have before us the central problem (and it is the most delicate and difficult one of all) of how and by whom are people to be selected and appointed to the status in question? Here again, it is not the part of a single, isolated individual to dream up an answer to this question and to put it forward as a serious and responsible proposal. But here, once more, there would seem to be no more effective way of bringing out the elements of the problem than by constructing some sort of a model and revealing, through this example, something of the challenges to which, in the drawing up of such a panel, one would have to respond. The following should be thought of in that way: as only one of what, I am sure, would be many alternatives, but as the one that would seem to this writer to have the fewest disadvantages.

Before going ahead to outline this proposal, I wish to point out certain of the dangers to be avoided. If appointments to this panel were to be made without geographical distinction, simply from among persons whose eminence and suitability for such designation were considered to be nationally recognized, this would leave unconsidered many others who might well have deserved the appointment but lacked national recognition. And since a preponderance of the nationally recognized ones would presumably be found to be residing in one or another of the major urban regions of the country, this would leave unscanned and untapped the resources of other regions. To avoid this, it would be important that any procedure for selection take account both of nationally recognized eminence and of a reasonable geographical distribution. The following suggestion is made with this in mind.

Let us suppose that Congress (from whose action, after all, this entire project of a Council of State would have to flow) were to invite each of the state governors to form a very small ad hoc committee, to consist of the governor himself as chairman, together with the state's highest judicial figure, and one layman to be chosen by the two of them. The task of this committee would be to identify the most distinguished of those of the state's citizens who could satisfy the criteria for eligibility, and appoint him or her to membership on the national panel. This would yield the number of fifty—half that of the present national Senate.

It may be asked at this point, Why duplicate in this way the existing Senate? Were its members not supposed, in the minds of the founding fathers, to be the most distinguished citizens of their respective states—men of wisdom, protected by their longer term of office from any of the sordid details of financial legislation, and thus well suited (as I am suggesting that the members of the Council of State should be) to look at the nation's problems from a more lofty and detached position than that enjoyed by their fellow legislators of the House of Representatives? And if so, why create a separate, nonofficial body for this purpose? This question is all the more natural because the Constitution originally envisaged that the appointment to the senatorial office should be by the action of the state legislatures rather than by popular election.

The answers are not hard to find. The senators, whatever they were in earlier times, are now elected officials and not barred from reelection. This places them in the very thick of that welter of considerations, hesitations, compromises, unavowable motives, special interests, and short-term electoral necessities that go with the elected office. This welter of pressures has been intensified over the years, in ways the founding fathers could scarcely have anticipated, by the growth in size and complexity of the federal government as well as by the latter-day revolution in communication. These factors have increased manyfold the burden and tempo of daily business for all men in public office, senators included. Persons in this situation, as already noted, are not likely to have the time, the detachment, or the reserves of energy that could permit them to stand off and look at things in the manner here envisaged. They are charged with an important share in the day-to-day governing of the country, with all the responsibilities this implies.

Beyond that, they stand in the thick of politics. The members of a Council of State, as here proposed, would be, on the other hand, advisers rather than lawmakers. This would not only free their time and energies; it would also unburden their vision, for this last would not be affected by the concerns and distractions of either electoral status or legislative office.

But to get back to the method of selection: these three-man gubernatorial committees would be ad hoc bodies. After the initial selection, they would be appointed and come into action only when a vacancy arose; and their function would then be only to name a replacement for a vacancy from their state's spot on the panel.

The appointment by this means of fifty out of the one hundred members of the panel would assure a reasonable geographical distribution of its membership. This would obviously be not only desirable but necessary if the public were to feel that the membership was adequately representative of all parts of the country. In the case of the nationally known persons, there would probably be, as mentioned above, a greater concentration of suitable candidates in some of the great urban areas than in other parts of the country. To take account of this factor, I would suggest that the remaining fifty be selected by a small national committee, which might be suitably composed of the Librarian of Congress, who would act as chairman, together with delegates from at least two of the great national cultural institutions (the American Philosophical Society and the National Academy of Sciences might serve as examples) of the country. (These last might rotate among other such institutions of this nature.) In the appointments by this last committee, geography would not be a factor—only national distinction. It might be provided that certain categories of persons—presumably, all ex-presidents and, possibly, retired members of the Supreme Court—would be considered as ex officio members of this section of the panel, unless they declined the honor.

It would be, then, out of the members of this panel of one hundred names that the president would, as and when vacancies presented themselves, make appointments to the nine-member Council. There might well be an age limit for this membership, and perhaps other arrangements for assuring the existence at all times of a vigorous and fully engaged membership; but otherwise, to assure continuity and soundness of judgment, the appointments should be, at the least, long-term ones.

Such, then, would be the nature and the composition of the proposed Council of State. Its judgments would normally be, like those of the Supreme Court (but without the binding quality of the latter), rare, deliberate, and (in the better sense) sententious ones. They would normally be self-inspired; but this would not preclude the possibility that they might, at the pleasure of the Council, be responses to requests by the president or Congress for an opinion.

It will be argued, of course, that elected governmental officials or bodies, not being bound by the judgments of the Council, would pay little or no attention to them. Perhaps so, initially at least; but if these judgments came to be surrounded with the dignity and prestige they ought to possess, they should make a deep impression on public opinion, and should come with time to constitute a factor which, in the long run, the president and the legislators would feel a certain pressure to treat with some consideration and respect.

For three years, from 1947 to 1950, this writer served as the first director of the Policy Planning Staff that was set up within the State Department by General George Marshall in early 1947. This staff, having no operational responsibilities, was purely advisory to the secretary of state. In the course of those three years, we submitted over half a hundred papers to the secretary of state, a large number of them containing advisory recommendations. It was inherent in the concept of this staff that it should endeavor, in confronting the various questions with which it occupied itself, to look at these questions in their long-term aspects, rather than in the short-term aspects that pressed themselves most heavily on the operative divisions of the Department of State.

Some years later, as a matter of curiosity, I glanced over these papers with a view to ascertaining whether—and if so, when—they had had any significant impact on official policy. What I found was that most of them, if not all, seemed to have affected official policy, but primarily only after a lapse of two or three years. Initially, most of them had encountered opposition or quiet obstruction at the hands of the operative divisions. This clearly was partly a matter of ruffled feelings over the fact that anyone in another part of the State Department had ventured to intrude on their particular domains. But in another aspect I derived a certain satisfaction from this opposition, because I thought it showed that we had generally done our job in looking at the long-term connotations of the questions at issue. And I take comfort in these observations when it comes to the probable effects of the advisory opinions of a body such as the Council of State that I have suggested. I can imagine that in many instances its opinions would, immediately upon publication, encounter a wide area of rejection in both the executive and the legislative branches of the government. But it would not, I think, be too much to hope that over a longer span of time they would begin to affect official as well as public opinion, and would eventually find some reflection in actions at the governmental level.

The Gravity of the Subject

The above suggestions, I repeat, are meant to serve primarily as illustrative of the problem to which they relate. There are other ways, and very possibly better ways, by which this problem could be tackled. But that the problem exists, and that it must in some way be met, remains my deepest conviction.

Many of the views and ideas set forth in earlier chapters of this volume will doubtless strike some readers as frivolous or extreme and worthy only of what I hope will be a kindly dismissal. What is said in this chapter falls into a different category. There are, as has been seen, a number of serious national problems the solution of which has been shown to be beyond the capacity of our governmental establishment as it now stands. The result has been, as I see it, something close to a major crisis in the life of the nation. In the question as to whether this deficiency can be corrected, it is nothing less than the adequacy of our form of government to meet the unprecedented challenges of the modern age that is at stake.

I confess myself unable to see any way by which this problem can be hopefully approached other than by the creation of some sort of an advisory body in which deeper forms of judgment about our national problems, and ones more clearly detached from political involvement than the ones that now proceed from the governmental establishment, can be evoked and given consideration by public and official American opinion. If this cannot be accomplished, I fail to see anything before us but a continued tragic deterioration of the quality of our society and its possibilities for constructive service to itself and to the remainder of the world.

This is why I hope that however the suggestions set forth in this chapter may be viewed, the seriousness of the problem to which they are addressed will be recognized, and that even if these suggestions are rejected, others will be advanced to take their place. It is nothing less than the quality of this country, as a major object in the history of our time, that is here on the line.

Epilogue

... despair, is only for those who see the end
beyond all doubt.

—J. R. R. Tolkien,
The Fellowship of the Ring

*I*t is with a certain wonder and curiosity that I look back on what was written above. I sometimes had the feeling, while writing it, of an affinity with the proverbial old lady who is supposed to have said, on one occasion, "How do I know what I think until I hear what I say?" I comfort myself with the thought that I can scarcely have been the first writer who learned what he thought only when he had looked at what he had written. But such is the case; and I find it necessary to review what I have done before offering any comments on it.

I see that in the first part of the book I have recorded, however primitively, my reasons for decisively rejecting any and all suggestions that mankind might be perfectible. This rejection, I found, placed certain limits on hopes, but was no cause for despair.

I went on, then, to offer what many will regard as a no less primitive concept of religious faith. I did this, not with the idea that this concept ought to be in any way compelling or authoritative for anyone else, but simply as a means of allaying the curiosity of any who might wonder whether there was a religious basis for any of the judgments brought forward in the remainder of the book.

Having done this, I proceeded to give my view of the nature of government, as an unavoidable component of human affairs, and also of politics, as an equally unavoidable concomitant of all governmental activity. I tried to make it clear that I do not blame those who participate in either the governmental or the political process. On the contrary, I commend them for their willingness to bear the attendant discomforts. God forbid that we should be without them! I only pity them for the moral ambiguities with which this participation confronts them; and I hope that at the day of judgment they will be forgiven for whatever troublesome compromises these ambiguities may have forced upon them.

I turned, then, in the fourth chapter, to the way peoples are organized both for the interior processes of government and for interaction with one another on the international scene. I pointed to the relative novelty and the uncertain political-philosophical basis of the modern national state, and questioned its adequacy as the sole recognized form of political independence. I attempted to suggest that the effort to build a formal structure of international relationships exclusively out of a large number of theoretically equal and sovereign national states, ignoring the many and drastic disparities among them, involved too many artificialities to be adequate for the purpose it was designed to serve. I noted that the spirit of modern nationalism, as a form of collective identification for large bodies of people in this modern age, was dangerous stuff, particularly in new countries where people were unaccustomed to the sense of national independence.

Turning to the somewhat puzzling subject of ideology, I gave my reasons for rejecting the Marxist form of it, particularly (but not exclusively) as demonstrated in the extremities of its application in Stalin's Russia. But I made clear, too, I hope, my doubts about the ultimate validity of any purely materialistic ideological commitment, including even those that inspire the humane European welfare state. With relation to the classic debate about free enterprise versus governmental *dirigisme,* I took a position squarely in the middle, recognizing that nothing could be worse than an effort by government to "manage" any part of the economic process, but maintaining that there are limits, environmental and otherwise, beyond which free enterprise should not be permitted to go, and that it is the duty of the government to make those limits clear and to insist on their observance. I expressed my skepticism about the values, per se, of economic growth and automation. And I tried, as best anyone could who knows very little about either science or technology, to give an idea as to where these aspects of human thought and activity, in which some profess to see the necessity and possibility of a new and more promising way of looking at many things, find, in a layman's view, their limits.

The first part of this book, addressed to universal rather than to national realities, represented an effort to call attention to certain congenital imperfections in human nature and to show how these affected, everywhere, the indispensable institutions of government and politics. The focus of the second part of the book was limited to the condition of American society. The views offered were dominated by the author's impression that the country was in a bad and even critical shape: that there were a number of serious domestic problems with which this government had shown itself unable to cope successfully, and that for this and other reasons the nation's affairs were seriously out of control. To have such thoughts about one's own country posed a challenge to the author's sense of identity. Eccentric as might be the figure he presented on the present national scene—esoteric in its social and cultural origin, slightly *dépaysé* by the many years spent abroad, and colored by membership in a generation now close to total disappearance—he still thought of himself as an American (what else could he be?) and felt some sense of responsibility in that capacity.

Consideration was given to certain long-term factors which lay heavily on the country's chances for working itself out of these difficulties. First—its very size. It seemed, looking around the world, that the great countries—the so-called monster countries (the United States, the Soviet Union, China, India, and Brazil)—were problems to themselves even where they were not problems to others. And I had begun to doubt whether the sound principles of American representative government could operate successfully in so great a framework—whether, that is, they did not require, for their successful application, a more intimate geographical setting—a less remote relationship between the ruler and the ruled.

These doubts were reinforced by what I could see of the effects on national problems of the rampant egalitarian currents in American thought. It seemed to me that Tocqueville's apprehensions about the centralization of political power and about the declining meaning of citizenship for the average citizen were being at least partially borne out by the facts of the present day. The illness of bureaucratization, which Tocqueville also foresaw, was now raging in the federal government and was in many respects out of control.

These evils, it seemed to me, might be diminished if the powers of government could be concentrated in smaller units. The existing states, as they had developed in the years since their establishment, did not seem to me to be adequate for this purpose. Some were too small. Affinities to neighboring areas were sometimes greater than those that prevailed among elements within the same state. State borders did not always coincide with the natural environmental configurations of the country, a factor now daily growing in importance in our political life. These were some of the reasons for my suggestion that the country might be more successfully governed if it were divided into a number of major regions, devoid of the defects just mentioned.

I advanced this suggestion with little hope that it would even be taken seriously within the foreseeable future. The existing political establishment was rooted in the existing federal structure of government. Those who occupied elected positions within that structure, providing as it did the framework for their political success, would be the last ones to approve of extensive changes in it. But I comforted myself with the reflection that in politics, as in science, thoughts do not necessarily have to have a visible immediate utility in order to have value. Seemingly useless discoveries, in which at the time no practical applicability could be discerned, have often ultimately turned out to be the groundwork for useful developments. One is permitted to believe that something of the same might hold true in the political-historical arena.

The two chapters just referred to were followed by one in which the effort was made to show, on two specific examples, how insidious, how deeply rooted, and how unfortunate in their effects were certain of the most widespread and cherished habits—even addictions—of the American population. It was hoped that this exhibit might bring home to some people the realization that if public authority in this country hoped to cope successfully with the nation's problems, it could not follow the path of least resistance and leave social, cultural, and educational changes exclusively to the workings of the free-enterprise system. It would have to take some interest, at least, in the way people in this country live, in the habits they are developing, and in the effects of all this on the vitality of American society. And this, too, might more easily be accomplished in political entities smaller than the present federal one. Here, while I saw many dangers and a great deal of instability, I saw nothing that could or should prevent us from devising and implementing a far-reaching program of internal reform, along the lines of what I was suggesting.

Before turning to what seemed to be the only possibly hopeful approach to these various problems, I thought it right to take account of the relationship of this country, political and military, to its world environment. It seemed to me that so long as we exhibited such helplessness in the face of our own internal problems, and so long as we continued to suffer from certain congenital limitations of our form of government for the conduct of foreign affairs, there would also be limits on what we could, even at our best, do for the solution of problems beyond our borders. A plea was advanced, therefore, for a modest and relatively self-effacing foreign policy, designed primarily to give us, to the extent world affairs might permit it, the possibility to carry out internal reforms with a minimum of outside interference and distraction. And to accord with this concept, I urged a military policy which, while taking due account of the dangers presented by a highly unstable world environment, would fit with a role in world affairs considerably less ambitious and grandiloquent than that which the experiences of the last half century had led many Americans to take for granted.

In what was said above about the need for internal reform, it was possible to advance only the vaguest suggestions about the direction such reform might take. There could, no doubt, have been other such suggestions, no doubt even better ones. It was clear, in any case, that the details of such changes, in substance and in the means of approach to their realization, were nothing that could usefully flow from the thoughts and pen of any single individual, and particularly of such a one as myself. To have real value, they would have to pass through the filter of many other minds, and preferably some of the wisest, most experienced, most thoughtful, most detached, and most honest that the country could provide.

This filtering was something the country's political establishment could not provide. That it could not provide it was not a fit subject of reproach to the persons that made it up. Their helplessness in this respect did not flow primarily from deficiencies of personal character. These, the legislators and the officials, were in this respect no better and no worse than the general run of their constituents. Their helplessness flowed from the situations into which they had been placed by a number of factors: by the obligations they had incurred in order to get elected in the first place; by their extensive dependence on the favor of special-interest groups and on momentary currents of public opinion; by the crushing ponderousness of the bureaucracies by which they were surrounded; by the tempestuous speed of modern electronic communication; by the importunities of constituents and other visitors; by the tyranny of their overflowing in-baskets; and by the intellectual and moral compromises they were compelled constantly to make in order to accomplish anything at all. If, therefore, farsighted but practical ideas were to come forward for moving this country in more hopeful directions, these ideas would have to be from minds and imaginations other than those of the elected legislators and officials. And in such minds and imaginations, the country was not poor. It remained only to find them—and to ask.

From these considerations were derived the ideas I put forward in chapter 11 for an advisory body, a Council of State, to stand at the side of both the executive and the legislative branches of the federal government, to point out for them the changes that were needed in order to put this country on a more hopeful path, and to outline for them the ways one would have to go to accomplish those changes. Unusual as these suggestions may be for much of American opinion (and the writer has no illusions on this score), they were put forward with seriousness and conviction, because the necessity of something along the indicated line was inescapably evident. There was simply no other visible way to go—no other way, at least, that would not undermine the principles on which the American system of government was founded, without which no efforts to improve American life could make any sense at all. There was, in other words, not much that could be done to correct the deficiencies of the official political establishment of the country as we know it today; but one of the things that could be done was to place at its side a voice greatly different from its own; a wise, thoughtful, independent, and detached voice, minatory but constructive, not detracting from the establishment's powers but loud enough to be heard above all the cacophony of political ambitions.

Are there, reflected in these intellectual efforts, any consistent philosophical principles? I suspect that there are at least some rather basic *preferences* which, whether one wishes to call them principles or not, are detectable in much of what has been written above. And I shall venture to suggest what some of them might be. There is a preference for the small over the great, particularly in the case of the human political community. There is a preference for the qualitative over the quantitative, for the personal over the impersonal, for the discriminate over the indiscriminate, and for the varied over the uniform, in most major aspects of social life. There is a very decided preference for the effort to distinguish and consider what is real, as distinct from the contrived imagery of reality, in the view contemporaries take of their own civilization. With particular relation to the habits and practices of governments, there is an aversion to the American tradition of the treatment of social and political problems by great, all-inclusive categories (that is, by abstract and rigid legal definitions with theoretically wide-ranging applicability) and a longing for intelligent discrimination in the treatment of both persons and situations, even where this requires that a single public servant be authorized to decide something on his own responsibility. Insofar as ethics come into the picture, there is an emphasis on the importance of a controlled and courteous outward behavior, of manners, and of common decency, as means of redemption from the demonic component in the physiological inner man. Implicit if not explicit in much of the above, there is a wistful plea for recognition of the relative importance of means over ends, not in the sense that foul ends are not reprehensible and unfortunate, but rather that even the noblest ends are likely not to be achieved or, if ostensibly achieved, to be deprived of most of their beneficence, if the means used to achieve them are foul ones. And finally, there is the belief that if we are to have hope of emerging successfully from the great social bewilderments of this age, weight must be laid predominantly upon the spiritual, moral, and intellectual shaping of the individual with a view to the development of his qualities for leadership, rather than on the prospects for unaided self-improvement on the part of leaderless masses. If humanity is to have a hopeful future, there is no escape from the preeminent involvement and responsibility of the single human soul, in all its loneliness and frailty.

These, I reiterate, are some of the lines of philosophical inclination (if one consents to call them that) which seem to the writer to run, like woven threads—here apparent, there concealed—through much of what has been written in this book.

Is it a dark and despairing view of the human predicament that emerges? The writer's answer is no—it could not be. No one—neither this writer nor anyone else who undertakes to comment on the human scene—can profess to stand outside the subject on which he is commenting. There is no detached Archimedean platform from which the subject could be viewed. Just as the scientist's observation of an experiment affects the very material on which he is experimenting, the humanist, too, makes himself a part of the problem he examines; and he assumes thereby at least a small share of responsibility for the image he describes. His words, after all, may be expected to have *some* consequences, however trivial; otherwise, they would not be worth uttering. But the measure and quality of this effect is never predictable; and, that being the case, the responsibility of the writer is all the greater.

I cannot too strongly emphasize the seriousness of this responsibility. If the commentator's words sow despair, particularly among younger people whose ability to act upon life has not yet exhausted itself or even reached its peak, he may, by his despairing words, have given discouragement where courage was needed. He may have created hopelessness where, even if he could not himself see this, there was no reason not to hope.

And that, as I see it, would be the unpardonable sin. The hour may be late, but there is nothing that says that it is too late. There is nothing in man's plight that his vision, if he cared to cultivate it, and his will, if he dared to exercise it, could not alleviate. The challenge is to see what could be done, and then to have the heart and the resolution to attempt it. Anything in the way of a comment on the human condition that weakened that heart or undermined that resolution would be an inexcusable abuse of the responsibility of the speaker.

The observations brought forward in this book are offered, then, however severe some of them may seem, with a view to encouraging others to take heart—not to lose it. But to take heart is to act. It is the writer's hope that this book itself, in its own small way, is an action, and will be received accordingly.

Index